Homage to Barcelona

COLM TÓIBÍN was born in Ireland in 1955.
He is the author of six novels, including *Brooklyn*, which
won the 2009 Costa Novel Award, *The Blackwater Lightship*
and *The Master*, both of which were shortlisted for
the Booker Prize, and a collection of stories,
Mothers and Sons.

Also by Colm Tóibín

FICTION

The South

The Heather Blazing

The Story of the Night

The Blackwater Lightship

The Master

Mothers and Sons

Brooklyn

NON-FICTION

Bad Blood:
A Walk Along the Irish Border

The Sign of the Cross:
Travels in Catholic Europe

Love in a Dark Time:
Gay Lives from Wilde to Almodóvar

Lady Gregory's Toothbrush

PLAY

Beauty in a Broken Place

COLM TÓIBÍN

Homage to Barcelona

PICADOR

First published 1990 by Simon and Schuster Ltd

This revised and updated edition with a new chapter published 2002 by Picador
an imprint of Pan Macmillan, a division of Macmillan Publishers Limited
Pan Macmillan, 20 New Wharf Road, London N1 9RR
Basingstoke and Oxford
Associated companies throughout the world
www.macmillan.com

ISBN 978-0-330-37356-2

A CIP catalogue record for this book is available from
the British Library.

Typeset by Intype London Ltd
Printed in the UK by CPI Mackays, Chatham ME5 8TD

Contents

Acknowledgements vii

1. Demons and Dragons 1

2. The Gothic Quarter 11

3. Nightclubbing 24

4. City Without Walls 30

5. A Dream of Gaudí 50

6. Picasso's Quarter 63

7. Miró in Barcelona 79

8. The Republic's Golden Age 96

9. The Civil War 107

10. Girona 130

11. The Catalan Summer 141

12. Food and Sex 159

13. A Fragile Country 171

14. The New Regime 183

15. Barcelona 1992 192

Select Bibliography 211

Index 213

Acknowledgements

I am grateful to Michael Loughlin, Evelyn Byrne and Simon Foran for their unstinting hospitality and kindness in Barcelona. I am also grateful to others who provided shelter: Catie Lenaghan, Donald Kuhne Linares, Encina Alonso and Ramon Viladomat. I am grateful also to Ramon Viladomat in his capacity as press officer of the Department of Culture in Barcelona Town Hall, as I am to the poet and publisher Lluis Urpinell who put his considerable knowledge of Catalan culture and society at my disposal.

I wish also to express my gratitude to the Catalan Generalitat, and in particular to Ricard Lobo of the publications department. I am also grateful to the staff of the Biblioteca de Catalunya for their patience and kindness, as I am to the staff of the library of the Fundació Miró.

Antoni Strubell i Trueta was my first Catalan teacher in Barcelona, and it was through him that I came to understand what was happening in the city after the death of Franco. His contribution to this book has been immense. I am grateful to his family, to his parents Michael and Amelia Strubell, for their hospitality, and to his brother Miquel Strubell i Trueta for his help and encouragement. I am particularly grateful to Michael Strubell Senior for his careful and painstaking reading of the manuscript; he is not responsible, of course, for errors or interpretations.

I also wish to thank Aengus Fanning, Anne Harris and Ronan Farren of the *Sunday Independent* in Dublin and Helen Costa, Aidan Dunne, Eamon Dunphy, Carme Ferré i Sanpera, Padraig Ferry, Quirtze Grifell, Conxita Hostench, Terry Keane, Jordi Llobet, David McKenna, Josep Palau i Fabre, Mary Raftery and Francesc Viçens. I am also grateful to Derek Johns who commissioned the book, and to Nick Brealey and Brian Perman of Simon & Schuster. I am especially grateful to my agent Imogen Parker of A. P. Watt for her constant and generous encouragement and commitment.

1

Demons and Dragons

I remember the strange humidity during that first September in the city. I remember the rancid smells and the constant noise as steel shutters were pulled up and down. I remember the sound of cars and motorbikes reverberating against the old stone buildings, the footfalls and voices which echoed in the narrow streets. It was 1975, two months before the death of General Franco. I was twenty years old and had just arrived in Barcelona.

The buildings on the Rambla, the long tree-lined walk between the Plaça de Catalunya and the port, were as different as each face which sized you up for a split second before it passed. The Rambla, busy all the time, was a whole new world to wander in and discover. The kiosks selling newspapers and books were open day and night. During the day one stretch had kiosks selling flowers, another had kiosks with animals for sale. People sat at the outside tables for hours on end staring at passers-by.

I knew no Spanish, but I understood that the Rambla had its own customs, its own rules. The prostitutes, for example, didn't seem to come up from the port beyond a certain point. Also nobody seemed to be going anywhere in particular. Most people seemed to be idly strolling. On Sunday mornings families filled the Rambla, walked up and down under the shade of the plane trees. I tried out each bar. I stood at the kiosks and tried to decipher the newspaper headlines and the titles of books.

One night, while close to the Cathedral, I strayed into a small square through a narrow alleyway. It was quiet and dark and hidden away. One of the walls had been badly damaged by shrapnel or bullets. Nobody came through the alleyway while I was there and there was no sound except a trickle of water from a small fountain in the middle of the square.

I began to haunt the old city. I could hardly wait for darkness to fall, when the lamps would be lit high up on the walls, and the streets would become shadowy, ghostly. This was the late medieval world of master craftsmen, stone-cutters, masons, sculptors and architects surviving intact in the middle of a city.

When I found work as a teacher and decided to stay for a while, I began to study the language and by January I was confident that I had made some progress. One evening I was invited for supper to a small flat in the Gothic quarter. My fellow guests were natives of the city. As the conversation went on I realized that I couldn't understand a single word they said. All the nights spent poring over the niceties and oddities of Spanish grammar had been in vain. It was only when someone apologized to me for speaking in Catalan, and thus excluding me, that I understood the problem.

They and their family and friends, they explained, all spoke Catalan as a first language, although they were fluent in Spanish as well. Most of them couldn't write the language, however, and few of them had ever read a book in Catalan. It wasn't merely spoken, they explained, in villages and remote places. It was the language of the prosperous classes in Barcelona. Franco had banned the public use of the language in 1939.

Catalan, I discovered, isn't a dialect of Spanish, nor of Provençal, although it has close connections with both. Some words (*casa* for 'house', for example) are the same as in Spanish; other words (*mangar* for 'eat') are close to French or Italian. Most of the words for fruit, vegetables and spices are completely different from the Spanish words. The way of forming the past simple is like no other language; the way of forming the past continuous is more or less the same as in Spanish; the way of forming the past subjunctive is the same as in Italian.

Catalan is a pure Latin language. There are no Arabic sounds. Thus the pronunciation of the word 'Barcelona' does not have the 'th' sound as used in the series *Fawlty Towers*. Catalan sounds are harsh and guttural. The language is full of short, sharp nouns such as *cap* for 'head', *fill* for 'son' and *clau* for 'key'; and similar-sounding verbs: *crec* for 'I believe', *vaig* for 'I go' and *vull* for 'I want'.

By the time I began to learn Catalan in 1976 I didn't just need it in order to follow the conversation at dinner parties, I needed it to know what the crowd was shouting in the streets, to read the writing on the walls. In that year the language which had been the preserve of the city's middle classes and which had, since the Civil War, been used mainly indoors now took to the streets with a vengeance.

By 1977 it was as though it had never been banned. The new Spain was prepared to allow Catalonia a certain autonomy and the Catalan language a certain official respect. In those years when I lived in Barcelona the Rambla changed from being the centre of life in the city to being a centre of political dissent, where the crowd ranged against the police, where tear gas and rubber bullets were fired, where there were baton charges. As I walked up the Rambla each morning to go to work, I had to pass jeeploads of police. Policemen dressed in grey stood with machine-guns pointed at passers-by. By the time I left the city, however, in 1978, the Rambla had returned to its former self, democracy was, for the moment anyway, secured, and the citizens of Barcelona could once more wander freely in the Rambla and fleetingly size each other up.

I went back to my own country, and returned to Barcelona on holidays a few times over the years. Every so often in Ireland I would come across someone who spoke Catalan. Hearing the language again would bring it all back: the beautiful old city, the graffiti in red on the Cathedral walls, the political ferment, the smell of garlic, the faces in a demonstration defiant against the police, the slogans, the sexual freedom and the heat.

In January 1988 I returned to Barcelona to write this book. I stayed there all year and since then, I have kept a room in the city. People asked me if the city had changed; some of the changes were obvious, such as the street names which were now in Catalan only. There was more crime. But I still wasn't sure. On the final Sunday in September 1988, the last day of the Mercè festival, which had not existed in the Franco era, I felt at ease enough in the city, at home enough again, to look around me carefully, to take notes, and maybe take stock.

You could hardly move on the Rambla that morning; the street was crowded as it had always been, but the stretch between the port and the Liceu Opera House was seedier than before. There was a sense that people who should have been in jail were walking about freely, a feeling that the police might swoop at any moment.

This was Picasso's stomping ground in the years when he lived in the city; this was where George Orwell, in May 1937, watched fascinated as the crowd built barricades with speed and skill. Now men stood around, watching and waiting while all around them street-sellers sold jewellery and rugs, cheap cassettes and Indian clothes.

The Rambla began as a small stream, a seasonal river whose channel was used in the dry season as a roadway. In the fourteenth century as the city grew it was included within new walls, and then in the eighteenth century the stream was diverted and became the street which Federico García Lorca hoped would go on for ever. Some of the buildings are from the eighteenth century: the Virreina Palace, near the market, was built in the 1770s, as was the Casa March, further down on the other side. But most date from the nineteenth century, including the Liceu Opera House, which was built in 1847, re-built after a fire in 1861, and re-built after another fire in 2000.

A few of the buildings were constructed in the style for which the city later became famous: using tiles, mosaics and floral motifs, mixing medieval images with the idioms of the Art Nouveau movement, with decoration and colour on the outside of buildings. L'Antiga Casa Figueres, for example, was first built in 1902, and is now restored and again in use as a cake shop.

Across the road one of the banks has bought and restored L'Antiga Botiga Bruno Cuadros, finished in 1885 with all the elaborate colour and subtle decoration of its original pastiche Japanese style. But these buildings stand out on the Rambla; by the time serious money was available for building in Barcelona, the Rambla had ceased to be fashionable, and was replaced by the Rambla de Catalunya and the Passeig de Gràcia.

The atmosphere changes once you pass the Opera House and the coloured tiles designed by Miró into the more stable and solid world of the flower-sellers. People walk differently, the clothes are smarter, no one wonders if you are easy prey. It is relaxed, as you walk past the bird-sellers' stalls, towards the Plaça de Catalunya.

As always, there was a queue that Sunday outside Agut, the restaurant behind the Passeig de Colom on Carrer Gignàs. It would be three o'clock before he could give us a table, the owner told us at half-past one. I put my name down and told him we would be back, having agreed with my companions that it would be worth the wait.

The owner is young, but he is earnest and grave; he takes his role seriously. In 1976, when I first went to his restaurant, his father was in control. His father's comportment has been described by John McGahern in a story called *The Beginning of an Idea*: 'the *jefe* who watched for the slightest carelessness, the red and white towel on his shoulder like an epaulet'.

By three o'clock there was a large crowd outside Agut; everybody seemed to believe that they were next in line and each time the owner came and called out a name from his list there were sighs and moans of hunger and desperation from everybody else. Eventually it was our turn. As we sat down the couple at the next table were having a dessert of lemon sorbet with champagne poured all over it. The food looked good, the people animated and content, the waiters constantly bringing more wine and shouting orders into the kitchen.

The fare was traditionally Catalan. Agut's *escalibada* was particularly good: onions and green and red peppers roasted on the outside and then peeled and soaked in oil. The free-range chicken cooked with prawns came next in an old-fashioned ceramic dish, followed by profiteroles for dessert.

As it approached five o'clock there was a sense of hurry in the restaurant, a sense of expectation. Notices all over the centre of the city announced the *correfoc* for seven o'clock, encouraging people to wear old clothes and headgear, and asking those who lived along the route through which the devils and dragons would pass not to throw water on the participants. 'Respect the devils and the dragons,' one sign read. These had been put up by the authorities.

The festival had begun on Friday with a speech by José Carreras, fireworks over the Town Hall and concerts in the old city squares at ten o'clock. Maria del Mar Bonet, who in the 1970s had written one of the classic songs in Catalan against

Franco's police, who had been arrested and held under the old regime, was now being paid by the municipality to sing in front of the floodlit Cathedral, its spiky façade dramatic against the clear sky. She sang in Catalan, medieval songs of the troubadours, songs from the twelfth and thirteenth centuries, and then her own songs, songs about love and friendship and her native island of Majorca. I looked up once, distracted by something in the sky, and saw a seagull, flying towards the Cathedral spire and hovering there in the floodlight, holding its wings perfectly still. It wavered there for so long that everybody began to notice it, and a small cry went up from the crowd.

On Saturday, in the late afternoon, the giants did their dance through the centre of the old city to the beat of drums. Every village and every district of the city kept its own giants and some took them to Barcelona for this festival. The giants' faces were wonderfully made, perfectly still and serene as they were marched through the streets: kings, queens, Moors, pirates, harvesters, noblemen, noblewomen, all of them more than fifteen feet tall, doing twirls and running for a stretch and then standing still so the small human carrying their weight could have a rest and a replacement could take over.

Sunday night was the highlight. Sunday night was going to be rough. You might get pushed and knocked over, or badly burned by the fireworks which would be attached to the dragons and the devils. The clock had been put back on Saturday night and by half past six, as the crowds went towards the Plaça de Sant Jaume, darkness was already falling.

The square had been fitted out with overhead cables laden with fireworks; in front of the entrance to the Town Hall a huge devil had been built of more fireworks. There were some old people in the square, and young children sat high on their parents' shoulders, but most of the people in the square were young, boys and girls in large groups, hats on their heads to protect themselves from the sparks, handkerchiefs at the ready to protect their lungs from the sulphurous fumes.

Five to seven: we waited close to the edge of things, away from the real centre of danger, not far from the van which the Red Cross had driven into the square. It was dusk now, and at seven it began: the whole square became a mass of bangs and small explosions, a line of fireworks caught and the noise zipped over our heads with a spray of sparks. The devil in front of the Town Hall lit up as though an electric shock had gone through it. And five minutes later it was over – the square was in darkness, the first bangs and thrills finished. Now it was time for the parade.

For one moment during the fireworks when the sound of the explosions was echoing against the old walls of the Plaça de Sant Jaume, I remembered the last time I had heard this square reverberate with explosions. In the years immediately after Franco died this was one of the places where the demonstrators would gather, and this was where the police would come in jeeploads, complete with batons and rubber-bullet guns and other weapons. I remembered this square in 1976 and 1977, the huge crowds gathering in front of the Town Hall, calling for amnesty, for liberty, for autonomy, the Communists, the Socialists and the Nationalists all united in shouting the same slogans. I remembered how frightened we were when the police would charge into the square wielding their batons, how everyone would rush to one of the exits only to find it blocked and then panic and rush towards another. I remembered one Sunday evening in 1977, how I kept looking behind me as I ran down towards Via Laietana and noticed that two policemen had fixed on me and were making ground. I darted towards Sant Just, and waited there, shaking with fear. I remembered another bright evening when I saw a circle of policemen in the square beating a young girl with batons, hitting her hard, with passion and temper, over and over. We all stood at a safe distance wondering what to do, no one brave enough to intervene.

During all the years of Franco's reign and for two years afterwards a plaque remained on the wall to the right of the huge door of the Town Hall, telling the citizens of Barcelona that '*La Guerra Ha Terminado*' – the Civil War had ended and the 'red army' had been defeated. Out of this very door, as we stood in the square fifty years later, now came dragons of all shapes and sizes, as though emerging from the jaws of death, breathing fire and making their way across the square. Sometimes they lunged into the crowd, who shrieked in terror and pushed back to avoid the flame. Gangs of youths then ran at the monsters as though to attack them, and tried to hold them back as the devil or dragon attempted to get by. Each time a new fiery monster appeared another mock feud broke out. Soon we became braver and moved towards the centre where we could watch each demon emerge, some of them huge and scaly, others multi-coloured with fierce faces out of comic books. We left ourselves room to run if one of these decided to come after us.

One by one they came out, a procession of horrible and grotesque creatures. Their minders, holders and protectors were armed with sacks of fireworks and were prepared to stop without any notice, fix new petards into their launchers and let them loose on the unsuspecting and excitable crowd. The procession was to end at Passeig de Colom, and at nine o'clock the last big display of fireworks would be shot into the air at the statue of Columbus to celebrate the tenth anniversary of the parade. This parade had begun in 1979, just as the city was getting on its feet again after the long rule of the old dictator.

When all the monsters had emerged we walked down and met the parade again at Passeig de Colom. Here the youth of the city came into their own; groups of them stood under buildings imploring people on the balconies to throw water down on them. '*Aigua! Aigua!*' they roared in Catalan and shouted with joy as bucketfuls of water were flung all over them. Others ran over to join the lucky ones who had found a willing balcony and they all revelled in the showers of cold water.

They were now attacking the devils and dragons with greater ferocity, and trying to impede the progress of those who carried the fireworks. But the parade was still making its way towards the statue at the bottom of the Rambla without much trouble, until they started to sit down in front of it shouting in Catalan '*no passareu, no passareu*', meaning 'you will not pass'. The torchbearers attacked them with their sparks and battles broke out, but these were mock battles: not once did anyone lose his temper or hit an opponent. Eventually, they were moved in time for the demons to get through to the statue of Columbus and see the fireworks shoot over the city.

The music started at ten. For the third night in a row bands played in the old squares and up on the hill of Montjuic which overlooked the port. There were crowds on the Rambla now, pouring down into the metro, or walking up towards the Plaça de Catalunya, just sauntering, idling, waiting for the concerts to begin.

To the right was the Plaça Reial; the much-maligned Plaça Reial, reputed to be the source of all the crime now in the city centre, the place where the handbag-snatchers and the dope dealers hang out, the square where tourists and thieves and touts meet, but which respectable natives of the city stay away from. The square was built in a French neo-classical style between 1848 and 1860; in 1879 Antoni Gaudí designed the lamps in the centre, one of his first commissions. A fountain has been added, and there are tall palm trees. On sunny winter mornings – the winter sky is usually clear and sunny in Barcelona – the square can be very beautiful and in the summer you can drink beer and eat *tapas* until after two in the morning. But still, the place is seedy. In the early 1980s the municipality tried to clean up the square and they have been doing so ever since, without much success. Then the authorities began to put on jazz concerts on a Sunday night; a trendy architect did up the buildings, and writers and singers were reputedly about to move into the square at any moment. Yet none of this has had the slightest impact on the indigenous population of the square, who haven't changed much since 1975. You still have to watch yourself there, and it seems that nothing will ever change in the Plaça Reial.

Yet on that Sunday night of the Mercè festival every seat at every outside bar was taken. For once the plan was working: the middle classes were sitting comfortably in the Plaça Reial. The waiter brought us glasses of beer, squid deep fried in batter and slices of lemon. All around us were Catalan voices. The same Catalans who had abandoned the Plaça Reial to the foreigners and the outsiders were back tonight, back in the downtown that they had learned to fear. This fear had been born not just in previous years when the sale of heroin had become rampant in the area, but in the years after the Cuban War at the end of the nineteenth century when there was desperate poverty; the years after the First World War when there was enormous unemployment and unrest; and the years of the Civil War, when the Anarchists held the city centre.

That Sunday night the Catalans were in the Plaça de Sant Jaume too, dancing to a band playing Viennese waltzes. There were more old people here; each generation seemed to have found its level on the last night of the festival. In the Plaça del Rei around the corner the music was more modern and cool, and this was where the fashionable people were, the people who would later move on to the fast-lane nightclubs, now standing in the fourteenth-century square swaying slightly to the music.

A bar on the corner, an old bar with upstairs windows overlooking the square, was half-empty now, although it was a hot night and the square outside was full. Catalans and the citizens of Barcelona in general have very little interest in alcohol, will seldom have more than one drink in a bar, and will often nurse a Coca-Cola for an entire evening.

All over the city the music went on. On Friday night 180,000 people had gone to the free rock concert on Montjuic and tonight there were 100,000 people up there again; earlier, an estimated 100,000 had watched the dragons and devils on the *correfoc*, and the same number of children had taken part in various events in the city over the weekend, all the events being paid for by the Town Hall. There had been no arrests, no fights. The city was stable now, at peace. The squares were full of people as midnight approached. Barcelona was having a good time.

2

The Gothic Quarter

The Gothic quarter is still dark now, and quiet. It is always quiet at night: you can hear only the hum of traffic in the distance and the soft noises which pigeons make as they settle in. Its topography is intricate. The dim light comes from old lamps high up on the walls. You can linger here at night, in the strange heart of the city, and wander undisturbed through this maze of grey stone. You can sit on the long stone bench in the Plaça de Sant Iu opposite one of the side doors to the Cathedral or on the steps of the Plaça del Rei, where Christopher Columbus, according to legend, was received by Ferdinand and Isabella when he returned from his voyage in 1493.

It is ironic that Columbus should have been received in Barcelona, and doubly ironic that his statue overlooks the port from its high pedestal – Columbus' discovery of the New World meant that Barcelona would never recover its power as a port, though its decline had begun almost a century earlier; his return was merely the last ring in its death-knell.

There is a rawness about some of the old buildings, each single stone bears a different texture, has weathered in a different way. It is easy to get an idea of the stonemason at work, to see how each stone has been cut and placed. The streets are so narrow that you are constantly aware of the stone, and not just its roughness, but its force and its power as well – because the Gothic quarter of Barcelona is not a crumbling set of medieval buildings, or old ruins being shored up and restored: the buildings are towering and strong, solid and immovable, monuments to the science and skill of the architect as well as to the art of the builder. There is a crude and forceful energy at work all over the Gothic quarter.

Barcelona is the only city in the world whose centre looks like this. It is the only city in the world which was powerful during the fourteenth century and not afterwards. There are only a few buildings from the sixteenth century here, buildings such as the Arxiu de la Corona d'Aragó in the Plaça del Rei. There was no widening of the streets to make way for new thoroughfares and more opulent palaces. Only later in the nineteenth century did they create a vista in front of the Cathedral, or build the few straight streets which cut through the old city, most of which was thus left intact and still stands in its dark medieval splendour.

But it is not a museum. Three of the Gothic churches are still used: Sant Just (1342–1363); Santa Maria del Mar (1329–1383) and Santa Maria del Pi (1306–1391). The Cathedral, begun in 1298, is constantly in use for Mass and prayer. Only the church of Santa Llúcia (1257–1368), beside the Cathedral, has the air of a church more honoured by tourism than by religious observance, and Santa Àgata in the Plaça del Rei (1302–1311) has long been a museum.

Similarly, the Gothic buildings associated with civil and mercantile power are still in daily use: the Catalan Government operates from the Palau de la Generalitat, which was begun in 1403; the city authorities run Barcelona from the Casa de la Ciutat, begun in 1373. The Stock Exchange still conducts its august daily affairs in the Llotja, begun in 1352. During the morning, the old city is full of buskers and businessmen, strollers and civil servants, in this fourteenth century city there is movement, activity, commerce all day.

The museum city, the site of the Roman city Barcino, is underneath the Gothic quarter. Traces of the Roman walls, built at the end of the third century, run through the Gothic quarter like a seam, appearing, for example, in the Plaça Ramon Berenguer off Via Laietana, again inside the Museu Marés in Carrer dels Comtes, where other Roman remains are on show, visible once more inside a shop on Carrer del Call, in a cheap restaurant at the back of the Plaça Reial, emerging elsewhere in small snatches on Carrer de la Palla and the Museu de la Historia de la Ciutat under the Plaça del Rei – where the old city is preserved *in situ*, complete with streets, walls of houses, mosaics, and jars for holding oil. Barcino was never an important centre of population such as Tarragona was. The area within the walls was small and made up of a considerable number of public buildings and monuments, dominated by the Temple of Augustus. It was, historians maintain, not so much a Roman settlement as a centre of government. Its remains, such as the three monumental columns surviving from the Temple of Augustus in the Centre d'Escursionistes de Catalunya in Carrer de Paradís, off the Plaça Sant Jaume, linger under the real city, but almost nothing is left from the period of the Visigoths, nor from the Moors, and very little from the Romanesque period. The only real ancient past was the Roman one, and that came to an end at the beginning of the fifth century.

The Moors had an impact, however, on the general history of Catalonia. It was the Moors who caused the Catalans to approach Charlemagne in the early eighth century and put themselves under his protection and in his power. The *Chronicle* of the Abbey of Moissac described how 'the inhabitants of the famous city of Barcelona, fleeing the cruel yoke of the enemies of Christ, approached us and freely gave or ceded their city to our authority'. So began what is known as the *Marca hispánica*, the Spanish March, which comprised territory on both sides of the Pyrenees, including Roussillon and Cerdagne, in what later became France, as well as Urgel, Besalú, Barcelona, Girona, Osona, and Empúries on the southern side of the Pyrenees in what would become Spain. With the help of the Franks, Girona was re-captured from the Moors in 785 and Barcelona in 801. Over the next hundred years, as Charlemagne's Empire weakened, Catalonia was to become increasingly self-reliant, with Barcelona as its capital and the Count of Barcelona as its overlord. By the end of the tenth century the Counts of Barcelona were, in the words of one historian, 'sovereigns in their own land', and by the end of the eleventh century Rome was persuaded to remove the Frankish control over the church in Catalonia, thus further consolidating its independence.

More than a hundred years later, by the time Jaume I came to the throne, the House of Barcelona had incorporated the poorer region of Aragon, and Catalonia had given up hope of expanding north to Provence, setting its sights on the Mediterranean. Jaume I took Majorca from the Moors in 1229 and also took possession of the other Balearic Islands, later taking Valencia as well. Catalonia's Golden Age was about to begin.

Jaume married his son Pere to Constance, heiress to the throne of Sicily. In 1282 Sicily was captured by Catalans, Constantinople was taken by Catalan mercenaries in 1303, Athens and Thebes in 1310, Corsica in 1323, Sardinia in 1324 and finally Naples in 1423. There were Catalan consulates in all the Mediterranean ports and market places. 'Catalan merchants,' wrote Jan Read in *The Catalans*, 'rivalled those of Genoa and Venice in the traffic of spices from Alexandria, and her sailors ranged from the Sea of Azov to England and Flanders.'

'From here we governed Athens', Jordi Pujol, President of the autonomous Catalan Government, proudly told an audience in the spring of 1988. 'And the Barcelona pound was one of the strongest currencies in the Mediterranean, then the centre of the European world. It was the culmination of a splendid period.'

'The industrial development of the country kept pace with its commerce,' Josep Trueta wrote in *The Spirit of Catalonia*. 'Iron works and textile factories reached a high degree of efficiency. Agreements with Flanders, Italy and England on the trade in wool, dyes and textiles were among the bases of material prosperity.'

But just as the fourteenth century was coming to a close, things changed in Catalonia. In 1381 a number of private banks collapsed in Barcelona and within a few years the golden florin, introduced in 1346, had gone down in value by seventy-five per cent. 'The Catalan economy,' Jordi Pujol told his audience, 'entered a crisis. And during that final part of the fourteenth century all of Catalonia began to fall apart. And this was how we entered a deep decadence which lasted centuries. The point arrived when Catalonia seemed dead.'

By the end of the fifteenth century, when Ferdinand and Isabella were ruling Spain, when the Moors (and the Jews) had been expelled, the Atlantic route would replace the Mediterranean as the highway of trade. Catalonia had no part in the Atlantic route; its brief flowering was over.

The city of Barcelona was left with two things: its solid, austere, stone buildings, mostly built in the fourteenth century, which would form its core, and a tradition of progress and freedom far in advance of the country which would now come to rule over it. The English writer, Richard Ford, writing in 1880, described the situation: 'The Catalonians, under the Aragonese kings, during the thirteenth century, took the lead in maritime conquests and jurisprudence, nor was trade ever thought to be a degradation until the province was annexed to the proud Castile, when the first heavy blow was dealt to its prosperity.'

This feeling that as intellectuals, humanists, inventors, writers and entrepreneurs they had risen above Spain would never leave Catalan consciousness. They came to believe that they had not been simply sailors, but cartographers as well; not merely writers but book collectors and translators; not only merchants and builders, but men of culture, who sought to impose order, peace and a system of law in place of darkness, chaos and piracy. They were, they believed, modern; while Spain was medieval.

Catalonia never had a king; it was ruled by the Counts of Barcelona, who in 1068, a hundred and fifty years before the Magna Carta, codified the law into *usatges* which dealt with the rights and duties of the sovereign. The *usatges* later became part of the nationalist dream which saw this early definition of rights as the beginning of the tradition of individual freedom of which the Catalans claim part.

The book – *El Libre del Consolat del Mar* – which governed the international law of the sea was originally written in Catalan. Other institutions such as the early parliaments ('This was the first democratic parliament in Europe,' the guide in the Consell de Cent building told me in 1988), the medieval universities and the legal systems haunted Catalonia over the next several centuries as a national identity began to take shape. In Catalonia even in the twentieth century this sense of past greatness lingers, and the idea that Catalonia was once part of a great European tradition of learning and innovation has left its traces in the minds and hearts of the Catalans. Thus, in the dark days after the Civil War, when the Catalan surgeon Josep Trueta was in exile in Oxford, his book *The Spirit of Catalonia* concentrated on this tradition, the life of the mind in medieval Catalonia, the great beginnings of a nation. 'For the sake of all nations,' he concluded, 'and especially of Spain, one may utter the fervent hope that Catalonia is witnessing the end of her tragic interlude.'

The life of Catalonia was to include several tragic interludes.

In 1624 the King's Chief Minister, Olivares, wrote his famous memorandum which said: 'The most important thing in Your Majesty's Monarchy is for you to become King of Spain . . . [you] should secretly plan and work to reduce these kingdoms of which Spain is composed to the style and laws of Castile.' Castilian imperialism had begun. Catalonia gained nothing from the War of the Reapers (1640-1652), which began as a peasants' insurrection but ended as a war over Catalonia's control of its own territory. By the terms of the subsequent Treaty of the Pyrenees, Catalonia lost its lands on the northern side of the Pyrenees to France, although they remained – and to some extent still remain – Catalan-speaking.

The Catalans also lost the War of the Spanish Succession. The siege of Barcelona lasted for a year and two months, ending on 11 September 1714 when all symbols of the Catalans' former autonomy were destroyed. The university was closed, all books published in Catalonia were burned, writing and teaching in Catalan was forbidden, nine hundred houses and eleven churches were pulled down by the victorious forces of Philip V and the Ciutadella fortress (now a park) was built. Civil servants were exhorted to 'take the greatest care in introducing the Spanish language, in which cause the most discreet and disguised ploys will be used, so that the effect though not the intention may be noted.' Catalonia was now part of Spain.

Those two events – the War of the Reapers and the War of the Spanish Succession – became central to the mythology of Catalan nationalism. The first gave Catalonia its national anthem which opens: 'Triumphant Catalonia will once more become rich and full' and is called after the Reapers (*Els Segadors*) who came to Barcelona seeking their rights in 1640. The chorus, sung with the right hand raised, can be translated as 'A good blow of a scythe, defenders of the land'.

The ending of the siege of Barcelona in 1714 gave the city its *Diada*, its national day, 11 September, whose celebration was consistently banned. In 1976 Franco had been dead almost a year when the day of the *Diada* loomed; permission was sought for a demonstration, and was withheld until late on the evening of 10 September. On the morning of 11 September 1976 the recently-published Catalan newspaper *Avui* confirmed the news: the *Diada* could be celebrated for the first time since the Civil War, not in the city, however, but in a suburb called Sant Boi, also the traditional seat of Barcelona's mental hospital.

Tots a Sant Boi, the slogans appeared all over the city. There were thousands of people there that day, some of them waving Catalan flags for the first time in forty years, others for the first time in their lives. They called for autonomy and liberty, they called for the return of their old rights. But more than anything, they sang *Els Segadors*, the banned national anthem. They sang it with vigour and fervour and fire in their eyes. And when the chorus came, they clenched their right fists and raised them to the sky.

Bon cop de falç, defensors de la terra, bon cop de falç.

It was clear that day that Catalan feeling had not died, nor fallen into the hands of hooligans or Anarchists. These were middle-class people, law-abiding, hard-working, respectable, who had kept quiet during the years of the dictatorship. It was clear, too, that the classical paraphernalia of nationalism could still wield power: the date, 11 September, the date of the Catalans' final defeat; the song, *Els Segadors*, commemorating a Catalan rising against Castile; the flags, four bars of red against gold, signifying four rays of blood made with four fingers placed into the heart of a dying Catalan warrior during the distant but tangible past. That day the forceful symbolism of Catalan nationalism made itself manifest again in the outskirts of the city.

*

In 1908 as part of the general reform of the city, Via Laietana was cut through the old quarter, right down through it like a huge tear in a delicate cloth. The new buildings were ugly, functional, overbearing, like the street itself, which carried traffic between uptown and the port, and opened up a view of the hills above the city from the medieval quarter.

The old city had been added to all the time, piecemeal, palaces appearing beside tenements, cobbled streets curling and winding, districts full of blind alleyways and arches. Now, however, with the right-angles of Via Laietana, there was order. Whole streets and squares were removed to make way for this new stretch of progress. Old photographs survive, and old names: Carrer de Jupi, Carrer del Bon Dia, Carrer del Oli, but now the old quarter of the city had been cut in two. Several buildings deemed to be important were removed stone by stone and reconstructed, including the Casa Padellas in the Plaça del Rei and the Museum of Shoes building in the Plaça de Sant Felip Neri.

In the area on one side of the new street you have the majestic buildings of the fourteenth century: the Cathedral, Sant Just, Plaça Sant Jaume, Santa Maria del Pi. On the other side are the Church of Santa Maria del Mar and the medieval palaces on Carrer de Montcada, and all around them old streets crammed with humble buildings, five and six storeys high, built mostly in the eighteenth century, but maintaining remnants of earlier houses and streets from as early as the thirteenth century.

If the Gothic quarter, the area around the Cathedral, is the heart of the city, then these small streets on the other side of Via Laietana are its mind, just as the Rambla is its central nervous system. They are corridors, caverns and passageways, called after the old trades: Carrer Corretgers, for example, was the street of the belt-makers, Carrer Flasserders was the street of the blanket-makers, Carrer Assaonadors the street of the spice-makers. The streets are noisy and busy, the side streets full of small artisan shops making furniture or mattresses, cutting glass, or repairing electrical goods. The main streets, Carrer Carders, for example, or Sant Pere més Baix, are full of shoppers from early in the morning, and, twice a day, full of school-children coming and going.

During the past ten years a few fashionable bars have opened in the area around Santa Maria del Mar, in the streets around Carrer de Montcada; a few yuppies have moved in, but not many. The area is still mainly working class, as it was at the time when the Anarchists were strong in the city. For most Catalans, it is too seedy, too down-at-heel. You don't live there unless you have to. So on Sunday morning you can wander around the Plaça de Sant Agustí Vell, the old crumbling square at the end of Carrer Carders, you can sit on one of the seats there, or at the outside tables at Bar Joanet, or inside the Bar Mundial, one of the best places for seafood in the city, and you can watch the people of old Barcelona on a day off, a living community within the old quarter which has not yet been gentrified.

However, the area itself contains its own gentry, often in the most unlikely places. I was invited to lunch one day by Catalan friends who lived in one of the streets around Santa Maria del Mar. The street was narrow and dark, the doorway of the house was depressingly drab, the stairway was narrow. But inside there were chandeliers and broad windows, books everywhere, old paintings, old furniture, large rooms. There was even a servant.

The most imposing street is Carrer de Montcada, which houses the one-time palaces of the merchant princes, where building after building exudes that rough, strong style so common in the city, where the stone seems gnarled in texture, yet enduring and imposing. Most of the palaces were built between the twelfth and sixteenth centuries. All of them have stone courtyards, with stone stairs rising to the main living quarters; all of them have been remodelled at various times, but they are built in that grey, tapestried stone which characterizes Barcelona. All of them, too, have old wooden gates, crusted with the centuries, guarding the courtyards from the street. To walk down there – the Picasso Museum is there, as is the Galeria Maeght – is to walk through the world of the medieval merchants, who built the Stock Exchange and the shipyards, the men who made their money from import and export.

To walk on further is to remain in their world. The Casa Meca on the Passeig del Born, although it has been refurbished on the inside, still has all the appearance of a fourteenth-century palace, with its gallery on the top floor and its arched windows, its solid stone, its stately presence on the wide, comfortable boulevard, which leads from the back of the Church of Santa Maria del Mar to the restored nineteenth-century market building. This is the rich core of the old quarter; all around it, however, are the artisan houses, narrow alleyways where washing hangs out to dry on the balconies. This quarter was built before the rich and the poor saw fit to move apart, into their own particular ghettos.

In the late 1970s it was almost impossible to rent a flat down here. Ten years later it was easier, ten years later it seemed that more and more foreigners were moving into the little streets around Santa Maria del Mar. Miracles happened. Friends of mine were loath at first to look at a flat on offer in one of the tiny streets between Carrer Carders and Carrer Assaonadors; the atmosphere seemed too dangerous and claustrophobic. You could put your hand across the street and pat your opposite neighbour on the head. What they were shown into, however, turned out to be the top two floors of a small eighteenth-century palace, complete with patio and two large balconies, with all the back rooms bright and beautifully furnished, everything tastefully restored and in working order. At the end of 1988 the rent was less than three hundred pounds a month.

By day the old area of Barcelona is bustling, full of shouting, hammering, drilling and shutters being pulled up and down. You listen out for sounds. If you want a replacement gas cylinder you wait for the sound of the delivery man hitting a cylinder with a piece of metal in the street. One flat where I lived had no door-bells, which is common in old Barcelona, and since I lived on the fifth floor I knew that five hammering sounds against the front door meant that I had a caller. There was no other way of getting through.

By night it is quiet. Once off the main streets you hardly meet anybody. When winter comes, and the darkness settles down on the city by half-past five or six, there is a special pleasure in wandering around, knowing that the old buildings are still open and that you can turn into the back door of Santa Maria del Mar from the end of Carrer de Montcada and suddenly catch sight of the interior of the church: the rising columns, that thin, stately, Gothic purity, the sheer beauty of its plainness. All the roughness of the outside has been transformed now into perfection. Its simplicity is the result not merely of the architects' design (Berenguer de Montagut, Ramon Despuig, Guillem Metge) but also of the Anarchists gutting the building in the anti-clerical purges of 1909 and 1936, and burning everything they could get their hands on.

In 1936, however, the Anarchists left Barcelona Cathedral alone as well as the monastery at Pedralbes, believing that they were of superior artistic value. The Cathedral is thus clogged up with a choir in the centre which obscures the monumental sweep of its columns. It is a shock to come into the Cathedral because the façade, built at the end of the nineteenth century, has none of the ruggedness of the usual Catalan Gothic style. It is spiky and pointy, over-rich, over-endowed with statues and ornaments. George Orwell, when he was in the city during the Civil War, took a real dislike to the façade, and suggested that the Anarchists had made a mistake in sparing it. It gives the impression that the Cathedral inside will be showy and baroque, so you are not prepared for the cool, sombre, shadowy building within, for its height, its strength and force, for the understatement of its colours, for its sombre atmosphere. The vegetation in the middle of the cloisters is lush and overgrown in the summer; all the year round a noisy flock of geese keep guard there, underlining the importance of this place, which was begun at the end of the thirteenth century on the site of a Romanesque church, added to throughout the fourteenth and fifteenth centuries, and is still standing now, immense, high-toned, solid, the most imposing monument in the old city.

You can move throughout the old city watching how the styles emerged, how the multi-faceted columns of the Llotja, the Stock Exchange, make it look like a church taken over by the forces of Mammon, more like a Gothic cathedral than a centre of commerce. You can examine the pastiche Gothic archway between the Generalitat building and the President's palace on Carrer del Bisbe which appears on all the postcards. Although it was built in 1928, it fits in well, perhaps too well, with its surroundings.

The real Catalan Gothic is so plain and unadorned that it is hardly open to pastiche. It can be found in the square façade and the ornate rose-window of Santa Maria del Pi, just off the Rambla. But the pinnacle of the Catalan tradition in architecture comes not in haunting, spiky building, but in the making of curves, in the round soft arches of the late fourteenth-century city. Elements of these appear in the Cathedral and in Santa Maria del Mar. The best examples, however, can be found in secular buildings such as Sala Tinell, in the Plaça del Rei, now an exhibition centre, held up by a set of graceful and wonderfully proportioned wide stone arches. These can be seen again in the Consell de Cent in the Town Hall buildings in the Plaça Sant Jaume. They lack opulence and drama, they have no medieval splendour nor any sense of pageantry about them. They were built to stand.

So too were the arches in the Drassanes, the Barcelona shipyard, at the bottom of the Rambla, built in 1375. There is nothing crumbling about the arches, the stonework, the steps, nor the span of the roof. The span of each arch, and the way it was constructed was, for its time, new, a part of Barcelona's contribution to the development of architecture.

The arches appear again in the old hospital of Santa Creu, on Carrer Carme, which is now the National Library. It is cool in the summer. Soft shadows are cast by the rough-cut stone. Like the Stock Exchange, it is filled with old nineteenth-century furniture and fittings. With its spareness and greyness, its high ceilings with their gradual curves, it is a perfect place to read, and a great example of what was known as *la volta catalana*, which architects (including Le Corbusier) would come to study in the twentieth century.

In front of the Cathedral on Saturday evenings at seven, the Catalans dance *sardanes*, their national dance. They join hands and form a circle, placing their bags or coats in the middle. The eleven-man wind orchestra sits on chairs on the steps of the Cathedral with the music in front of them, all sober-looking men. The music, when it begins, could be café music. It is light-hearted, occasionally shrill, becoming jolly; but always, after a short time, a melancholy tone will enter into the soul of the music, one of the reed instruments will soar, playing a tune which is plaintive and thin, and then it will fade, re-appear and fade.

The dance is graceful and slow. It looks easy until you try it. John Langdon Davies wrote a whole book about it in 1929 called *Dancing Catalans*. 'The music goes on,' he wrote, 'sometimes grave and gentle, later becoming cheerful and faster.' He understood, too, its political overtones, quoting Enric Morera: 'The *sardana* is Catalonia', and Aureli Capmany: 'To dance the *sardana* imperfectly is to commit a sin against art; it is to insult Catalonia.' It took Langdon Davies a seven-page appendix to describe the intricacies of the steps.

The dancers in front of the Cathedral are divided into the young and the old. The old people, who appear to be in their late seventies or even older, take it easy, join hands and do the steps more slowly than the young. Each group has a leader who shouts out instructions. Everyone is serious and intent. Although each girl has a boy on either side and vice versa, there is nothing sexual about the choreography of the *sardana*; it remains deeply demure, despite the rise and fall of the women's breasts.

If it is the winter, the façade of the Cathedral is floodlit. On one side at right-angles stands the Casa de la Canonja from the fifteenth and sixteenth centuries, opposite the Casa de l'Ardiaca from the same period. Behind is the Hotel Colon and the architects' building with Picasso's murals of the *sardana* on the façade.

Suddenly there is a lift in the dance. The music becomes louder and more joyful. You watch the faces of the old people, knowing that in the years after the Civil War, when they were in their twenties and thirties, this dance was banned by Franco. *'Amunt,'* somebody shouts and the dancers begin to soar. The young in their circle have the energy for it. They fly, carefully preserving the grace and sweetness that they have built up. The music rises above the square, loud and full of joy, and the dancers go with it until it comes to an end. *'Visca!'* they shout together as the last note plays.

3

Nightclubbing

A city shows you your age as the seasons remain the same but the nightclubs change. One day in the late 1980s in the waiting-room of an estate agency I got talking to a fellow about the city. He didn't go out much, he said, but when he did venture out it was late. He saw no point in going out before two in the morning: that was the time when the city was at its best. It wasn't, he intimated, cool to go out before then; only the over-eager went out before midnight and it didn't pay to be over-eager.

The names of the places he went to which I wrote down in a notebook belong to history now, but just then, in those years, they were the places that attracted young people from all over Europe. The night city was cool and modern and open all night. It was civilized; there were no undertones of violence and drugs were easy to get. Slowly as the 1990s wore on new names became trendy. Nic Habana, KGB and Autozut were replaced by La Boite, Sala Bikini and Jamboree. Only a few places – Up and Down, for example or Karma – remained in vogue.

I remember Zeleste Nou, a warehouse turned nightclub in the middle of nowhere. Along with Martin's, the gay emporium at the top of Passeig de Gracia which is still there, it was my idea of fun. It didn't do to look nervous or shifty, or stand around a bloke from a provincial Irish town, when you were trying to get past the doorman in Zeleste Nou without paying a cover charge. Your job was to look the part, slide past, appear as if you knew where you were going. And above all, if you were really stuck, you needed to talk Catalan and talk it really fast as if you were born talking it. It wasn't the money which mattered; it was the humiliation of having to pay it.

I remember how much I loved getting into a taxi on the Rambla or Via Laietana and saying the magic word 'Zeleste' and then being driven around the Parc de la Ciutadella into the nowhere world of lorries and trucks packed on the side of the road; no traffic, no blocks of flats, just warehouses and silence. And then the taxi would stop at one of the least likely buildings in the whole quarter.'

Often there were concerts. Big groups came to Zeleste Nou; the place could hold 2500 people. It still looked like a warehouse; but it was easy to find air, easy to get out to one of the passageways along the roof. You could stand with a gin and tonic and look at the moon. Close to one of these passageways was a room the length of the warehouse with white curtains and soft light, with sofas and armchairs and table service. At half-past three in the morning you could sit there with a bottle of *cava*, the Catalan champagne, while the clients of Zeleste downstairs danced the night away you could sit undisturbed by the loud music, the sweat, the crowds and all those young people.

Zeleste Nou is gone, and I can tell my age by the fact that I remember it. But there's worse. I remember its predecessor, called simply 'Zeleste', in the 1970s when it was just beside Santa Maria del Mar. That is how I know I am middle-aged. I was at the Maria de Mar Bonet concert there in January 1976. I remember the heavy curtains, the dark furniture, the old-fashioned appeal of the place. That was when the new ruling class, the men and the women who later came to run the city, used to meet in the years before they took power. Zeleste was the place where the young designers and architects, painters and writers, politicians and journalists had discussed matters of mutual importance late at night in the last years of the dictatorship. This was the home of that special cool which Catalans had made all their own.

Zeleste was set up by a man called Victor Jou. I went to talk to him when the new version of the club was in its heyday. The fact that he was fifty didn't stop him talking about counter-culture and the channeling of energy. His was the first nightclub in the city. There were flamenco clubs and bars, but nothing like the places he had seen in London in the late 1960s and early 1970s. He set up in an old clothes shop in 1973. He was interested in music, in offering a venue to more marginal and left-wing

groups, to jazz bands, and to people who wanted something new
and different.

Barcelona was still a dangerous place for such people. The
police had a fixed idea of what happened in places like Zeleste: it
was where men brought prostitutes and got drunk. But there was
something funny going on in Zeleste in the early 1970s and the
police couldn't work out what it was. There were no prostitutes
and no drunkenness and no flamenco music. There was just talk.
Often there were live acts, but mostly the young professional
people of the city sat and talked in Catalan and had one or two
drinks. What were they talking about? The police were desperate
to know. They suspected the worst. This was without precedent,
this nightly business down by the church of Santa Maria del Mar,
of up to three hundred people talking. They must be talking about
politics. They must be plotting something.

Twice during the early years of Zeleste the police came in vans
and arrested the entire bar – all three hundred clients – and took
them in for interrogation. They checked each one out: name,
address, age, profession. Most of those whom they had disturbed
from their drinks were young, Catalan and professional. In a
few years, once Franco was dead, they would come to control the
city, but at the time they were a new phenomenon. The police
were deeply puzzled by them. Up till now the Catalans had stayed
at home and talked to each other in private. Now they were
preparing for power. They were the early signs of what became
known as the Transition, the peaceful change from Franco to
democracy. A new class was emerging: their parents had put their
trust in their businesses and their families and had known never
to congregate in bars; their children were now ready to design,
build, inform, entertain and generally manage the new Catalonia.

*

Some things never change. The Catalans do not drink and move
around in groups like the Basques; they do not love drink and
music and the night like the southerners. They are melancholy
and distant. So that as the city developed its name for a fast-land
nightlife, Catalans in Barcelona would relish telling you that they
hardly ever went out. It was normal for them to shrug their

shoulders and purse their lips and disparage the whole notion. There is an abiding phrase which most Catalans love: it is *molta feina* and it means *a lot of work*. Everybody had *molta feina*; not having *molta feina* meant that there was something dreadfully suspect about you. *Molta feina* was the excuse for everything, in particular it was the excuse for not going out, for knowing nothing about the nightlife of the city. Having *molta feina* put you above all that.

And right through from the 1970s to now, it was common for people to shrug their shoulders and announce that they were from Gràcia. Gràcia had once been a village, just off the Eixample. It was close to town, it was old, it was well kept. It was trendy to live in Gràcia, but it was even better to be *from* there.

People from Gràcia didn't leave Gràcia. All their social and sexual activity was down with the boundaries of their *barri*. Instead of exploring the big, bad world of the city, they promised to take you on a tour of the old bars of Gràcia some day, they gave vivid descriptions of a cheap meal they'd had in a local restaurant. They wrote you out long lists of all the places you should go to in Gràcia. 'Now this is the real place to go, only real Gràcia people go here,' they would say, and add a further restaurant to the list. And then the nightclubs, they said, Gràcia was great for nightclubs too, but it wasn't like the rest of Barcelona. In Gràcia, you see, everybody knew everybody. Gràcia was where it was all at.

And even if you weren't from Gràcia, the Plaça del Sol there was beautiful. On Friday nights when it was warm the bars on the square would be all full, the tables outside all taken, and the pavements crowded with people. The streets around were busy with traffic, but the square had no cars, so when you walked in, it was like arriving at a rich and glamorous private party, everybody dressed up and cheerful, the hum of voices rising in the hot night. The houses in the square were opulent in their stately nineteenth century way, and there was a great feeling of comfort as the children of the middle classes basked in the Plaça del Sol. There were other such squares in Gràcia too, less talked-about, less crowded, where you went if you wanted to be out of the mainstream, somewhat left of centre. Here you could have a local bar and, if you needed it, a local dope peddler.

Being in with the Socialists was a considerable social asset in Barcelona. People were pointed out to you and introduced to you late in the night: they were, it was whispered 'in' with the Socialists. There were others who were in with Convergència, the ruling Nationalist party in Catalonia, led by Jordi Pujol. But the Socialists, even after they lost power in Madrid, continued to control the city of Barcelona and they were more glamorous than the men from Convergència. Convergència stood for rural values, old traditions and Catalan pragmatism. Convergència people had their roots in nineteenth-century nationalism. The Socialists stood for the greatness of Barcelona, for the Olympic Games and for the twenty-first century.

In the few years leading up to the Olympic Games, Javier Mariscal was one man who had benefited hugely from being 'in' with the Socialists. His doings were followed closely by the clients of certain bars in the city. Mariscal had entered the magic circle of power and influence and fame, someone told me late one night. Mariscal was a designer. He had been commissioned to design the Olympic mascot; and he had not only agreed to do so, but he had gone home to his native Valencia and announced to a barful of people that Catalonia would be a far, far better place without the Catalans and that the President of Catalonia, Jordi Pujol, was a dwarf. When all this appeared in the newspapers, he was forced to retract, eat his words and look shifty for the cameras, but this didn't take away from his status in the city.

You could buy Mariscal curtains, you could sleep between Mariscal sheets (both of which you could buy in Vinçon on Pesseig de Gràcia), and when summer came, you could dine in a special Mariscal creation with an enormous prawn over it down by the Moll de la Fusta, which was all the rage until the mid-1990s when it ceased to be all the rage. Opinions were divided on Mariscal. People hated his Olympic mascot, thought that it looked naive and foolish, a child could do it; people disliked his *faux-naïveté*. But he symbolized the future of the city, he stood for innovation, imagination; he was bright and clever and original. He was everything Barcelona wanted to be. In November 1988, his retrospective *Cien Años de Mariscal* – A Hundred Years of Mariscal – opened in the old Stock Exchange building in Valencia, attended by the Mayor of Barcelona and the Mayor of Valencia. Mariscal had it made. In 1989 his show arrived in Barcelona in an old ship which docked in the port for two months.

I watched him carefully at the opening of the big exhibition of new projects for the Olympic city one Saturday evening in October 1988. It was in the restored waterworks building on Carrer Wellington, beside the Parc de la Ciutadella. Those whom the writer Manuel Vasquez Montalbán had called *la generación de 92* were in full attendance, the people who were going to make money and reputations from the Barcelona Olympic Games in 1992, out of designing new buildings, out of the public relations, out of the vast organization which would be required. Most of them were young, formally dressed, talking quietly and intensely, sipping champagne. Scruffiness was not in vogue. These were the young who were going to inherit the earth, and they were leaving nothing to chance.

Mariscal moved among them, a wry expression on his face, talking to a few people. He was dressed formally too. He seemed nervous, slightly sheepish. He stood at the bottom of the stairs waiting for the King and Queen of Spain to come down with the Mayor of Barcelona and the President, Jordi Pujol. Most of the guests were kept away from the stairs and the place was tense with security men. But Mariscal was hovering near the bottom of the stairs. And suddenly it struck me why: he was waiting to be presented to the King and Queen, just as he would a few days later be on the list to attend the party on the royal yacht *Britannia*, when the Queen of England came to Barcelona, Javier Mariocal, top designer, with all the young trendy architects and designers around him, stood waiting while the King and the Queen came down the stairs. And when they reached the bottom he was the first they met. The photograph flashed as he shook hands with Jordi Pujol, the man whom he had called a dwarf. He was cool and respectful as he shook hands with the King and Queen.

This was the homecoming of a whole generation, the men and women who had been hauled out of Zeleste in the 1970s by the police. This was their apotheosis.

4

City Without Walls

Against the grey traditional houses all round it, the Palau de la Música Catalana, the city's concert hall, has all the appearances of an aberration, a dream building paid for by a mad king, or a capricious count, designed by an architect with more imagination than good sense. Somehow, it doesn't look serious.

Yet it remains a central point in the city's architectural and cultural development. Its architect was a conservative nationalist, twice elected a Member of Parliament, deeply respected among his own profession. It was paid for by the Orfeó Català, a choral society made up of the city's middle classes.

The style is known as Modernisme, and it was taken up by Catalan architects at the end of the nineteenth century as a national style from a number of sources, Art Nouveau and William Morris' arts and crafts movement being among them. In 1903, just two years before the Palau de Música was begun, the leading Barcelona architect Josep Puig i Cadafalch, wrote: 'the most important thing we have done is that we have made a modern art, taking our traditional arts as a basis, adorning it with new material, solving contemporary problems with a national spirit.' The national spirit had taken over everything by the turn of the century, culture and politics winding themselves around each other so that art, architecture, poetry and the Catalan language became as important politically as tariff rates, protectionism and industrial expansion.

The Catalan economy had begun to expand at the beginning of the nineteenth century, after the Napoleonic Wars. The textile industry began to grow, the first steam-powered machinery being installed in 1831 and the first automatic looms the following year. Catalonia became the fourth largest cotton textile producer after England, France and the United States. In 1848, the first railway line on the peninsula was built between Barcelona and Mataró, and in 1861 Barcelona established a rail link with Saragossa.

The wine and cork industries also flourished, the former greatly boosted by the phylloxera pest in France, so allowing Catalan wine merchants to double the price of a cask of wine. The steel industry also began to grow and flourish. Thus, towards the end of the nineteenth century and the beginning of the twentieth, Barcelona witnessed a display of capitalism at its most euphoric, its most prodigal and its most explosive.

The city simply burst open. There were too many people within its walls. As early as 1821 a French visitor wrote: 'The people do not fit in Barcelona'. The only solution was to knock down the walls and expand the city: the Passeig de Gràcia was, at that time, green pasture; Gràcia and Sarrià were villages outside the city, the buildings of Barcelona went no further than the Plaça de Catalunya.

The problem, as usual, was Madrid. The central government refused permission for the expansion of the city (which had a population of 115,000 in 1800, 175,000 in 1850, 346,000 in 1880 and 533,000 in 1900). During civil disturbances in 1854 the people of the city began to knock down the walls themselves and by the end of the 1850s it was agreed to put out tenders for a plan for the new city. The plan selected by the authorities in Barcelona was rejected by Madrid which chose a design for the expansion of Barcelona by the engineer Idlefons Cerdà. This proposed a grid-shaped system of streets, each block representing an octagon, with long sides – the streets of the new quarter – and shorter sliced-off corners.

This area became known in Spanish as the Ensanche and in Catalan as L'Eixample, meaning literally, 'the Extension'. It became the fashionable quarter of the city, to which the new merchants and the professional classes moved, having abandoned the old narrow streets of the Gothic quarter and the area around Santa Maria del Mar. These streets were wide, and the new apartments were well-ventilated, well-lit. The shops on the ground floor were the best in town. Cerdà designed the new city for the new class, who began to compete with each other for the most opulent and stylish new building, the most expensive and luxurious block of flats. From now on the architects would take over as the high priests of the bourgeois city.

More than a hundred years later the Eixample is still the core of the fashionable city, where the best shops are, where the best firms have their offices, where prices of flats are high and getting higher. If you don't mind the noise of the traffic pouring up like torrents of water from the street, it is a good place to live. Even the buildings which are dreary on the outside, too square and solid, too grey and functional, may have Art Nouveau plasterwork inside, or Modernista furniture, or huge windows at the back giving on to a balcony which catches the winter sun.

One of the earliest Modernista buildings in the Eixample and one of the most famous was done by Lluís Domènech i Montaner between 1881 and 1886, on Carrer d'Aragó 255, the headquarters of a publishing house. It had all the Moorish flavour which Domènech i Montaner and others, such as Gaudí, would use in later buildings. (Domènech i Montaner also designed El Palau de la Música.) It used brick, wrought iron and stained glass around an iron frame and exudes that vague medieval quality which so much of this style strives for, not merely innovative but Catalan as well.

The Eixample is full of such experiments and strange graftings from the tree of Modernisme. While some of the hallways are sombre, with unplastered stone walls and marble floors, others are bright with tiles and coloured glass, columns made of glass and wrought iron with floral designs in ceramics at the base, and arches in medieval style.

Gaudí became the most famous exponent of the new style, but there were others who belonged more to the mainstream of Modernisme such as Josep Puig i Cadafalch whose buildings can be found throughout the Eixample. His style moved from the strident neo-Gothic to the more gentle Germanic; the most striking example of the latter has become the Museum of Sport on the corner of Carrer de Buenos Aires and Carrer de Casanova. Many of his buildings culminate in spiky towers, amongst them the Casa Serra at the corner of Rambla de Catalunya and Carrer de Corcega, or his Casa de les Punxes at the corner of Diagonal and Carrer de Bruc. His work kept harking back. Just as a modern composer might quote Bach, Puig's work continued to use central motifs from Gothic architecture and the medieval world. Even the two family houses he designed in the first few years of the new century on Tibidabo, the hill overlooking the city, were exercises in pastiche, using modern techniques.

His first important building in the city had all the elements he was to play with until he was forbidden to practise as an architect at the end of the Civil War: he designed the Quatre Gats building in Carrer de Montsió where Picasso and his friends used to drink in the early years of the century. It, too, was full of medieval flourishes, ornate sculptures, Wagnerian iconography, but it used brick and wrought iron to complete the Modernista picture.

His best-known building is probably the Casa Amatller on Passeig de Gràcia beside Gaudí's Casa Battló and a few doors down from Domènech i Montaner's Casa Lleó i Morera. This block of houses on Passeig de Gràcia became known as la Manzana de la Discordia, the block of discordance, owing to its set of ambitious buildings, all of which were designed in a different variation on the Modernista style. Puig i Cadafalch's building here is as neo-Gothic as the rest of his large-scale work in the city, its façade is sumptuously decorated, the windows on each floor are done in a different shape and style, the symmetry coming only in a castellated roof. Again, he used wrought iron on the outside, adding to the fairy-tale medieval quality of the building, making it look even more like something out of a picture-book than Gaudí's building next door. Inside he combined Art Nouveau stained glass with the Gothic atmosphere of the palaces on Carrer de Montcada.

After the breath-taking innovations which both Gaudí and Puig i Cadafalch made on the façades of their buildings on la Manzana de la Discordia, the building on the corner looks dull, drab, not worth stopping for. It is only when you go inside Domènech i Montaner's Casa Lleó that you get some idea of what an important addition this is to the general level of discordance. This is much sweeter, much less severe than the general run of his work. The walls and ceilings are decorated in a brightly coloured Art Nouveau floral pattern and at the back there is a huge room in stained glass, with patterns of red and yellow flowers. It is a rich study in Modernista opulence.

His Hospital de la Santa Creu i Sant Pau, which eventually replaced the medieval hospital buildings in Carrer Hospital, is more austere, and on a much greater scale – the complex includes twenty-six buildings – but his stamp is still there in the use of brick, tiles and wrought iron, in the use of decoration and colour. Of all the architects who designed the new buildings of the Eixample, Domènech i Montaner was the most hard-working and influential. He was involved, for example, in three buildings which are almost side by side on Carrer Mallorca (the Palau Montaner, the Casa Iglesias and the Casa Thomas). Perhaps the best and most accessible of his buildings is the restaurant, still functioning, of the Hotel España on Carrer de Sant Pau, behind the Liceu Opera House. Every element in Domènech i Montaner's exotic and fanciful iconography comes into play in the restaurant: the colourful tiles, full of heraldic allusions as well as references to mermaids and the sea; the carved ceiling inlaid with patterns of fruit and flowers; the huge wrought iron lamps; the arched door-ways; and set against all this, the plain unadorned wall between the tiles and the ceiling. Here he left out nothing. His restaurant remains untouched, locked in the time warp of Modernisme, and more than eighty years after it was built it still looks wild and wonderful, beyond belief.

Lluís Domènech i Montaner was also one of the main architects involved in the Great Exhibition of 1888, which set about putting Barcelona on the map of the world, now that the walls had been knocked down, now that the city had gone through the years of enormous prosperity known as the gold fever. Paris and London had held exhibitions: Barcelona was now ready to declare itself. The site chosen for the Great Exhibition had its own significance as a symbol in the city: it was the site of the Parc de la Ciutadella, where Philip V had knocked down hundreds of houses to make a fortification in 1714 after the siege of Barcelona. It was a symbol of the oppression of Catalonia, and now it would be the arena in which the city's new wealth and flair and modernity would be paraded.

Just thirty years before, Barcelona had been the most insanitary and congested city in Europe, more like Calcutta than the Paris it would now come to admire and copy. In the months before the

Great Exhibition feverish building went on: the people of the city came down to stand and gape at the construction of the Gran Hotel International on the Passeig de Colom which was going on by night as well as by day, with the help of electric light.

It would be built in fifty-three days by what one writer would call 'its army of high-spirited workers one to two thousand strong'. It had all of Domènech i Montaner's hall-marks and made use also – for this Great Exhibition was to be about progress above all – of new materials such as light ironwork frames, hollow brick walls, and prefabricated structural and ornamental elements. Some of the hotel was built on a floating platform over a ruined embankment in the port.

Part of its curiosity value was that it would be knocked down as soon as the Great Exhibition was over. The young Puig i Cadafalch, fifteen at the time of the Great Exhibition, couldn't believe his eyes. The Gran Hotel Internacional was his 'first vision of that great Barcelona for which we are all working'. Such visions were appearing all over the city. In that same year Gaudí's Palau Güell in Carrer Nou de la Rambla was under construction, the previous year the Palau Marcet at the corner of the new Gran Via and Passeig de Gràcia was built; all over the Eixample the solid five-storey buildings were being put up. The Casa Maria Robert on Gran Via was built that year, as was the market complex on Carrer d'Aragó and the medieval-style Casa Antoni Roger on Carrer d'Ausiàs Marc, designed by Enric Sagnier i Vilavecchia, whose Casa Juncadella on Rambla de la Catalunya was also under construction in this *annus mirabilis* of 1888.

After the Great Exhibition, visited by two million people, the city would never be the same again. The Columbus statue at the bottom of the Rambla, full of frills and decorations, was put up; the Arc de Triomf on Passeig de Lluís Companys celebrated the triumph of Catalan enterprise after years of Catalan defeat and humiliation. Close by, a statue was raised to Roger de Llúria, one of the Catalan mercenaries of the fourteenth century who had taken the Mediterranean by storm. In the Park itself an *Hivernacle* and an *Umbracle* were built using modern techniques to grow exotic plants and flowers. Domènech i Montaner also designed the Café Restaurant of the Great Exhibition which would be known as the Castell dels Tres Dragons. This building, on the Passeig de Picasso side of the park, had great influence on the young architects of the city (Domènech i Montaner also taught at the new school of architecture, set up in 1875) in its use of a steel frame and brick walls, in its reference to the Catalan heritage, in its insistence on traditional craftsmanship and a conservative, nationalist imagery. After the Great Exhibition Domènech kept the building in use as a workshop for the artisans who had come to the city.

The economic boom brought with it other cultural developments, in particular the literary movement known as La Renaixença. There had been very little literary activity in Catalan in the sixteenth, seventeenth and eighteenth centuries. After 1714 the language was no longer allowed to be taught in the schools or used officially. It was a private language, used colloquially. After centuries of silence a number of long poems published in Catalan in the nineteenth century re-awakened interest in the importance of Catalan in the past and its possibilities as a contemporary literary language. The medieval poetry competition, the *jocs florals*, was reinstated in 1859, the same year as the Eixample was begun. Many of the poems which emerged in the new literary revival were deeply patriotic in tone. A newspaper in Catalan was established in 1879.

In the 1870s a great interest developed in the Catalan landscape and the movement known as Excursionisme began. Groups of Catalans would wander through the foothills of the Pyrenees or the mountains of Tarragona province, rediscovering their heritage; the movement had deep nationalistic overtones. At the same time, a group of Catalan painters moved out into the countryside and worked in the open air. Certain places, such as the mountains of Montseny and the Canigó, became sacred repositories, special places where it was thought that the spirit of Catalonia could be found at its most intense.

But it was music which most moved the national soul. Among the workers in the new factories a choral movement began, led by Josep Anselm Clavé, a militant Republican, who became a Member of Parliament in 1873; by 1861 there were eighty-five workers' choirs in Catalonia. The Liceu, the city's opera house on the Rambla, was opened in 1847 and rebuilt in 1861 after a fire. The city became addicted to the operas of Wagner; the march from *Tannhäuser* was first sung in Catalonia by a workers' choir in 1862. Wagner's medieval myth-making, the bloated rhetoric of his orchestral settings, the scale and ambition of his work suited the new merchants of Barcelona who, as the century moved to a close, matched it with their Modernista buildings. Between 1901 and 1910 working libretti of Wagner's operas were published in Catalan.

During this period the ballads were written which would stir the hearts of the Catalans, which glorified the Catalan tradition, the Catalan flag and the Catalan landscape, and which would in future years become rallying cries. The Orfeó Català was founded, a choral society, which performed the great choral works such as Bach's *Mass in B Minor* and Beethoven's *Missa Solemnis* in Catalan. At the turn of the century this society commissioned the Palau de la Música.

'Barça', the football club, was also founded at the turn of the century, and quickly became a crucial factor in the city's culture, a vehicle for integrating the new immigrant workers into the life of Barcelona. In times of political difficulty it took on all the force of a political party, an unarmed army. Its victories were political victories, its games mass meetings.

Almost everything was in place. Catalonia's former greatness was being conjured up and exploited by the nation's poets and architects; the fact that Catalonia was great once more was being proclaimed by her leading sons; the language was finding new adherents and it too would soon be as vital and expressive as the new buildings of the Eixample. The Catalan landscape was being reinvented for the new generation. There was only one ingredient missing and that was politics. By the end of the nineteenth century, the new prosperous classes, the Catalan entrepreneurs, industrialists and bankers found it increasingly difficult to function under the dead weight of Spanish centralism and they made constant demands on Madrid, which saw Barcelona as more and more unruly and troublesome. The national sentiment was thus matched by a national grievance. The men who organized the Great Exhibition of 1888 now put their considerable weight behind forging

a new political identity for Catalonia. The battle which would
end in the Civil War was underway.

Until the end of the Civil War two separate forces operated in
the city of Barcelona, one representing the men of property, the
new class of Catalan merchants, the other representing the new
class of factory, artisan and immigrant workers. They constantly
misunderstood, disappointed and provoked each other. The
problem was that both forces sought radical change: the former
group wanted modernization and economic and political autonomy, while the latter, in the end, wanted revolution. Just as the
first force had embraced Modernisme and made it the emblem of
its brave new world in the Eixample, the working class of the city
embraced Anarchism.

*

The architect Lluís Domènech i Montaner became one of the
leading voices in the chorus of industrialists and intellectuals calling
for a federal Spain and an autonomous Catalonia. As early as 1869,
when he was nineteen, Domènech i Montaner was a member of
La Jove Catalunya, a nationalist group. He was among those who
founded the Lliga de Catalunya in 1887, the party which represented, as the Lliga Regionalista, Catalan bourgeois interests over
the next forty years.

An account of Catalan grievances and demands was presented
to Madrid on several occasions such as the *Memorial de Greuges* in
1885 and the *Bases de Manresa* in 1892. But it was the loss of
Cuba in 1898 which galvanized Catalan opinion. In the Catalan
countryside, the eldest son inherited everything, leaving the
younger males of the family to go into business, or to go abroad.
Great fortunes had been made out of Cuba, and Catalans had
come to see Cuba as a Catalan preserve rather than a Spanish
colony. They deeply resented what they saw as Spanish incompet-
ence in losing the island.

The Lliga, representing this resentment, thus triumphed in the
elections of 1901. Domènech i Montaner was one of the new
deputies elected to the Cortes in Madrid. The Republicans came
second. That same year both parties took power in Barcelona's
City Council. The Lliga, according to the historian Isidre Molas,

'encouraged traditionalism and was a lever for the conservative classes, who never identified fully with it, but supported it as the strongest defence against movements of the left.'

The Lliga's main achievement, besides consolidating and controlling Catalan bourgeois interests, was the *Mancomunitat*, which was set up in 1914 as a confederation of the four provinces of Barcelona, Girona, Tarragona and Lleida, with responsibility for local administration. It managed to improve local services and founded a number of important cultural institutions, such as the Institute of Catalan Studies. It also established Barcelona's reputation as a capital city. When Prat de la Riba, its first President, died in 1917, he was replaced by Josep Puig i Cadafalch, the architect, who had been first elected to the Cortes in Madrid in 1907. Thus two of the city's leading architects, Puig i Cadafalch and Domènech i Montaner, who had attempted to forge a national style in Catalonia, had become leading politicians. In those years in Catalonia, culture, capitalism and politics were inextricably connected.

While the Catalan merchants were busy building a national spirit on one hand and disposable hotels on the other, the working class of the city lived in great poverty and misery. In 1856 a married man with two children living in Barcelona was said to need 4000 reals a year to live on; yet an unskilled worker's average yearly wage was less than 2500. The pattern of low wages in the city continued. In 1900, for example, when the city was swelling with unskilled workers who had come from all parts of Spain to satisfy the demand for labour in Barcelona, a family of four was said to need 14,50 reals a day for subsistence; an unskilled worker in Barcelona earned only ten reals.

It is not surprising that serious and powerful radical movements would emerge in the city. The Catalan economy during these years went through a considerable number of crises and collapses. No one's position was secure, no worker's wages were safe. In 1885 a metal worker earned five pesetas a day; by 1900, after the loss of Cuba, it had gone down to four. The Catalans who wanted imagination and innovation in their buildings and their politics remained stubborn employers.

The emerging nationalism in Catalonia didn't hamper the

development of radicalism in the city. Many workers, who came from elsewhere, were hostile to Catalan, or were bemused and puzzled by the new language and culture; others, born in the city, were affected more deeply by their exploitation by their fellow Catalans than by any shared national identity. Other groups combined left-wing politics with nationalism.

Trade unions had been founded by the city's textile workers as early as the 1830s. When unions were banned by the central government in 1855 there was a general strike in the city for nine days, the first of its kind in Spain. Many of the factories in Barcelona remained small, some no larger than workshops; many were undercapitalized and badly managed. Housing conditions were poor, the people unhealthy.

The first disciple of Bakunin arrived in Barcelona in October 1868 and travelled from there to Madrid. His name was Giuseppe Fanelli. He made conversions in Madrid. 'Spaniards,' wrote Gerald Brenan in *The Spanish Labyrinth*, 'had long been waiting for this moment . . . Fanelli, whose money was running low, took the train to Barcelona. He left behind him copies of the statutes of Social Democracy, the rules of a Geneva working-class society, a few numbers of Herzen's *Bell* and various Swiss and Belgian newspapers, containing reports of speeches by Bakunin. These were the sacred texts on which the new movement was to be constructed. At Barcelona his success was repeated . . . Within the space of less than three months, without knowing a word of Spanish or meeting more than an occasional Spaniard who understood his French or Italian, he had launched a movement that was to endure, with wave-like advances and recessions, for the next seventy years and to affect profoundly the destinies of Spain.'

Anarchism had taken a hold in Barcelona, among the workers and the trade unions. 'The next twenty years,' Gerald Brenan wrote, 'are the most obscure and ill-defined in the history of Spanish Anarchism.' Small groups formed in villages; 'millenarian fervour', in Gerald Brenan's phrase, would lead to a mass demonstration or strike, and then there would be nothing; groups joined together and broke away from each other; Anarchism had intellectual adherents as well as small groups who believed in random acts of violence.

Thus the closing year of the century could produce in Barcelona a magazine such as *Acràda* on the one hand, and bomb-throwers on the other: both believing in the theories of Bakunin, both looking forward to the great day when man would no longer be a slave to capital, when the Church, the Government, the Army and all others who sought to govern their fellow men would be cast aside. *Acràcia* was carefully and subtly written, dealing with complex issues of politics, economics, demography, morality, revolution. Its tone was thoughtful, while its content was strictly Anarchist. During the years when it appeared Barcelona became known as The City of the Bombs.

The first attack was in 1891 at the headquarters of the Catalan Employers' Federation. In 1892, there was an attempt to assassinate General Martínez de Campos in Barcelona. The assailant, Paulí Pallàs, was later executed, and in reprisal, another Anarchist, Santiago Salvador, threw two bombs into the stalls of the Liceu Opera House during a production of *William Tell* in December 1893. One exploded, killing twenty people and wounding others. (The other bomb survived intact, and photographs of it, round and shiny with spikes sticking out, would appear regularly in the Catalan press.) The Liceu was the heart and soul of fashionable Barcelona; the Anarchists were now at war with Catalan bourgeois society.

The police and the city authorities did not understand what was going on. Police intelligence had not expanded with the city's Anarchist population. Thus each outrage would be followed by the arrest and torture of large numbers of trade unionists, Anarchists and workers' leaders, most of whom had nothing to do with the crime. The historian H. B. Clarke wrote in 1906: 'Holders of advanced opinions, though peaceable citizens, might if they fell into the hands of the police be treated like wild beasts.' David Hannay, the British Vice-Consul in Barcelona, later wrote: 'The memory of the torturings in Montjuic [of Anarchist prisoners] has done more to excite the social hatred of the poor against the rich – a sentiment once hardly known in Spain, but now too common.'

During Corpus Christi 1896 the next bomb was thrown at the religious procession moving along Carrer dels Canvis Nous to Santa Maria del Mar. Six people were killed, and the usual suspects were rounded up and tortured. The bomb, wrote Jan Reed in *The Catalans,* 'was used as a pretext for arresting union leaders in no way concerned with the attacks; but instead of breaking the unions, as employers had hoped, it simply swelled the ranks of the Anarchists, while the workers, for whom conditions had not materially changed over the past century, were still further estranged from their employers.'

In the new century the general strike replaced the bomb as the main Anarchist weapon against the yoke of capitalism. The new century also saw the growth of the Radical Party in Barcelona, a grouping led by Alejandro Lerroux, who at that time, before his later conversion to the Conservative cause, espoused anti-clericalism and opposed Catalan nationalism. In 1900 the first piece of social legislation since 1873 was passed by Parliament, which included a workers' compensation act, and laws limiting a woman's working day to eleven hours and banning work for children under the age of fourteen. There was also a general strike in the textile industry that year. In the following year, 1901, Francesc Ferrer published his periodical *La Huelga General* which proposed industrial action as a prelude to revolution. There was a general strike in the city during the first week of May. Ferrer also founded the Escola Moderna in September, a school which taught Anarchist principles. Within four years there would be forty-seven such schools in Barcelona. Among Ferrer's admirers was one Salvador Dalí, father of the painter. In 1902 a metal workers' strike in February became a general strike. In the subsequent strife between the police and the workers there were ten deaths and more than 350 arrests. Workers' centres were closed.

'Barcelona', Gerald Brenan wrote, 'now and for the next twenty years became the scene of extraordinarily complicated and unscrupulous manoeuvres: radical Republicans contested elections with the secret support of Conservative Madrid: gangsters were taken into the pay of the Government, the Anarchists were provoked or egged on and the police themselves laid bombs at the doors of peaceful citizens in an endeavour either to intimidate the Catalan Nationalists or to produce a state of affairs in which the constitutional guarantees could be suspended.'

In July 1909, when the Spanish Army was defeated in

Morocco, the Government called up the reserves in Catalonia. The reserves had to come from the lower classes, as anyone with money bought himself out of the Army. In the Cuban War a great number of soldiers had been killed and mutilated, and now nobody wanted to go to war so that the commercial interests of the Spanish merchant class would be protected. The situation wasn't improved when a number of rich women from Barcelona, bearing holy medals, scapulars and tobacco for the soldiers, appeared at the port as the first ship of troops was due to leave. Mass meetings were held to protest. In Terrassa, one leader spoke against sending 'useful citizens to the war who are indifferent as to whether the Cross triumphs over the half-moon, when you could form regiments of priests and monks who, as well as being directly concerned with the success of the Catholic religion, have no family, no home and are of no use to the country.'

Gradually, over that week in July 1909, the target of protest in the city ceased to be the State, the Army or the rich, and became the Church. The Anarchists had always been anti-clerical, as had the Radicals under Alejandro Lerroux. ('Enter and sack the decadent civilisation of this unhappy country!' Lerroux had said. 'Destroy its temples, finish off its gods, raise the skirts of the novices and elevate them to the status of mothers!') In five days the union leaders and Anarchist leaders lost control and mobs ruled, twenty-two churches and thirty-four convents were burned, members of the clergy were killed, tombs were desecrated. The reprisals were equally bloody; figures vary as to the number of workers shot on the streets but it was certainly close to a hundred. Five Anarchist leaders, including Francesc Ferrer, who edited *La Huelga General* and had founded the Anarchist schools, were executed. Ferrer had taken no part in the violence. The Lliga Regionalists, representing the Catalan middle classes, supported the Government in the harsh measures taken against the Anarchists and Republicans in the city. The Republican leader, Lerroux, had taken no part in the events of what became known as *La Setmana Tràgica* (The Tragic Week), and many of his disillusioned followers moved to the Anarchist camp.

The First World War made things worse. After the boom in production, which was considerable, came the slump. By the end of the war there were 140,000 workers unemployed in the city, which had become in the words of Gerald Brenan 'the refuge of every sort of international criminal'. Between 1914 and 1920 inflation ran at 190 per cent, while wages rose by only 115 per cent. Barcelona was becoming increasingly chaotic as both employers and Anarchists made use of assassination squads.

The central organization of Spanish Anarchism, the CNT, was formed in 1911. By 1917 it had 714,000 members. Between 1910 and 1923 there were 800 strikes in the city. The largest strike came in 1919 when the workers of the electrical company, 'La Canadiense', went on strike. When a large number of union leaders in the city were arrested, and military law was declared, a general strike began, and lasted for two weeks, with 100,000 workers participating. The city was crippled, the stoppage was total. This time the Government gave in, offered an eight-hour day and obligatory pensions for workers. But it was not to be the pattern: a second general strike failed that same year and by August 1919 there were thousands of trade unionists in prison in Barcelona.

The Catalan employers demanded that the Government impose order on the city and demanded the banning of the CNT, to which eighty per cent of the workers in Barcelona belonged. They continued to employ private hired assassins, and the workers continued to retaliate. In sixteen months 230 people were shot in the streets. As the Lliga moved further to the right, new national-ist parties were founded, encouraged greatly by the shake-up in Europe after the First World War. 'Some were deeply impressed by events in Ireland,' wrote the historian Isidre Molas, 'and Ire-land became a symbol for the most radical workers of Barcelona.' One of the new parties founded was called Nosaltres Sols, a direct translation of Sinn Fein. But by far the most important was Estat Català, established in 1922 to offer policies which were both nationalist and radical.

The coup came in September 1923 when the Captain General of Catalonia, Miguel Primo de Rivera, declared himself Dictator and took over power in Spain. The Catalan bourgeoisie supported the dictatorship; the architect Puig i Cadafalch, as President of the Mancomunitat, lent his support to Primo de Rivera, believing that he would impose order on the city's workers and assist the cause of Catalan nationalism.

The Dictator responded by banning the Catalan flag and insisting that the Catalan language was for use in the home only. He saw bourgeois nationalism and radical trade unionism as equally dangerous. In 1924 he dissolved the Mancomunitat and declared the CNT illegal. In 1925 he banned the Orfeó Català, still the main choir in the city, and closed the Barcelona football club (the crowd attending a football match had booed the Spanish national anthem). The Catholic Church supported him and ceased to use Catalan in churches and seminaries.

*

The Lliga lived to write history; the Anarchists' dreams came to dust. The class who built the Eixample came to be remembered for their Great Exhibition of 1888, for their Modernista buildings, for their patriotism. The fact that they paid less than subsistence wages to the workers who carted the stones which fulfilled their dream of a great new city did not become part of the myth, nor that they employed assassins to gun down trade union leaders, nor that they supplied both sides in the First World War, nor that they were prepared to support the dictatorship of Miguel Primo de Rivera. These men, as time went on, would be held high in the esteem of their compatriots.

The world they gave birth to, Catalan-speaking, conservative, bourgeois, still survives in the city. Eighty years after it was built, their Palau de la Música Catalana is still breath-taking in its daring and its style. This is where on a Saturday night, for the weekly concert by the city's orchestra, you will find Catalan bourgeois society at its most refined. The building is rich in colour: indeed the tiles, the mosaic-work and the stained glass look almost garish. 'Yet in its opulence, the force of its imaginative structure and texture, it is a symbol of the city's arrival from the darkness into the light of prosperity, the light of culture. The concert programme notes are now printed in Catalan only, and Catalan is the predominant language of the audience. The Palau de la Música has never been an exclusive club or a fashionable venue, everyone enters by the same door, when the lights go down, and you feel that hush of an audience settling down in their beautiful building full of flourish and fantasy, you get close to the core of the Catalan bourgeois dream.

Until the fire in 1994, the Liceu Opera House was like the kingdom of heaven, except the other way around. The rich came in by the main door; the others entered by the side. If you sat with the rich, you felt uneasy, as though another anarchist bomb could at any moment land on you from on high. If you sat above in the cheap seats it was often hard to see and uncomfortable. The public bars were in bad repair, dark and dingy; the private bars had fine murals by Ramon Casas. The great singers continued to come. In 1988 both Placido Domingo and Joan Sutherland sang here, as well as Montserrat Caballé and Jose Carreras. The building itself had nothing of the Palau de la Musica's florid turn-of-the-century sumptuousness. It was a big, grand nineteenth-century opera house in the Italian style. People did not come to it to be seen; it was a part of their tradition, they came for the music. The opera house was privately owned by a large number of shareholders who inherited rights to certain seats in the theatre. These old Catalan families go back a long time. The Barcelona bourgeoisie are one of the few non-disturbed owner classes in Europe outside Switzerland. They took part in neither world war, nor, to any extent, in the Spanish Civil War. They have survived intact. The descendants of the families who built the Liceu and re-built it after the first fire in 1861 could be seen on Gala nights with their children and their grandchildren coming to hear Wagner once more, as they have done all their lives.

After the fire in 1994, as the Town Hall and the Catalan government and other official bodies set about re-building the Liceu, these families had to give up most of their ancient rights. Negotiations with them were lengthy and difficult. The opera house was a great symbol of their power and wealth and culture. Eventually, they ceded ownership and the money from the insurance. In return, they have priority booking for their old boxes and seats. It was decided to re-build the theatre as it was. It was decided also to destroy some of the buildings around the opera house and evict their tenants to add offices and better rehearsal space. This addition to the Liceu is one of the ugliest new buildings in Barcelona. In 2000, when I pointed out to one of the best-known architects in the city that the Liceu extension destroys the vista as you walk towards the Rambla along Carrer Ferran, he shrugged and said that it was unlikely that the architects had taken that into account.

The new Liceu, which opened its doors in 2000, has none of the grandeur mixed with shabbiness of the old Liceu. The old porters and ushers, doddery in their ancient uniforms, have been replaced by young people, all shiny and bright. All the public spaces are shiny and bright as well. And the auditorium and stage is now a massive and state-of-the-art television studio, created in the knowledge that opera can only pay for itself through television and video rights. The first time I went there was to see Montserat Caballé in *Tosca*. My seat was cheap, but no one told me when I was buying it that the only way I could get to see the stage was to lean forward and put my hands on the shoulders of the people in front of me and then lean forward some more. I had the courage to do this only once – for the climax of 'Vissi d'arte' – because the people in front of me went crazy. Now the big campaign was to let the ordinary taxpayer know that the Liceu was for them too. The new glossy brochure called the Liceu 'un teatre de tots' (a theatre for all). It has been called many things in its long history, but this was new. It was as though the fire had purged the class hatred and the class history that had made the Liceu a symbol of Catalan life over so many years.

*

The men who founded the city left us the Eixample. It is at its best, perhaps, on winter evenings at six o'clock, when the shops are still open and business is still going on. Passeig de Gràcia and Rambla de Catalunya, the two main shopping streets of the Eixample, have a glamour to be found nowhere else in Barcelona, in the faces, the clothes, the hairstyles. But always there is a sense of purpose, people carry briefcases and files. Everyone seems to be on their way somewhere. In the last two hours of the working day the Eixample buzzes with business and purchasing power.

There is a special pleasure in using these buildings, in doing business in these offices, or visiting apartments in the Eixample.

The dimly lit hallways, the mysteries of ceramic and glass, tiles and wrought iron, with the carved wood of the lifts, the floral patterns, the outrageous mixtures of colours and elements create an extraordinary atmosphere. And then the odd building which looks as though it missed all the fun is sober and grey on the outside, and inside yields up new designs within the constellations of Modernisme. The chemist shops look like sets for Wagner in street after street of the Eixample; most of them are still perfectly preserved, open for business now at seven in the evening; the woodwork, the tiles, the colours are all part of a dream which began with the generation of 1888.

As 1992 and the Olympics come closer, these are the people the city looks up to: the men who dreamed the great capitalist dream in Catalonia, the architects who put that dream into stone. These are the men the city sought to commemorate in 1988 on the hundredth anniversary of the Great Exhibition. Domènech i Montaner's building at the entrance to the Parc de la Ciutadella housed a new exhibition to commemorate the Great Exhibition; special ramps and walkways were placed between the Arc de Triomf and the park; nearby, a special exhibition was held of the projects for 1992, showing what the future held for Barcelona.

The big commemoration, however, was held in the summer. On one of those sweltering nights in July, one hundred and fifty thousand people gathered in the avenue between the Arc de Triomf and the Parc de la Ciutadella to hear the Barcelona tenor, José Carreras, sing. The concert was free, but those who gave money to the charity which Carreras had nominated received a card explaining that this concert was an act of homage to the men who had built Barcelona, the men of 1888. It was also an act of thanksgiving, as this was Carreras' first concert since his recovery from a serious illness. The Queen of Spain was there, as was the President of Catalonia and the city's Mayor.

Towards the end of the concert, after he had sung his light Italian drinking songs and his songs by modern Catalan composers, Carreras stopped and consulted with the pianist. We could see him on huge screens which had been placed at the sides. Both performers searched through the music, looking for something. And then they seemed to find it, the pianist settled down, and

Carreras stood ready to sing. When the first notes sounded, the whole avenue began to cheer. I didn't recognize the opening notes, and when I turned to the man beside me and asked him, he answered me with a kind of exasperation: '*L'Emigrant*,' he said impatiently.

There was silence now, as the piano introduction continued, waiting for the voice: *Dolça Catalunya pàtria del meu cor*. For the crowd, it was not just a song, it was a national hymn. They lit their cigarette lighters as the song went on, and held the flames in the air in solidarity with the spirit of the song. All around us the city's middle classes stood with tears in their eyes and lumps in their throats.

In their emotion, however, there was more pride than anger, more self-satisfaction than hatred of the traditional oppressor. So when Carreras began the Italian opera arias, he was greeted with delight: this too was central to the Catalan tradition, part of the reason they loved their country. They knew these songs. At the end, for the second encore, another great Barcelona singer, Montserrat Caballé, came on stage with roses in the shape of a heart which she presented to Carreras, and they sang together. He started the toast from *La Traviata*; she stood beside him and listened, we could see her face clearly on the screen, we could see her acting out the part of the diva who had been caught unawares, pretending she wasn't going to know the words.

And then the time came, and her voice was startling in its strength and force, loud and clear in the hot night. When the chorus came, she urged the crowd to sing, she and Carreras stopped, and left the people of the city on their own. Everyone seemed to know the words and the tune, everyone around us sang it out, the toast from *La Traviata*, as though they had known it all their lives.

5

A Dream of Gaudí

The old man left no memoirs. He gave no interviews, nor did he have any intimate friends. He disliked being photographed, so the few images we have of him – as a good-looking young man with a beard, as an old man carrying a canopy in a religious procession – appear over and over in the many volumes written about his life and his work.

Most of our information comes from a few books written by young architects who came to know him in the last decade of his life, the years when he was living in a small house in the grounds of the Park Güell. He would get up at seven in the morning and walk to Mass in Gràcia; he took communion every day; after Mass he walked to his beloved Sagrada Família on which he worked exclusively between 1909 and his death in 1926. So much to be solved: each stone, each piece of sculpture, each shape had to fit his grand plan. All day he would work there, figuring out his huge building. He would cross the street to watch as a new flourish was added to the rising towers of the church. He would change his mind, come back, order it to be removed, and start again.

'He existed in his private world', wrote one of his collaborators, 'with essentially nothing in common with those who surrounded him.' His Sagrada Família, the crowning glory of the new Barcelona, was to be a church more than double the size of Saint Mark's in Venice, sixty-five feet higher than Saint Peter's in Rome, with five longitudinal and three transverse naves, a lobe-shaped apse, nine chapels and two winding staircases. It was designed to hold 13,000 seated people. It was, he said, to be a pauper's Bible; it would tell the whole story in stone.

Why, a visiting bishop asked him, did he trouble himself so much about the tops of the towers? After all, no one would ever see them. 'Your Grace,' he said, 'the angels will see them.' Daily he faced the most complex problems of weight and stress, but he never lost sight of the aim: his Sagrada Família was to be an expiatory temple 'to induce the powers of heaven to have pity on Catalonia'.

Detail was vital to his design; he gave each small thing equal importance. He made a model for a pew which would be comfortable only when sat on correctly: crossing one's legs in church was not part of his dream. He was famous for his austerity, his old clothes, his long fasts, his vegetarianism. He ate lunch in his workshop and continued working until six or seven in the evening when he would walk to Passeig de Sant Joan and then down towards the Cathedral. He would make his way to the Plaça de Sant Felip Neri to attend evening devotions in the church.

The city is studded with his work, done during its period of prosperity and expansion. A hundred years later, the buildings he designed are still daring and original, yet also lurid and fanciful. His Casa Vicens, hidden away in a side-street in Gràcia, is still startling in its use of Moorish elements and styles, in its colours and in its use of wrought iron and ceramic decoration. Gaudí was twenty-six, just out of architectural college, when he designed it. Like everything else he did, Casa Vicens seems to have its roots in something deeply personal, its iconography and shape coming from within him as though he were a painter or a poet rather than a house-builder.

Gaudí was born in the province of Tarragona. His family, like Joan Miró's, were artisans. He spoke only Catalan for most of his life, refusing to speak Spanish. He seldom left Catalonia; once, in 1878, in the company of other Catalan nationalists, he visited Carcassonne, which the architect Viollet-le-Duc was in the process of restoring. But in general he had no interest in anything outside Catalonia. Like his colleagues Puig i Cadafalch and Domènech i Montaner, he saw his work as essentially political when young, as he would later come to see it as spiritual. He tried to invent an indigenous Catalan architecture.

He was lucky to have graduated at a time when the city was hungry for architects with new ideas, when the newly rich Catalan industrialists were anxious to embrace all that was innovative. In his twenties he worked on the fountain in the Parc de la Ciutadella;

he also designed the two large lamps in the centre of the Plaça
Reial and the street lamps in the Plaça del Palau. They still stand,
full of the sense of the medieval which characterizes Gaudí's work.
The metal of the lamps looks like carefully wrought armour, spiky
and menacing.

He believed, according to one of his associates, that the best
way to get to know a man was by spending his money, and judged
that the industrialist Eusebi Güell, for whom he worked between
1885 and 1914, was 'a gentleman in every sense of the word'. He
built him a house in Carrer Nou de la Rambla between 1885 and
1889 when other architects were busy on the Great Exhibition.
The house is now a centre for the study of the dramatic arts, and
is open to the public. From outside, the building is plain, less
imposing than the Casa Vicens which Gaudí finished in 1880.
The doors, however, have all of Gaudí's hallmarks: the shape of
the two entrance gates is parabolic, the iron is twisted into different
textures, the upper parts close to Art Nouveau, the lower more
patterned and forbidding. In between, also in wrought iron, is the
Catalan flag, crowned by an eagle.

The house looks more like a fortress than the palace of a
Catalan merchant prince. Perhaps for good reason: its neighbourhood is still one of the poorest and most deprived areas of
Barcelona. In a room opposite, ten years after Güell's house was
built, Picasso painted his Blue Period paintings. Picasso had no
time for Gaudí. He disliked his puritanism and his conservative
Catholicism. From Paris, he sent a postcard to a friend which
mentioned one of Gaudí's collaborators: 'If you see Opisso tell
him to come here as it is good for saving the soul – tell him to
send Gaudí and the Sagrada Família to hell.'

The style inside the Palau Güell is exquisitely incoherent,
clearly designed by an architect crazy about his materials, exulting
in the different uses to which they can be put: the stone and
wrought iron outside; inside, the marble, the wood, the ceramic
tiles, the brick, and again the wrought iron. From the first floor
up, the building is a study in marble, iron and wood. The wood
is inlaid, plain, or gilded, there are carved wooden animals in small
panels or in large settings: wooden floral designs or abstract,
vaguely Arabic patterns. So, too, the wrought iron is used in every

possible setting: on the interior balconies, staircases, door panels, window frames, ceilings. It is made to look like a pattern of briars and brambles around the doorway, or like the branches of a tree over a fireplace with lightbulbs emerging from each branch. The centrepiece of the house is the salon on the first floor which has a domed ceiling with holes to resemble stars and ethereal Pre-Raphaelite paintings on the walls. All of the rooms in the palace seem to flow out of this. It is clear that the architect's taste is for the exotic, the overworked, the over-expressed.

By the time Gaudí had finished Palau Güell, he was one of the most successful and fashionable architects in the city. He was already working on the Sagrada Família. He was made its chief architect in 1883 when he was thirty-one. He lived well. He travelled in a covered carriage from site to site, often giving instructions to the foreman without getting out. He dressed well and attended cafés and concerts and opening nights at the Liceu Opera House. But over the next ten years his religious feeling deepened; he began to avoid society and opening nights at the Liceu; became ascetic and puritan in his personal habits and more and more dogmatic, more temperamental, more dictatorial.

The idea for the Sagrada Família came from a rich Catalan publisher, Josep Maria Bocabella, who was concerned about the spread of revolutionary ideas in the city. He set up a society dedicated to Saint Joseph, patron of the worker and the family: the aim was to build a new church in the city to expiate the sins of the revolutionaries. Gaudí inherited the original architect's plans for a modest neo-Gothic church, but he began to imagine a construction on a much vaster scale, with an elaborate inner harmony. He saw it as a great monument for a profoundly Christian Catalonia. 'The man without religion,' he said, 'is a man spiritually ruined, a mutilated man.'

By 1894 Gaudí had formed the habit of going on long fasts. Towards the end of Lent that year he had been absent from the Sagrada Família for several days. On the Sunday before Easter some of his collaborators visited him. One of them, Picasso's friend Opisso, described the scene in Gaudí's flat in the Eixample: 'As soon as we had stepped through the door, we stopped, astounded by the squalor of the room. The wallpaper was peeling, because the architect had apparently forbidden anyone to touch it. His furniture consisted of nothing but a sagging bed and an uncomfortable cane sofa.' Gaudí was completely clothed, with an old coat thrown over him as a blanket. His colleagues called in Bishop Torras i Bages, an old friend, to persuade the architect to end his fast.

Güell, Gaudí's patron, travelled extensively, and it was through him that Gaudí came to see books and magazines about art and architecture outside Catalonia. It was through Güell, for example, that he became acquainted with the work of William Morris and his English contemporaries. In 1909 Güell commissioned Gaudí to design a park on the outskirts of the city, on which Gaudí worked sporadically for the next fourteen years. The original idea was to produce a colony of houses for rich people, but this never happened, and the park was later bought by the city for public use.

The Park Güell can be reached by taking the metro to Lesseps and walking along Travessera de Dalt. As you turn left and walk up the hill, the first ceramic pillar which comes into view, full of curves and dips, could only be by Gaudí, who seemed throughout his life to see the right-angle as a kind of aberration to be abhorred. There are no straight lines in nature, he said. He was in his element here on this hill above the city, letting art loose on nature. He reflected the wildness of the place in the wildness of stone. Everything here curves just as nature curves, the stone pillars look like tree trunks, the textures seem random and natural. He hated evenness.

On the steps inside the gate a huge stone frog squats, covered in coloured pieces of broken ceramic tiles, with water flowing out of its mouth. Despite the apparent innocence of the idea, there is something unsettling about what one commentator called 'the alarming Hansel and Gretel atmosphere' of his work here on the steps of the park. At the top of the steps is a plaza surrounded by a whirl of benches, also covered in broken and left-over pieces of ceramic tiles, each of them a different shape and colour. The benches are shaped like waves of the sea, curving and flowing, like something out of a dream. They seem to melt in the light above the city, the shattered ceramic scraps stuck together according to some indiscernible plan; they shine and glisten in the sun like something unfinished, something still growing. Under the plaza are groups of columns like a petrified forest, holding up the plateau above, growing into it.

There are long stretches of park, however, which Gaudí left alone. Small paths lead into bush and thicket while other sections are more formally laid out, like public gardens anywhere. It comes as a shock in the middle of this to find stone columns textured like trees rising at odd angles from the ground, leaning against a wall of stone, also at an odd angle to the ground. As you walk the length of the columns until they curve and twist around the shape of the hill, it is like being in a hall of mirrors. And as you look back the trees and vegetation in the park begin to look like human constructions and Gaudí's stonework like nature, what has always been there.

*

Gaudí's first building on Passeig de Gràcia was the Casa Battló, which he remodelled between 1905 and 1907, designing a new façade, the first floor and the roof. 'Architecture,' he had written, 'is an ordering of light.' Casa Battló seems to glisten and soften in the sun, looking as if it might fade away, evaporate. Like everything Gaudí did, it appears menacing; the first floor windows have columns shaped like bones, its shape disdains logic and sense, it looks more like an outburst than a building. And yet the detail is there again, painstaking in every aspect.

Further up Passeig de Gràcia on the opposite side stands his Pedrera, or Casa Milà, which many architects view as his greatest achievement. Here he replaced the ethereal with the geological and followed the shape of waves and the shape of the molten rock of the mountain of Montserrat. He used cut stone, with hammered surfaces which appear to be the result of natural erosion. He dispensed with interior load-bearing walls, so no two apartments are the same; he was the first architect to design a garage in the basement of a building. He worked out each detail, from servants' entrance to door handles to banisters.

The roof can be visited by the public each day now since the Casa Milà was bought by one of the city's savings banks. Here Jack Nicholson and Maria Schneider played games in Antonioni's film *The Passenger*. The roof, too, curves and waves. Pillars and chimneys stand like masked figures, phallic shapes. All around the city's new rational buildings can be seen, glass and steel, right-angles, straight lines.

The house is still lived in; none of the apartments has yet become a museum piece. Some of the tenants are said to pay low rents, fixed years ago. In the summer, in one of those blazing days of heat, a designer friend who had decorated one of the apartments in La Pedrera borrowed the key from the owner. We promised not to stay too long.

Gaudí's details were instantly apparent: the door handle was designed to be opened with the left hand, since the right hand would be turning the key.

Inside was a cave of light. A corridor circled the inside court-yard of the building; a door led into a huge living area with a ceiling whose plasterwork looped and curved in melting layers. It seemed to pull in the light from Passeig de Gràcia and play with it. Nothing was straight; each column on the balcony was different. The original floor designed by Gaudí was still in place, made of triangles in wood of different textures and shades. I had never been in a room like it before; it was softer, more comfortable and not as forbidding as the outside of the building suggested. The walls in their curve and flow decorated the room rather than defining its limits. Two other rooms led off the main one. Further down the corridor there were other quarters, which were cooler in the summer; each flat was designed with a winter and summer section. The bathroom was full of white light.

The flat was lived in; books and records lay about the place. A huge, modern, steel contraption with wheels for holding a stereo and a television set stood in the main living room; it fitted in perfectly with Gaudí's space as did the colours, a dark green and a dark blue in which the rooms had recently been painted, and the specially designed furniture and the painting by Miquel Barceló. That day it was like standing inside a work of art. This was the pinnacle of fashion, a specially designed pad in Gaudí's La Pedrera.

As Gaudí worked on the building he came more and more to see it as a shrine to the Virgin, the waves of stone culminating in a huge statue, four metres high, of the Virgin and Child with Saints Michael and Raphael. He also planned to have the opening words of the *Ave Maria* inscribed on the building. But it was not to be: in July 1909 Barcelona revolted, and what ensued became known as *La Setmana Tràgica*, during which churches and convents were burned. The Milà family, who had commissioned Gaudí, became alarmed, fearing that the building in which they had invested so much money might become a target for Anarchists in any future uprising. They instructed Gaudí to remove any external signs of religious devotion from the building. He was outraged and travelled to Blanes on the coast where Rosario Milà was staying: but she would not relent, telling Gaudí that religion was a private matter and did not call for external signs – 'even less so under the circumstances'. Gaudí was disgusted. He resigned from the job, leaving its completion to one of his assistants. He would never again accept a commission from a member of the Catalan bourgeoisie. He went back to his church in 1909 and devoted his energy to the Sagrada Família.

He spent the day among his papers and models. There was a bed where he slept sometimes. He joked that people, friends, avoided him when they saw him coming, in case he would ask them for money for his Temple. He often ran out of funds completely. For his façade of the Nativity, he used real models for the figures which were to decorate the stone: Picasso's friend Opisso was in charge of finding models and photographing them. Gaudí used a system of mirrors to capture the model from all angles and worked out a way of enlarging figures and changing perspective. Christ was a thirty-three-year-old worker, who was placed naked, except for a loin cloth, on a cross and photographed. The caretaker was used as Judas, a goatherd for Pilate, the grandson of one of Gaudí's collaborators for the infant Jesus, a local spinster for the Virgin. Gaudí made mad and inspired choices for his figures. For King Solomon he chose a rag-man from the Eixample, for a Roman soldier he found a barman from Tarragona who had six toes; Gaudí insisted that there be six toes on the statue as well.

Plaster casts were made of animals. In order to verify that the casts of the chickens were realistic, Gaudí ordered a chicken coop and placed the casts among the chickens to check that the attitudes

were correct. He also made casts from his human models. Poor
Opisso was to be the fourth herald angel: 'I undressed down to
my underpants, and Gaudí imperiously ordered me to assume the
pose he had in mind. The sculptors Llorenç Matamala and Ramon
Bonet covered my body with plaster. All of a sudden I was over-
come by such a bad cramp that I fainted.' The donkey for *The
Flight into Egypt* was cast from life. When Gaudí saw it kicking,
he ordered it to be hoisted into the air in a girdle. 'As soon as he
felt himself suspended in the void,' Gaudí said, 'he remained calm,
and it was thus possible to cast him easily.' Casts were also made
of plants and flowers. But the scorpion which tried to sting the
master was excluded from the façade.

He was still thinking and experimenting as his towers rose in
the sky. One of his detractors, Eugeni d'Ors, said that he went
home at night and prayed and then acted on the Virgin's advice.
'He didn't make plans,' said Joan Miró, who admired him, 'he
made gestures.' He was concerned about the bells of the Sagrada
Família, about which way the wind would blow and on certain
days he would arise at dawn and travel to various parts of the city
to observe the direction of the winds in the early hours of the
morning.

He remained a convinced Catalan nationalist, being held by
the police in 1924 on 11 September, Catalonia's national day,
during the dictatorship of Primo de Rivera, for trying to take part
in a commemoration in the Gothic church of Sant Just. The police
insulted him, calling him a *sin verguenza*, a man without shame;
he was released after a day, but this arrest was seen as another
example of the persecution of Catalonia.

By 1926 he was living in the workshop at the Sagrada Família.
He had been a misogynist all his life; he also disliked people
who wore glasses. He looked like a tramp, and was known now
in the city for his unworldliness. On 7 June he went as usual to
the Church of Sant Felip Neri to attend devotions. He was
crossing the Gran Via in the Eixample at six in the evening when
he was hit by a tram. No one recognized him, his clothes were
held together with pins, and the taxi drivers at first refused to
take him to the hospital. Eventually, he was taken to the public
ward of the Santa Creu in Carrer Hospital and moved to a private

room when they discovered he was the architect Gaudí. He lived for several days, the words 'Jesus My God' constantly on his lips. He died on 10 June.

A few days before his accident the first tower on the Nativity façade had been completed, and in the ten years following his death the three other towers were finished. He had been working for years on a model of the church, since he knew that he would not live to finish it: he would leave others to solve the problems of support and buttressing which so preoccupied him.

But his name and his great project, like everything in Catalonia, were associated with politics, with conservative, Catholic nationalism. Thus when the Civil War broke out in July 1936 the Anarchists came for his building. They destroyed and burned his workshops, the models, the casts, the archives, the plans, they smashed what sculptures they could find and destroyed the crypt. They opened and desecrated the tomb of Bocabella, who had wanted to build his expiatory temple, and of his wife. They opened Gaudí's coffin and it remained open until the war was over.

*

The best way to see the Sagrada Família now is to travel there by metro: you come out of the ground to be confronted with this enormous shock of stone, so rough and full of detail, so deeply original in its shape and conception.

There is nothing inside: just two façades out of a huge and complex design have been completed. Only a tiny part of the church has been built, and the eight towers which you can see from the hills around the city will be dwarfed in the end by what is to come. You notice immediately the difference between the towers which Gaudí oversaw and the recently-completed towers. The sculpture on Gaudí's façade is, for the most part, still there in all its strange lifelike detail, down to the animals, the flora and fauna and the Holy Innocents. You can stand back and take in item after item from Gaudí's menagerie, Gaudí's version of the Nativity. The sculpture on the other façade is done in a modern expressionist style; by comparison it is, to say the least, bland.

Gaudí's towers include internal staircases which rise to the top, so the whole city as well as the whole site can be surveyed. As you go up, you can see that each ledge has been separately designed, you can observe at close quarters the spiky shapes, the sense of nature trapped in stone which Gaudí worked on for forty years. His intransigence too can be experienced: it is difficult not to feel uneasy at how close some of the steps come to open ledges, it is difficult not to contemplate sudden death as you move from one staircase to another. Gaudí would have approved.

There are drawings on show, a model and various photographs, but nothing tells you that Gaudí's plans and models were destroyed in 1936 and that nothing remains except photographs of drawings, done mainly by Gaudí's associates. Nothing tells you that the architects have no idea how to proceed, that all they have is Gaudí's vision of what the church would look like in the end, but no idea of how he wanted it built. Nothing tells you that they are working from clues, that the church remained untouched between 1940 and 1956, that these years were spent trying to piece together the smashed model.

There has been pressure on them to stop, to leave what Gaudí did as a relic to be preserved but not added to. In the early 1960s Le Corbusier, Walter Gropius and others signed a letter calling on those in control of the Sagrada Família to leave it alone. There is in the city now an enormous argument over what should be done to the Sagrada Família: you can almost tell someone's politics by the view they take. The fashionable architects commissioned by the Socialists to design the sports facilities and living accommodation for the Olympic Games believe that work should stop on the Sagrada Família, or the job should be handed over to one great architect of stature equal to Gaudí's. They claim that the work going on now has nothing to do with Gaudí's vision, that it is 'mediocre architecture, superficial imitation'. Gaudí, one leading architect and Gaudí scholar points out, was there every day, watching, working out solutions. These men, he says, referring to the present architects, are using simple solutions and modern, cheap construction methods. They are using reinforced concrete where Gaudí used stone. The sculpture now being put in place on the new façade, he says, is inferior, far from Gaudí's view of what sculpture should be.

Those who support the building of the church are equally

trenchant: 'The architects who oppose us are like flies around shit,' one of them told me. There is a great deal of money available now for the church from private donations, legacies, entrance charges, and from Japan where people have a particular interest in the construction. More than one and a half million pounds was donated in 1988. The Sagrada Família could be a goldmine for an architect now; some of its supporters believe that the Socialist architects in the city would like to get their hands on it.

Joan Bassegoda i Nonell, Professor of Gaudí Studies in Barcelona, and a supporter of the completion of the Temple, admits that there are very real problems. Gaudí didn't work with drawings, being more of a sculptor than an architect. He was trying to develop a new language for architecture, based on natural shapes and forms. Of course, Gropius and Le Corbusier wanted work to stop on the Sagrada Família, Professor Bassegoda asserts, they were the architects who would least understand what Gaudí was trying to do, they were rationalists. Do I understand, he asks, what the word 'expiatory' means? The building of the Temple was to expiate the sins being committed in the city, so it is more important to build it than to finish it. The team of architects are simply trying to work out the problems Gaudí had left, and are using whatever methods are available now. The critics of the Sagrada Família don't understand, he says, that it is a church, a house of God, and not a simple building that is under construction. It can't, it won't, be abandoned.

Jordi Bonet, the chief architect, whose father worked with Gaudí, explains again that the Sagrada Família is an 'expiatory' temple, and that each day's work on the church is another step in atoning for the sins committed in the city. Building it is a sacred task even if the model is an 'enormous puzzle', even if the master 'didn't leave any plans on how to make the towers', even if they are working only on 'general lines'.

Soon the nave will be ready. Gaudí had worked out ways of using sloping columns to hold up the roof, he was trying to solve once and for all the problems of the buttressing of Gothic buildings. Jordi Bonet says they are still conforming to the shape of Gaudí's plan, but they are using reinforced concrete now. A computer is working out the problems of weight and stress.

He knows that the four towers he has built, the Façade of the Passion, look different from Gaudí's four towers. He agrees that he used quicker and easier methods. But Gaudí, he says, didn't plan everything to look the same. He wishes that the intellectuals and artists who attack him, who call the Sagrada Família a folly and an anachronism, who insist that the quality of the work going on there is a travesty of Gaudí's vision, he wishes they would come and see what the nave will look like. He stands in front of a plan of the nave and shows me how the columns will make it look like a forest. 'Look how the light comes in,' he says. He is passionate and enthusiastic.

Work will go on, then: it took forty years to build the first four towers, twenty years to build the second four, by the early 1990s the nave will be ready. But that is only the start. With modern methods of construction they can move more quickly; the men who control the church are determined, their vision is not simply architectural, but religious as well. They know their enemies and will keep them at bay. When will it be finished? I asked Jordi Bonet. It wasn't important, he said; he didn't know, couldn't tell. People used to ask Gaudí the same question and Gaudí would answer, cryptic as ever: 'My client is not in a hurry.' His client was God.

6

Picasso's Quarter

Along the waterfront are the shipping companies, the trading firms, the offices which specialize in import and export, the places which deal in customs clearance. And over to the right, presiding over the port of Barcelona, is the statue of Christopher Columbus.

Picasso painted the statue of Columbus in 1917 during his last extended stay in the city: he caught the shimmering blue-green light from the sea against the solid commercial port buildings of the nineteenth century. He painted a world of shifting perspectives which included a city balcony, some trees, the Spanish flag, the mast of a ship and the hot sun over the city.

This was the world Picasso knew then, rather than the new city being built by the architects. In all his years in the city he never moved more than two or three streets away from the waterfront. He painted the port, the beach at Barceloneta; he painted the narrow streets of the old city and the maze of rooftops. This was the city which formed him as a painter.

His family first came to Barcelona in 1895 when he wasn't yet fourteen. His father had found a job at the Fine Arts School, the Llotja, in the Passeig de Colom, where Gaudí had studied architecture, where Miró would later study. It was on the top floor of the fourteenth-century Stock Exchange building. Picasso was enrolled as a student there in the autumn of 1895.

He managed to complete in one day what it took normal entrants to the Llotja one month to do. His drawing style was harsh and direct and utterly sure of itself. He was the small boy who for fun threw pebbles down at passers-by from the rooftop of his studio in Carrer de la Plata, which his father rented for him. He was the small boy who ran and hid when he was identified as the culprit. But he was also the painter who in the same year, when he was only fourteen, worked on the large canvas called

Science and Charity in which he was solving complex problems of tone and composition while also managing to conjure up a sense of compassion and pain.

He was let loose in the city, the city of Anarchists and bombs, the city of capitalists and merchants busy building the Eixample. His family lived at first in Carrer de la Reina Cristina and then around the corner in Carrer Lauder; both streets gave on to the port. Soon after their arrival the Ruiz Picasso family moved to Carrer de la Mercè, one street back from the waterfront, to a second floor flat at number three, a building which has recently been demolished.

His parents weren't strict, he wasn't even obliged to go to Mass. When one of his biographers asked him when he had his first sexual experience in Barcelona, he put his hand flat at the level of his shoulder to signify that he was very young indeed. All the time he drew, filling notebook after notebook: street scenes, cityscapes, academic studies and his father's lean face, over and over his father's face, haunted, severe, disappointed, the face of someone who has failed.

Picasso was younger than the rest of the students at the Llotja, five years younger than his best friend there, Manuel Pallarès, with whom his friendship would last for more than seventy-five years. There is a photograph of them taken in 1957, two healthy-looking, bald, old men outside a building in Antibes, Pallarès slightly taller than Picasso. There is another photograph of them from the same time which Picasso has painted over to make them look like epicurean old Roman senators. Pallarès lived in a *pension* in Carrer dels Escudellers, close to Carrer de la Mercè where Picasso's family lived. He came from a village in the province of Tarragona, close to the Ebro, Horta de Sant Joan. He spent a great deal of time in the Picasso household and Picasso would refuse to go on family outings unless Pallarès came as well. They wandered around the old city together, drawing the artistes in the music halls off the Rambla, or making sketches in the Parc de la Ciutadella where less than ten years previously the Great Exhibition had been held. When he was still fourteen Picasso did an oil painting of Pallarès as well as several drawings. In 1898 he went to Pallarès' village in Tarragona where he stayed for eight months.

The streets where they lived and worked were in the 1980s the places in Barcelona where drugs are bought and sold. The names of the streets – Escudellers (where Pallarès lived in a *pension*), Carrer de la Plata (where Picasso had his first studio), Carrer de la Mercè (where his family lived), Carrer dels Escudellers Blancs (where he had his next studio), Carrer Nou de la Rambla (where he created some of his 'Blue' paintings) – these names are more likely to appear on a map of the city showing where crime – drug dealing, mugging, assault, robbery, pimping, prostitution – is at its most intense, rather than on a guide to the old artistic and Bohemian quarter of Barcelona. If you go down there, they say, you're looking for trouble, even though the restaurant Agut is close by, even though Los Caracoles, one of the most popular tourist restaurants, is on Carrer dels Escudellers itself.

Just as the winter of 1988 was coming to a close I was wandering around these streets one Monday evening. Over the weekend six people had died in Barcelona from overdoses of heroin, including two gypsy brothers. The newspapers were full of stories of bad heroin for sale. In one of the side-streets off Carrer d'Avinyó, where Picasso is reported to have spent time in a brothel, I noticed a crowd who had gathered at a doorway. They were shouting, I couldn't make out what they were saying. With a few others, I stood and watched for a few moments. Suddenly a black man ran out of the doorway. A cry went up from the crowd and they began to follow him. I stood out of the way when I noticed that the crowd had sticks; they were dark-skinned and badly dressed and it was only when I read the following day's newspapers that I realized that they were gypsies who had come to the city seeking revenge for the deaths of the two gypsies over the weekend. They were searching the area for blacks whom they held responsible.

I saw the look of terror on the face of one black man as he ran past; the gypsies, about thirty of them, had found others in a restaurant. Over the next half an hour, until the police came, they toured the narrow streets behind the Plaça Reial looking for vengeance. The shops stayed open, ordinary life went on, people looked for a moment, shrugged and continued on their way.

★

For the painters in Picasso's Barcelona Paris was the capital. His friend Jaume Sabartés would later say: 'The idea of going to Paris was like an illness.' The two men who dominated the artistic life of the city, Ramon Casas (1866–1932) and Santiago Rusiñol (1861–1931), had been back and forth to Paris a great deal in the 1890s, and been much influenced by new developments in painting there. Rusiñol wrote articles for the newspapers in Barcelona about his trips to Paris, including an account of a friend running into his studio one day shouting that he had found two El Grecos for sale: 'Two Grecos! Two big Grecos!' Rusiñol bought them for a thousand francs and took them to Sitges, forty kilometres south of Barcelona. There, in the summer of 1894, the year before Picasso's arrival, at the second of his Art Nouveau festivals, he had the paintings carried through the streets of the village in sacred procession, escorted by Catalan poets and artists.

Poets read from their work that day, including Joan Maragall, one of Gaudí's supporters and grandfather of the Socialist politician who would become Mayor of Barcelona in the 1980s. Rusiñol made a speech: 'We prefer to be Symbolists and mentally unbalanced, nay even mad and decadent, rather than debased and cowardly; common sense stifles us, prudence in our land is in excess . . .'

Rusiñol could afford to be stifled by common sense; he and Casas came from rich Catalan families. Both of them owned apartments in Passeig de Gràcia, Casas living next door to Gaudí's La Pedrera, on the first floor of a house which was equally extravagant and modern, whose dining room had an enormous mock medieval fireplace complete with marble griffins and a wrought iron fender. His apartment can be visited now, as it has been incorporated into the design shop Vinçon. Rusiñol divided his time between the Cau Ferrat in Sitges and a luxurious flat in Paris.

Neither painter became an Impressionist; their work is closer to Whistler than Renoir. Their landscapes are softly lit, their gardens are ordered and picturesque, the faces of the women they painted are tender. What they brought home with them from Paris, besides a style of painting which emphasized light and mood, was a sense of the cosmopolitan world beyond the Pyrenees. They became leaders, trend-setters. They offered Picasso a context in which he could flourish, a context not available anywhere else in Spain. Rusiñol dressed elaborately, played the role of the artist, gave parties (Manuel de Falla and Erik Satie would be guests at the Cau Ferrat in Sitges, among many others); he wrote travel books and involved himself in current fashions; in 1899, the year when Picasso first met him, he was being treated for morphine addiction.

Casas was less flamboyant, less interested in colour and decoration and more in tone and texture. His range was broader than Rusiñol's and included a number of remarkable political paintings, one of a public garrotting which caused a sensation when it was first exhibited in Barcelona, another of an army charging against a crowd. He painted murals and portraits of fashionable women, he painted the King. Like Rusiñol and Picasso, he painted the port of Barcelona.

Rusiñol became a collector of paintings, ironwork, furniture and bric-à-brac. His house still stands above the sea in Sitges, a museum now, complete with his two El Grecos, a number of small early Picassos which he bought in Barcelona, a painting by Carles Casagemas, who would become an important figure in Picasso's life, and work by himself and Ramon Casas. The rooms of the Cau Ferrat have all that sense of the medieval which permeates Catalan architecture. In the early years of the century Picasso came here with Carles Casagemas to see the El Grecos and later Dalí and Lorca would be among the artists who would spend time in Sitges.

Sitges stands out as an old seaside resort. The streets are narrow and some of the buildings are done in the Modernista style with Art Nouveau flourishes. At the turn of the century, it was an important place for those interested in new movements in painting. Now Sitges is a bustling seaside resort, one stretch of beach reserved for gay people. At weekends in the summer the village and its beaches are crowded with day-trippers from Barcelona, but during the week, even in summer, it retains something of its turn-of-the-century glamour. On summer nights people move up and down the thoroughfare known to the locals as Sin Street, while others watch from the tables outside the bars. The sun-tanned young wander the streets, watching and waiting, the bars throb with fast music, the discos are full of people gathered for the holy sacrament of sex. The mad and decadent world which Santiago Rusiñol proposed in 1894 goes on in Sitges until the dawn.

*

When Picasso came back to Barcelona in 1899 after his stay at Horta de Sant Joan, the fever for building was still going on throughout the city. Over the next ten years the Palau de la Música went up, Gaudí's two houses on Passeig de Gràcia were built, Via Laietana was cut through the old city. Catalan nationalism was going from strength to strength. Picasso remained an outsider, an Andalusian in a Catalan city, taking advantage of its pleasures but remaining untouched by its chauvinism.

Paris had Le Chat Noir, a meeting place and exhibition space for artists. So, too, Barcelona would have Els Quatre Gats on Carrer de Montsió off Portal de l'Angel in a building designed by Josep Puig i Cadafalch, which is now a restaurant. The phrase *Quatre Gats* means in Catalan 'very few people, a handful, a minority'; literally, 'four cats'. Rusiñol and Casas were among the founders when it opened its doors on 12 June 1897; it was run by Pere Romeu who had come back to Barcelona from Paris. The interior was designed in true Modernista style with tiles, arches and wrought iron, and soon to be adorned with a painting by Ramon Casas of himself and Pere Romeu on a tandem bicycle. Over the next seven years the bar was to become a major focal point in the artistic life of the city.

In 1899 and 1900 Picasso became acquainted with at least thirty Catalan painters and sculptors at Els Quatre Gats, most of whom would move back and forth between Barcelona and Paris. None of the younger generation was rich: most came from the lower middle classes, were shopkeeper's sons, or farmers' sons who became deeply influenced by the work of William Morris, Cézanne and Toulouse-Lautrec.

Picasso did not exhibit at Els Quatre Gats until February 1900; this show included nothing from his stay at Horta and only one oil painting. It consisted mainly of drawings of figures in the Bohemian world of the city, especially the clients of Els Quatre

Gats, most of whom were older and better known than Picasso. It included Rusiñol and Casas. Picasso's drawings were close in style to those of Casas, who had previously drawn Picasso in Bohemian clothes.

During this period in Barcelona, between February 1899 and his first journey to Paris in October 1900, the painter to whom he became closest was Carles Casagemas, a young, melancholy, romantic Catalan whose father was American Honorary Consul in Barcelona. He rented a studio with Picasso in Riera de Sant Joan, soon to be demolished to create the square in front of the Cathedral. They had no money to buy furniture so they decorated the walls with paintings of the tables and chairs which they couldn't afford. Picasso added a life-size butler and a maid. Casagemas had his first exhibition at Els Quatre Gats a month after Picasso.

They decided to go to Paris. Pallarès agreed to go with them but he was decorating the church in his native village so they left without him in order to see the Paris Great Exhibition of 1900 before it closed. Picasso and Casagemas installed themselves in an apartment in rue Gabrielle, previously inhabited by the Catalan painter and client of Els Quatre Gats, Isidre Nonell. When Pallarès arrived a few weeks later he found them there in the company of two models, Germaine and Odette.

Although Picasso was looked on by his fellow painters as Andalusian, his first months in Paris were spent exclusively with the painters he had known in Barcelona, including Ramon Casas, with whom he visited the Great Exhibition. He worked hard, his hunger to draw and sketch never leaving him. He made contact with gallery-owners and dealers. Casagemas, however, did little; he had fallen desperately in love with Germaine. His portrait of her is in a private collection in Barcelona. She is wearing a large hat and is wrapped in a huge cloak. She is in profile, her black hair cut short, her lips painted, her face delicate. The overall effect is chic and glamorous: Barcelona looking at Paris. Casagemas' love became obsessive. He spent his days drinking and talking about suicide.

Picasso took him back to Barcelona at Christmas and then to Malaga for the New Year. They spent two weeks together in Malaga where they drank a great deal and wandered about, to the consternation of Picasso's family. Eventually they parted company, Picasso going to Madrid while his friend travelled alone to Barcelona and then to Paris.

In Paris on 17 February 1901 in a café, in the company of Pallarès, Odette and three other friends from Barcelona, including the sculptor Manolo Hugué, Casagemas tried to shoot Germaine who fell to the ground, uninjured; he then shot himself in the head. He was twenty-one.

No one's death would affect Picasso's art as much as the death of Casagemas. He was still in Madrid when he heard the news. He was asked not to tell anyone how his friend had died, as Casagemas' mother believed that he died of natural causes. He had done drawings and paintings of Casagemas before: there are two drawings, for example, from 1900, both with the head bowed, one in profile, the eyes closed as though in prayer. Now the dead Casagemas began to appear in his work.

There are several paintings from 1901: a mythical evocation of Casagemas' funeral, daring in composition and colouring; a more realistic portrait of the mourners with the body in the coffin below them; a painting in blue of Casagemas in his coffin; and a more vague, ethereal portrait, also in blue, similar to a self-portrait which Casagemas had done some time before his death.

He used his art to conjure up his dead friend. There are at least twenty drawings and seven oil paintings in which Casagemas appears. The most striking of these, later called *Life*, Picasso worked on for several years and didn't finish until 1904 in Barcelona. In the early drafts there is an easel in the background and Picasso has placed himself on the left in the foreground, naked, being embraced by a woman, while another woman and child stand on the right. But in the finished version, the figure of Picasso has been replaced by the figure of Casagemas standing there, being comforted, his body naked and vulnerable, his face grave and tender.

In the June after Casagemas' death Picasso returned to Barcelona where he had an exhibition with Ramon Casas at the Sala Pares in Carrer Petrixol. The magazine *Pèl i Ploma*, founded and funded by Casas, had come to replace the publication known as *Els Quatre Gats*, to which most of Picasso's friends had contributed;

it included an article on Picasso's work as well as five reproductions and Ramon Casas' portrait of him. 'Picasso's art is extremely young,' the magazine wrote, 'born of a spirit of observation which refuses to pity the weakness of his contemporaries, we can see in it even the beauty of what is hideous.' Santiago Rusiñol bought four drawings and a gouache from the show.

By this time, however, Picasso was back in Paris. He had his first show there at the Vollard Gallery in the summer of 1901 where he exhibited seventy-five paintings. He stayed there until December, when he returned to Barcelona to his parents' house at Carrer de la Mercè, and to a studio at Carrer Nou de la Rambla, beside the Eden Concert, one of the best known music halls of the city. Here he did the first of the 'Blue' paintings in Barcelona, in the period when some of the troops back from Cuba still hung around the city, miserable, penniless, unemployed.

His career, up till now, had been typical of every artist of his generation in Barcelona, including his decision to paint the poor and deprived of the city. The similarities between Picasso's early career and that of his contemporary Isidre Nonell, for example, would be uncanny were they not both adhering to a prevalent pattern of work and movement. Nonell was a shopkeeper's son from Barcelona – there's a plaque on the house where he was born in Carrer Sant Pere més Baix off Via Laietana – who also studied at the Llotja. Both painters rejected the Llotja's dry academicism, both felt liberated by extended stays in the Catalan countryside, both exhibited at Els Quatre Gats (Nonell a year before Picasso), and both looked to Paris, where Nonell exhibited in the 1890s in a group show with Gauguin, Toulouse-Lautrec and Van Dongen. In Paris, both exhibited at the Galerie Vollard, both lived at 49 rue Gabrielle; in 1903 they shared a landing at number 28 Carrer del Comerç in Barcelona; both began to paint women in states of solitude and desolation in the early years of the century.

There were differences, however. Nonell's portraits are more firmly rooted in the particular. He had found a style to work in; his style never changed. 'I show my work to my friends,' Picasso wrote to Max Jacob, 'but they find that it has too much soul and not enough form.' Picasso was restless, constantly changing and discovering, about to leave Barcelona behind. In the autumn of 1902 he went to Paris again and returned in the winter to the studio in Carrer dels Escudellers Blancs, which he had also shared with Casagemas just a few years before. During his previous stay at the studio, another Catalan painter, Jaume Sabartés, remembered being told of this seventeen-year-old Andalusian genius. He remembered being sceptical before he was taken to the studio and saw Picasso at work for the first time; he remembered drawings, cuttings, paintings everywhere.

In his book on those years, Sabartés wrote that Picasso generally got up late in Barcelona and went to the café for breakfast. He was well dressed by the tailor Soler, who made his clothes in exchange for paintings. Picasso carried a cane in 1902 when he had a studio in Carrer Nou de la Rambla, Sabartés remembered him poking people with it.

He would walk up and down the Rambla in the evening after dinner, often the last to leave the table at Els Quatre Gats. He would stroll up to the Plaça de Catalunya with anyone who was free, and, later, when he was on his own, he would play the money machines, convinced that he had a winning system. In company he wouldn't talk much, particularly if the talk was of literature or politics; he would, Sabartés remembered, 'listen and say nothing, as if he was thinking about something else.' He was capable of becoming completely absorbed in himself in the middle of a conversation and leaving suddenly, going home on his own.

In Escudellers Blancs he continued to work on his 'Blue' paintings, including *La Celestina* (The One-Eyed Woman) and *The Old Guitarist*. But there were too many visitors to the studio and at the beginning of 1904 he moved to a quieter place at 28 Carrer del Comerç.

Jaume Sabartés rented a studio close by, on the top floor of number 37 Carrer del Consultat, opposite the Llotja, in an ancient building which still stands at right-angles to the street. There was whitewash on the walls, which were made of a baked clay brick – badly baked, according to Sabartés – and Picasso came to decorate the walls, just as he had done in the studio he shared with Casagemas. He worked, according to Sabartés, like a man in a trance, paying no attention to Sabartés who felt that a secret force was driving Picasso's hand, lifting it to pursue a line which only he could see. He painted an enormous arm along one wall, as well as a nude and a bull's head. On the wall opposite the window, he painted a half-naked Moor hanging from a tree, complete with erect penis. One of the man's shoes had fallen off and the other was hanging loose, his legs were arched slightly forward, and below, on the ground, stood a naked couple making love. Years later, Picasso's Catalan biographer Josep Palau i Fabre knocked on the door, but the owner wouldn't let him in and kept shouting '*No hay nada*', (meaning 'There is nothing'); he was used to visitors looking for Picasso's murals.

Picasso and Sabartés saw one another at least once a day over that year. Sometimes they wouldn't talk much; Picasso occasionally hated the company. 'What imbeciles!' he would say, but the next day he would talk to the denizens of the Els Quatre Gats as though nothing had happened. During that year he would often invite Sabartés to his studio and paint his portrait – there is a formal portrait in blue, and a portrait of Sabartés as a decadent poet, among many others – working at first from life and then finishing the painting quickly on his own the following day.

By the end of 1903 Els Quatre Gats had closed its doors and the magazine *Pèl i Ploma* had folded. In April 1904 Paris called again. Picasso's time in Barcelona was coming to an end; this time his departure would be more or less for good.

He would not live in the city again until 1917, when he came with the Russian Ballet, in which his future wife Olga Koklova was dancing. He had designed *Parade*, which Jean Cocteau and Erik Satie had devised for the Russian Ballet, and which was running at the Liceu. Picasso stayed on in the city for some months to paint and avoid the First World War. His work during 1917 had the elements with which he would juggle over the next fifty years. His *Harlequin* is almost a poster, it is so colourful and graphic; his *Woman With a Mantilla* is done in a sort of pointillisme, but left unfinished and jagged at the edges. *The Balcony*, his first painting in which the world is viewed from a window, plays with perspective, but is, to some extent, realistic. His drawing of an injured horse, its great neck stretched up in the air and its legs buckling under it, clearly prefigures *Guernica*, done twenty years later, in its sense of violence, disruption and pain.

His style shifts during this period of intensive work to a more abstract and modern painting where slabs of flat colour are placed against each other, where the human form is worked out in straight lines and angles, in curves and circles. Neither in style nor in tone do they bear any relation to the other paintings done in the same few months in the same city.

*

Beyond the city, there were two places in Catalonia which were important in Picasso's development. He would always say of Horta de Sant Joan: 'All that I know I learned in Pallarès' village.' He went there for the first time on his return from a short period in Madrid, in the summer of 1898. He returned in the summer of 1909. He also spent the summer of 1906 in the village of Gósol, close to the French border in the province of Lleida.

To get to Horta Picasso and Pallarès took the train to Tortosa on the Ebro where they were met by Pallarès' brother; then they took turns on the mule all the way along the rocky and tortuous path to Horta. The journey to Horta now takes about three hours from Barcelona by car, and once you cross the Ebro you are in a world of winding mountain roads, quiet villages and sudden panoramic views of rolling fields with mountains in the distance. Horta is on the very edge of Catalonia; like the other villages around it is still Catalan-speaking. Picasso was seventeen then and while he was there Spain lost most of her colonies, including Cuba.

I made my journey to Horta in December when the days were still warm and the sky over Tarragona was a clear, picture-book blue. On both sides of the road on the way from Tortosa to Horta there were orange groves, the oranges ripe and sweet, big bags of them for sale at the side of the road. It was like a spring day when we first saw Horta rising like a small rock above the plain. The village was modest and quiet: there was a square with a few bars, and steep hills to a second square with arches and a medieval church of honey-coloured stone, and an old town hall. The names of those who had died on Franco's side in the Civil War were still listed in stone on the side of the church, and in a square at the very top of the village there was a monument to the division of the Italian Army which had taken Horta for Franco on 5 June 1938.

Picasso stayed in the old village, first in Pallarès' house in one of the narrow, winding streets, and then later, when he returned to Horta with Fernande Oliver in 1909 to spend the summer, in a *pension* close to the church in the street which is now called after him.

Picasso and Pallarès explored the world around Horta, staying in a cave nearby, or at farmhouses in the surrounding mountains, sketching and painting all the time. They attended festivals; Picasso learned Catalan from the people in the area. He stayed until the following March. By the time he revisited Horta in 1909 he was a Cubist painter, however, no longer interested in painting scenes of country life. He had made *Les Demoiselles d'Avignon* two years previously. What intrigued him during his second visit was the cubic nature of the village, how it seemed to rise to a point in sets of squares and rectangles.

In the Bar Agustí, owned now by the nephew of Manuel Pallarès, they will show you reproductions of the work Picasso did during his Cubist phase at Horta. They will open a book and show you *Houses on the Hill*, *The Reservoir* and *The Factory at Horta del Ebro*, all done in the summer. 'This is the bar you're in now,' they will say, pointing to a shape. They will show you the painting of the village done from the square. Each section of tone and shadow in the painting will correspond to a feature of the village. They will explain the chimney in one of the canvases.

He used a water trough to reflect the shapes of the rising houses and streets of Horta. He added a palm tree to one of his village paintings, his only departure from the real, as there has never been a palm tree in Horta. He painted portraits, including one of the grandmother of the woman who now runs the Bar Manolo in the main square. Already foreign artists are buying up the old houses in the village, using them for part of the year, while natives are constructing brave new houses for themselves on the outskirts of the village with a view of the mountain. The mountain is deserted now, no one lives there. In Picasso's time there would have been at least twelve big, thriving farmhouses. Now there are vultures, pine trees and at least two thousand wild goats. It has been abandoned.

In 1969 the Mayor of Horta and the local chemist went to the South of France to see Picasso. They couldn't believe how much he remembered after sixty years: each place in the mountains, each family, each street in the village. He spoke to them in a mixture of Catalan and French. 'Horta,' he kept saying, 'are you really from Horta?'

*

Earlier in the year on a Saturday at the beginning of June I went to Gósol in the province of Lleida, the village where Picasso and his girlfriend Fernande Oliver spent the summer of 1906. The bus took me from Barcelona to Berga, two hours' journey, and then I waited for a jeep to take me the rest of the way. It had been grey and cloudy as we climbed towards the Pyrenees, the cloud dissolving like smoke over the peaks in the distance. I was the only passenger for Gósol, the driver told me in that reserved, gruff tone you hear the further you move out of the city in the Catalan countryside.

A few miles from Berga we came across a large cluster of new houses on a ridge facing down towards the road and looking over the lake below in the valley. The driver said that these had been built five years previously for the people who had lived in the village below, which was now under water, having been flooded for a new hydro-electric station.

Did the local people feel bad about it? I asked. They certainly did, he told me. Was there a church, I asked him, did they flood the church as well? He pointed towards the hydro-electric station in the distance. If I looked down now, he said, I would see the church on a small island, still above water level, as it had once risen above the level of the village, while the houses of its former congregation rotted and fell apart slowly in the water. In the light of the late afternoon the water was a deep cold green under the darkening sky, and the church could have been a monastic settlement, a sanctuary away from the world. Last summer was dry, the driver said, and the drowned houses began to appear again. The people were able to look down and catch a glimpse of the places they had once inhabited until the lake filled up again and their houses returned to their watery place of rest.

It had begun to rain now as we passed several villages and made our way through tunnels under the mountains. From Paris, Picasso and Fernande had gone first to Barcelona. She wrote that as soon as he crossed the border he was 'gay, less shy, more brilliant, animated, taking an interest in things with assurance and calm, in fact at ease. He gave out an air of happiness in contrast to his usual attitude and character.' After a few days they set out for Gósol. This part of the journey, which we were taking by jeep, they had done on mules. We passed two rocks, like huge humps, which could be made out in the distance, despite the mist. This was called Pedra Força, the driver said; it was a popular place now for outings.

It was a wet month for May, the driver said, which explained the greenness of their fields in the valley and the abundance of flowers in the meadows. We passed a sheer mountain wall, rising on the left. The driver had told me about the pollution from the electricity station and the nearby coalmines, so I asked him if the eagles had disappeared. He had seen one that morning, he said, hovering and circling over these hills.

He knew about Picasso and Gósol, and told me that there was a plaque on the wall of the house where the painter had lived. Gósol had originally been built on the slopes of a hill where there were still ruins and an old church on the summit. Now, however, the village rested at the bottom of the hill, well sheltered. Behind the main square were farmhouses, with sheds and byres for the animals. There were a few bars and shops and a *pension*.

His summer here was the summer before he painted *Les Demoiselles d'Avignon*; soon he would cease to discover and begin to invent. The orange he used over and over in the Gósol paintings was close to the colour of the earth, the marl which gave the landscape all around its rich colour. He painted Fernande; he painted peasant life and local people. The work from Gósol was classical and simple, line and colour were more important here than the poses and theatrical effects of his work with circus people and harlequins from the previous year. In a few months he produced a large amount of work, a number of paintings hinting at *Les Demoiselles d'Avignon*, including one called *The Harem*, in which a number of female figures and one male appear against an orange background. The work from Gósol, with its serenity, its calm painterliness, its insistence on proportion and line, is like the peace before the war, the false stability before the Revolution. 'It is,' Roland Penrose wrote of Picasso's Gósol paintings, 'the transformation of the human form which is most striking . . . after Gósol the nudes, often composed as two figures facing each other, are statuesque in the simplicity of their heavy modelling . . . They have moved from the classical into a new atmosphere where preconceived rules of proportion are abandoned. It is these studies of the human form that foreshadow the great events that were about to occur and the birth of a new aesthetic conception – Cubism.'

Among the drawings Picasso did at Gósol was a study of the old man who ran the *pension*, wearing a traditional Catalan hat. A copy of it now hangs in the upstairs room of that house in Gósol where he and Fernande used to take their meals. The window overlooks the small square and beyond can be seen the long plain and the mountains in the distance. He liked it here, he enjoyed talking to the smugglers who made their living from the frontier close by, he went on a few trips with them. He translated a section of a poem by Joan Maragall from Catalan into French. But when he heard that there were a number of typhoid cases in the village, Picasso wanted to leave immediately. They packed up and hired mules once more, going straight over the mountains to France, rather than returning to Barcelona.

Catalonia had been useful to him, but it could no longer claim him. He was a French painter now, but he was also an outsider, just as he had been an outsider in Barcelona, belonging to no movement and no place. In the years to come, he would create the painting *Guernica*, a great cry of pain for what had happened in his country. He refused to allow the painting to be shown in Spain until democracy had been restored, but in the last years of his life he began to donate work to Barcelona. This work formed the basis of the city's Picasso Museum in Carrer de Montcada.

7

Miró in Barcelona

In the early years of the century Joan Miró's father would walk with him on Sunday morning from their flat in the centre of Barcelona to the Museum of Romanesque Art in the Parc de la Ciutadella. Later, when Miró became a painter, he would remember how important those early images were for him: he admired the flatness of Romanesque art, he liked the way each object, from a small plant to the human face, was given equal importance. The small collection on show in the Arsenal buildings, today the Catalan Parliament, gave him his first view of what could be done in painting. Romanesque art was in his blood, he would later say.

Catalonia, too, was in his blood. He had no time for Spain; he wrote and spoke in Catalan, and then in French; he remained all his life an ardent Catalan nationalist. His relationship with the city of Barcelona, where he was born and where he lived for almost half of his life, was more complex, however. He followed the pattern set for him by Picasso and Picasso's generation: he looked to Paris as his capital and as he moved into his twenties he became desperate to get out of Barcelona. Like Picasso and others, he found inspiration in the Catalan countryside, away from the city.

But Miró was different from Picasso: his roots were different and his psyche, too, was different. He had none of Picasso's prodigal talent, none of his precocious genius. Miró was deeply rooted in his Catalan heritage, in the world of his paternal grandparents in the land south of Tarragona and of his maternal grandparents on the island of Majorca. His sacred places were those villages in Tarragona he associated with his childhood: Cornudella, Mont-roig, Prades, Ciurella; and the island his mother came from, where his grandparents lived when he was a child. Both his

grandfathers were artisans, his Majorcan grandfather was a furni-
ture-maker who in his youth had travelled as far as Russia on trains.
His grandfather in the village of Cornudella was a blacksmith.

In the 1820s Carrer Ferran was cut through the old medieval
quarter of the city between the Rambla and the Plaça de Sant
Jaume; only one old house and a church fitted the alignment of
the new street. Ferran was, for a while, the most fashionable street
in the city. The original plan for elegant and uniform buildings
came to nothing, but small signs of the street's former glory can
be seen: the high marble hallways, for example, in the buildings
around the Hotel Rialto; the chandeliers still hanging from the
ceilings in some of the first floor salons; the globed street lamps.
In 1826 the first tram-line in the city was built along Ferran.
Thereafter, two further streets were constructed – Jaume I and
Princesa – and the old houses were knocked down to make way
for this new direct route from the Rambla through the Plaça de
Sant Jaume to the Parc de la Ciutadella. In the 1850s the Plaça
Reial was begun, thus giving the city the Parisian uniformity and
elegance which it had failed to achieve in the new streets. The
area remained in fashion until the Eixample was begun, when it
declined, but it continued to flourish as a commercial centre, as
it still does, and it was here on the corner of the Plaça Reial and
Passeig de Medoz, which leads on to Carrer de Ferran, that Miró's
father opened a jeweller's shop in the 1880s. Miró was born in
1893 in Passeig del Crèdit, a new block of houses off Ferran, close
to the Plaça de Sant Jaume.

The area between Ferran and the port still maintains something
of its village atmosphere. In 1895, when Miró was two years old,
the Picassos moved into Carrer de la Mercè a few streets away
from Passeig del Crèdit. Miró's mother and Picasso's mother thus
became friends, although their sons, twelve years apart in age,
didn't meet until 1919.

Miró's first surviving drawings date from the age of eight. In
the Fundació Miró in Barcelona, the building where a great deal
of his work is held, there is a tortoise with each square on its back
painted a different colour; there are landscapes from Tarragona
and Majorca. Miró went to school in the city in Carrer de
Regomir and at the age of fourteen began a three-year course at

a commercial school while also attending the Llotja, where Picasso and Gaudí had studied. His main interest was colour, but he had no facility for drawing, no natural ability. He was not encouraged to stay at the Llotja.

At the age of seventeen he began work as a clerk in a drug company in Barcelona. He worked six days a week from eight in the morning until nine in the evening with a few hours' break in the middle of the day. He hated it. After more than a year he suffered a nervous depression followed by typhoid, and left the job. The previous year, his parents had bought a farmhouse between the sea and the village of Mont-roig, which means literally 'red mountain', just south of the city of Tarragona, close to Cornudella where Miró's father was born. His parents sent him there to recuperate.

Between 1910 and 1920 Miró experienced what he would later describe as several enormous shocks to his system. The first occurred during those months alone in Mont-roig as he started to draw and paint again, his parents finally accepting that their only son was not going to become an accountant. Nature caused the shock: the trees at Mont-roig, the colour of the rock, the grass, the sky, the beach. His feet, he said, became rooted at Mont-roig, and the force entered through his feet.

Between 1912 and 1919 he divided his time between Barcelona and Mont-roig. He began to study art again at a school run by a Catalan called Francesc Galí, but he still couldn't draw, couldn't, in his own words, tell the difference between a curved line and a straight line. Galí worked with him, tried to make him do still-lives of objects without colour such as a glass of water or a potato. Miró invariably made them look like sunsets. He liked Galí, Galí was open to the new movements in art, and everything was done through Catalan. Galí played music for the students, read poetry to them and took them on trips in the countryside.

He found a trick to teach Miró to draw: he covered his eyes, made him feel an object, or perhaps the head of a fellow student, and made him draw it from what Miró later called 'the memory of my hands'. This experience with Galí, he believed, was the origin of his sense of volume and his interest in sculpture.

Miró didn't talk much: everyone who knew him said that he

was reserved, taciturn. But all his life he showed a great capacity for friendship. Here, at Galí's academy he met Enric C. Ricart and Josep Llorens i Artigas. In 1915, as Barcelona was going through one of its economic booms, he shared a studio with Ricart in Carrer Sant Pere més Baix, near the house where Isidre Nonell was born. Ricart and he would paint portraits of each other, Miró's full of that stiff formality and interest in line, detail and decoration which characterizes his early work. Thirty years later he began making ceramics with Josep Llorens i Artigas, by then a well-known ceramicist, which would result in a long and fruitful collaboration.

During the First World War, Miró began to study drawing at the Cercle Artístic de Sant Lluc, where the ageing Gaudí was a member of the same drawing class. The Cercle Artístic had been founded with the intention of combatting decadent influences on young Catalan artists. Another fellow student was the art critic Sebastià Gasch, who later became a significant figure in the art world of Barcelona, writing the first articles about Miró, Dalí, Lorca's paintings and the work of Antoni Tàpies. Gasch observed Miró coming into the drawing class in those years during the war. Miró looked like a child, small, plump, with a wrinkled jacket and a red face. His expression, according to Gasch, suggested a mannequin's false smile. Only when he spoke would the cardboard child disappear and Miró would display the brightness of what Gasch called, in a subsequent memoir, 'an antediluvian glow-worm'. He would walk quickly into the drawing class, without looking at anyone or saying anything. He kept apart, according to Gasch, and gave the impression when he was drawing of someone who suffered a great deal, sticking out his tongue like a child who struggled to trace out the first letters of the alphabet, and 'sweating like a slave with pain and fatigue,' he would fill the blank page with deep lines that were sharp and incisive, but bearing scant relationship to the model he was trying to reproduce. His nudes, Gasch wrote, looked like untidy sacks of potatoes. He talked very little and when he did he said things which were totally banal.

Just as the young Picasso had toured the Barri Xinès, the red-light district and the seamier side of the city with his friend Pallarès, so too Miró and Gasch wandered around that area of

Barcelona to the right of the Rambla as you go down towards the port. Miró had warmed to Gasch after the latter had entered an abstract painting in a group show which had caused considerable mirth among the public. Miró was developing a great dislike of the philistine public of Barcelona. He and Gasch spent time walking around Carrer del Migdia, Portal de Santa Madrona, Carrer del Cid, L'Arc del Teatre and Carrer de Sant Oleguer, the down-at-heel, dirty, half-deserted streets. Miró and Gasch liked the bars; in particular the Bar Navarro in Carrer de Santa Monica and the Bar Roure in Carrer del Migdia. The walls of the latter were painted with tropical landscapes; the style was remarkably naïve and colourful. The two artists became intrigued by these scenes and found work by the same painter in other bars in the area. They discovered that he was called Documentos, but no one knew who he was, or where he could be located.

They were down near the port one day, in a bar called The Red Lion when they heard a woman shouting at an old man, referring to him as Documentos. He was, Gasch wrote, small and skinny with sparkling eyes and 'the face of a kindly crook'. He drank all the time and was unbelievably loquacious. He invited the two young art students to come and inspect a fridge in the Bar Navarro which he had just finished decorating and he accompanied them to the Bar Roure to look once more at his tropical panels. He had been to America and Venezuela – his name had arisen from perennial problems with his papers – and his view of the function of painting was to re-create the colours of tropical places he had visited. His lack of good taste and his lack of interest in perspective intrigued Miró, according to Sebastià Gasch.

Miró was working all the time, drawing the port of Barcelona just as Picasso and Ramon Casas had done, developing a Fauvist style, canvases full of thickly-applied dark colours, dark greens, dark purples. In 1912 he had seen a Cubist exhibition in Barcelona with work by Léger and Duchamp, including the first showing of Duchamp's *Nude Descending A Staircase*, and in some of his sub-sequent drawings and paintings over the next few years the Cubist style is apparent.

The Cubist exhibition of 1912 was organized by Josep Dalmau, the man who because the great force in the Barcelona art world over the next ten or fifteen years, and who would launch both Miró and Dalí. Miró called him 'a sort of genial fool who managed to exploit artists and look after them at the same time.'

Dalmau was a bearded Catalan in his forties who had lived for some years in Paris. His gallery in Carrer Portaferrissa became a meeting place for the artists and critics in Barcelona during the war years. Miró, despite his shyness and reticence, became friendly with Francis Picabia, one of the leaders of the Dada movement who had taken refuge from the war in Barcelona from where he published his magazine *391*. Picabia and Miró met every evening at seven o'clock. Miró had come to agree with Picabia's view of the Barcelona character: 'When you talk with a native of Barcelona you never know to whom you're talking, at the same time he could be a politician, an intellectual, or someone involved in commerce.' Picabia shared Miró's love for the Catalan Romanesque tradition. Miró, by this time, had begun to show his work to the mercurial Dalmau, who promised him a one-man show if he persevered.

Dalmau, too, was involved with the big French exhibition in Barcelona which ran from April to July 1917. For Miró it was another shock, as intense an experience as his first extended stay at Mont-roig. He had never been outside Catalonia, he had never seen the work of the French Impressionists except in reproductions. Now this exhibition came, with works by Degas, Bonnard, Matisse, Monet, Vuillard, Cézanne, Courbet, Daumier, Gauguin, Seurat, Sisley, Toulouse-Lautrec. He was stunned, particularly by the Monets. (Gaudí, it should be said, saw the show as well and disliked it intensely.)

In the same year Picasso came back to the city. Miró saw the *Parade* which Picasso designed for Diaghilev's Russian Ballet. He was at first too shy to call on him, and by the time he did so Picasso had left. Picasso's mother took him upstairs to show him the bathroom; Picasso had used the shaving soap to make a drawing on the wall which she had left untouched.

Miró continued to spend time at Mont-roig. He wrote to his friend Ricart about his relationship with Mont-roig and the landscape around the village. He wrote about the blue and golden light there and the love he felt for the things all around, the small things, the leaves and branches of trees, the grass, the animals. He wrote about his spiritual life among the people, the intensity of his work, his great happiness.

His landscapes were painstaking in their detail, the colour childish and unreal; the style was completely individual, each small plant and blade of grass delineated as carefully as each swirl of cloud and each mountain range in the distance. 'With the exception of the primitives and the Japanese,' he wrote in 1918, 'everyone has painted only the great masses of trees and mountains, without paying any attention to the small flowers and the blades of grass.'

'That which interests me above all else,' he wrote, 'is the calligraphy of a tree or the tiles of a roof, and I mean leaf by leaf, branch by branch, blade by blade of the grass.'

He had come to loathe Barcelona where a new fashion in art known as Noucentisme was current. This movement, led by Eugeni d'Ors, who later, when the time was right, went over to Franco's side, wanted a withdrawal from the mad innovations of Gaudí and his sort and a return to the classical, the more balanced values of the Mediterranean. 'I must tell you,' Miró wrote in 1918, 'that if I have to live much longer in Barcelona I will be asphyxiated by its atmosphere.' He had his first exhibition at the Galeria Dalmau in February 1918, selling hardly anything. Barcelona was too conservative, too inward-looking. He needed to get out, now that the war was over 'PARIS! PARIS! PARIS!' were the only words in a note he sent to Josep Llorens i Artigas at this time.

Before he left for Paris early in 1919 he went to see Picasso's mother who gave him a cake to take to her son there. This offered Miró the introduction he needed. Over the following years Picasso introduced him to dealers, talked about his work to others and bought paintings from him. They spoke in Catalan, sometimes in French, and remained friends until Picasso's death in 1971, although Miró feared the demon in Picasso, and suspected his precocious facility as a painter.

Miró was shocked by the people around Picasso, 'the most stupid people in the world', he later told an interviewer, 'dreadful people, imbeciles from all over the place.' But the main shock was Paris itself; he was twenty-six years old, out of his native element for the first time, and, he realized, out of his depth. He couldn't believe Paris: the very air, the buildings, the atmosphere.

He stayed in a hotel owned by a Catalan family who didn't charge him much and invited him to eat with them on Sundays. The Catalan poet Salvat i Papasseit was there as well, as was E. C. Ricart, and the novelist and travel writer Josep Pla. Llorens i Artigas found Miró a studio which belonged to the Barcelona painter and sculptor Pau Gargallo, whose comic head of Picasso is in the Museu d'Art Modern in Barcelona. Gargallo taught in Barcelona in the winter and lived in Paris in the summer. Like Picasso, Miró spent his early years in Paris exclusively in the company of Catalans. But in these early months he could do no work. He spent the mornings in the Louvre and the afternoons visiting the galleries, and when the summer came he went back to Barcelona.

At Mont-roig he began to paint again. He worked hard for the rest of 1919 in the old farmhouse his parents owned; he did the second self-portrait which Picasso later bought, he did *The Nude by the Mirror*, he did some landscapes of Mont-roig and a painting of the village itself. The detail in the work became more stylized and controlled, more strict in its embroidery and its odd angles and decorations.

In 1920 Dalmau organized an exhibition in Barcelona of work by the French avant-garde painters and included work by Miró. Miró's life began to develop a pattern: he spent the summers at Mont-roig and the winters at Gargallo's studio in rue Blomet in Paris. In 1921 he had his first Paris exhibition, organized by Dalmau once again, but it was a complete disaster: nothing sold. That year Miró began work on his huge, ambitious painting *The Farm*. He began it in Mont-roig, continued working on it in his parents' flat in Passeig del Crèdit, then took it to Paris. It was the culmination of the work he had been doing over the previous five years, overwhelming in its detail, fastidious in its inclusion of each object: lizards, snails, rabbits, a dog, a donkey, all depicted as objects from a child's picture-book. He worked on it for nine months. He carried grass from Mont-roig with him to Paris so that the detail would be right. He went to the Bois de Boulogne and collected more grass to bring back to his studio.

But when he finished the painting in 1922 no one would buy it. He was penniless in Paris; one dealer suggested that he cut the painting up into smaller sections as people were living in smaller apartments now and couldn't buy large paintings. Miró was outraged.

On the other side of the partition in Miró's studio at rue Blomet was the French painter André Masson. They became friendly and Masson introduced Miró to young writers and poets in Paris, among whom were André Breton, Robert Desnos and Antonin Artaud. Miró began to mix in the literary and artistic world of Paris. He made the acquaintance of James Joyce, whose *Ulysses* was published in the same year as Miró finished *The Farm*. His studio was visited by Ezra Pound. Hemingway became his sparring partner; both he and Miró were interested in physical exercise. In 1923 Hemingway got together some money and bought *The Farm*.

By then, Miró's style had begun to change under the influence of the Surrealists. The first sign of this is a painting called *Ploughed Earth*, done between 1923 and 1924. His flat-coloured sky is still there, as well as his farmhouse and his animals, but new effects have been introduced: oddly surreal shapes, such as spires and triangles, have appeared. The following years he painted *Harlequin's Carnival*, the first painting in the style we have come to recognize as his, in which musical shapes and images from dreams are let loose side by side. '*Harlequin's Carnival*', he later said, 'expressed my hallucinations brought on by hunger. I came home at night without having dined and noted my sensations on paper. At the time I was living on a few dried figs a day.'

Miró found a French dealer, Pierre Loeb, who organized an exhibition of his new work in Paris in 1925. The opening was carefully stage-managed; it was to occur at midnight and the invitation was signed by the chief Surrealists such as Eluard and Aragon who had at last found their painter. The show sold out, and Miró was to be seen that night dancing a tango in his own peculiar style – step by step as though he had learned it from a book.

From then until 1928 he showed his work to nobody, continued his annual sojourn at Mont-roig, and moved in 1927 to more salubrious quarters in Paris, sharing a street with Hans Arp and Max Ernst. In 1928 his exhibition of forty-one new paintings opened at the Galerie Georges Bernheim in Paris; this show was also a success. The following year Miró married Pilar Juncosa in her native Majorca; they returned to Paris where the international slump forced Miró to rent a small flat with no studio. They began to spend more time in Barcelona and in 1931 their only child, Dolors, was born there.

In the 1930s Miró's fame began to spread; he found an American agent, Pierre Matisse, son of the painter. Between 1932 and 1939 he had twenty exhibitions in Europe and America, but none in Barcelona. Until the Civil War, he stayed in the city, working in an upstairs studio at Passeig del Crèdit where there are now two plaques to his memory, and going to his studio at Mont-roig, which he kept absolutely clean with smooth white walls onto which he hooked here and there the new work he was doing.

*

In the middle of April when the weather was beginning to improve and the sky was clear and blue over the city, I took a train to Mont-roig, a few stops south of Tarragona on the way to Tortosa. All the way down I could see the new buildings right along the coastline, all from the last twenty years, and, where there had been gaps left, now there was construction – every square inch of ground would soon be covered. In the winter Miró used to walk on the beach here; he enjoyed finding the curious things which the sea threw up.

The village of Mont-roig is seven kilometres from the beach and the railway; I set out walking, having to cross two busy motorways before I was on the right road to the village, facing what Miró called 'the vinegar-red rock of Mont-roig'. The town was quiet; there was only the tiny sound of the bell of the church which he painted so many times. The square is called after him. I went into a bar where young people were sitting without talking much, half-finished drinks in front of them, the silence broken by a tape on a video-machine. After a few minutes the barman turned off the video and told us to finish our drinks. It was closing time in Mont-roig.

I found a small *pension* for the night and got something to eat. Two bars in the main square stayed open until close to midnight, and outside a monument to the Nationalist dead in the Civil War, the men who died on Franco's side, still remained. I had seen a similar monument in Horta de Sant Joan, where Picasso had lived, and in Bot, the village next to it. As I stood in front of the monument in Mont-roig, a few men came to the windows of the bar and looked out curiously.

Miró's house was back towards the sea. In the morning, under a weak sun, I walked towards it along a road lined with olive groves. Behind was the jagged red rock over the village and the small hills, each one different, one slightly wooded, rising to a sharp cone, another just bare rock; the stone of the houses, the church and the castle at Mont-roig seemed pale against what Miró called 'the formidable red' of the rock. 'The land of the interior was what interested me,' he told his interviewer Georges Raillard. 'I always went back to these houses, to the church, the beach, to the mountain.'

The branches of the olive trees seemed dry, brittle, curled and gnarled, almost rotten. The leaves of the younger trees were a lighter, silvery colour. The sun was becoming hotter now in the mackerel-patterned sky. As I got closer to the first motorway I could look back and see the sheer white rock of the mountains further south.

Miró's house was sandwiched now between the two motorways. It seemed bigger than the farmhouse which he had painted. But the painting had not included the house, merely the outhouses and stables, which remained now almost exactly as they were sixty-five years ago when Miró painted them. Workmen were repairing one of the sheds; a woman walked past them and went into the stable which had been converted into living quarters.

Miró came here very little in his last years, but his family still own the house and the land. The woman told me that his grandson is studying in Barcelona, and doesn't like the city, so comes at weekends. Her own son appeared, he had been working in the fields. He was wearing a T-shirt with a map printed on it of Els Països Catalans, the Catalan countries which Nationalists feel should be united into one political entity: Catalonia, Valencia, the Balearic Islands and the Catalan-speaking south of France. We stood in front of the eucalyptus tree which Miró had painted in *The Farm* and looked back at the outhouses which he included in the painting: the hook over the top window was still there, but the door had been replaced by a window. The reddish-brown earth was the same. They grew fruit now, the woman said, they were just getting ready to harvest the peaches.

*

Miró's Foundation in Barcelona, his gift to the city he grew up in, looks over the city from Montjuic. It was designed by his old friend Josep Lluís Sert, one of the early Rationalists and followers of Le Corbusier in Barcelona, who designed the Spanish Pavilion in the Paris Trade Fair in 1938 and Miró's studio in Majorca in 1954 (by which time Sert had become Professor of Architecture at Harvard). Another old friend from Miró's Barcelona days was Joan Prats, who had the biggest private collection of Miró's work. His father owned a hat shop in Carrer Ferran around the corner from Miró's father's shop. 'When I see his collection,' Miró said, 'I think of all the hats he has given me.' Miró, in return, gave him paintings. Prats took over his father's hat business and later moved it to a more fashionable address in the Eixample; he became a great promoter of modern art in the city. His gallery in Rambla de la Catalunya is still one of the most powerful and successful commercial art galleries in Barcelona. He donated his collection of Mirós to the Foundation where it is housed in a separate room. His donation is important, as is that of Miró's widow, because they both include early work, while most of Miró's gifts to the Foundation date from the last fifteen years of his life. His family, he said, understood his need to allow as many people as possible to see his work. He also had an idea that in the future work such as his could not be kept in private hands. He looked forward to that time.

The Foundation building itself is beautiful; its very whiteness seems to breathe in the light. Each room is shaded from the direct glare of the sun; the light which comes into each room is guarded and intense, making the galleries seem like a shaded sanctuary against the world outside.

The first room tells the story of Miró's life, shows E. C. Ricart's painting of him and his of Ricart when they shared a studio together in the early days. The work in the next room is from the 1970s, one wall filled by the *Tapestry of the Foundation* from 1979. Miró's sculpture is spread throughout the gallery, including a few planks stuck together with a gaping red hole for a mouth entitled *His Majesty the King* and another plank beside it with a few nails driven in called *Her Majesty the Queen*.

The earliest work on show is the drawing of a tortoise from 1901; there is also a peacock from 1908 and nudes and landscapes from the next ten years. The room where the Prats collection is held includes the Barcelona series of lithographs done between 1939 and 1944. Also included is a collage he made for Prats in 1934, when he was living in Barcelona, of hats and a feather and a sign in English saying: 'Prats is quality'. Miró's friend Alexander Calder made a mobile for Prats' shop window.

In the Foundation, too, there are works by friends – a big Calder mobile, a Matisse drawing by Miró's dealer Pierre Matisse, a Philip Guston, a Sam Francis, a Henry Moore and an Antoni Tàpies. But the richest works are the big Miró paintings such as *The Fireworks Triptych,* full of Miró's personal calligraphy and iconography, surreal, naïve and musical, suggesting a whole underworld of electricity, reverie, dream, memory, imagination; ideographs moving from dark, atavistic nightmares to whimsy and humour. All the time as you move from room to room in this strange muted light, these big paintings are exhilarating in their confidence and colour, as though the world in here were the real world and the one outside merely its reflection.

Yet each time you come to a passage-way or a stairwell, or a window leading onto a balcony, the light hits you hard – the light which comes to these white buildings on a hill over the Mediterranean. You can walk out on to the roof, where some of the sculpture is on display, and see the city down below, the towers of Gaudí's Sagrada Família, the steeples of the Cathedral and Santa Maria del Mar, the trees in military file on avenues in the city, the hills beyond the city and the new blocks of flats running as far as the eye can make out.

*

'This is our masterpiece.' Carme Farré is standing looking up at
the Christ of Taüll in the Museu d'Art de Catalunya in the Palau
Nacional on Montjuic, above the Plaça d'Espanya. When she
talks about 'our' masterpiece, it is clear she is not simply talking
about the magnificent museum where she has been working for
twenty years, but the Catalan heritage, going back to the twelfth
century.

This is what has become of the museum Miró visited as a boy
in the Parc de la Ciutadella. It now houses the largest collection
of Romanesque wall-paintings in the world. Carme Farré knew
Miró in his last years, when he was setting up his Foundation, and
visited him in Majorca. She tells how he pointed to the veins
running up his arms to show her how essential the tradition
represented by this collection was for him.

Earlier in the day we wandered around the outer reaches of
the Palau Nacional, constructed for the Great Exhibition in 1929
when Mies van der Rohe built his German Pavilion and designed
his Barcelona chair. The Palau Nacional, however, has nothing in
common with Mies's functional style. It is a bloated, grandiose,
neo-classical building, built to impress. The Great Exhibition of
1929 had been planned for many years; at first it was to be held
as a celebration of electricity, but eventually it became a trade fair
patronized by the King and the Dictator, as a result of which the
hill of Montjuic, once a preserve of the military, became a site for
public parks and buildings. A Spanish village was built, as well as
various pavilions.

The Palau Nacional is a display of grandeur at the top of a
long series of steps from the Plaça d'Espanya. The stairways of the
palace, the high ceilings everywhere, seem designed to remind us
that we are small and servile.

It was built during one of the major periods of immigration
from poor parts of Spain to Barcelona. At one point 40,000
workers were engaged on the buildings for the 1929 Exhibition.
The following year the city's population topped the million mark
(it had been 640,000 in 1918). And in 1930, 37 per cent of the
city's population had been born outside Catalonia.

In 1934, when the fuss of the Great Exhibition had died
down, the Palau Nacional was designated as the home for the

Romanesque and Gothic collections. The opening day, 6 October 1934, coincided with Lluís Companys' declaration of a Catalan state; Companys was imprisoned and did not see the museum until his release and return to power in 1936 when he came there with Ventura Gassol, his Minister for Culture. They were addressed by the Head of Museums: 'You have here work which is totally ours; because only with the energy of the Catalans has it been created.'

The collection of Romanesque murals was created in 4000 small churches in Catalonia from the eleventh century to the thirteenth century. Nothing is known about the artists; but the work was done in a time of peace, a time when money – tribute – could be charged to those who wished to use Catalonia as a trade route. Most of the churches still stand, dotted throughout the country, often on isolated hilltops, sometimes forming the core of a village. They are rough, plain churches, low and squat. In Barcelona the Church of Sant Marcus on Carrer Carders, close to the Picasso Museum, is an early example of the Romanesque style and Sant Pau del Camp, on Carrer de Sant Pau is the largest in the city and the most imposing. The cathedral in Tarragona is half Romanesque; the Cathedrals of Girona and Tortosa have Romanesque cloisters.

In the eighteenth century Romanesque murals were plastered over throughout Catalonia and remained hidden until various organizations dedicated to the study of the Catalan heritage began a search for them. At the turn of the century as Catalan nationalism was developing, the murals became part of the dream of the sacred richness of the past: work done at a time when Catalonia was undisturbed, peaceful and prosperous, when the rest of Spain was in the grip of the Moors.

Josep Puig i Cadafalch, the architect and politician, became an expert on the Catalan Romanesque period, and his book is still one of the authoritative texts on the subject. At that time early in the twentieth century, Italian techniques were being perfected for the removal of murals, using wax. It was essential to gather the Romanesque murals into one place and safeguard them. There were plans, however, by private collectors, to export the murals to the United States. In 1924, they were purchased by the Town

Hall in order to keep them in Catalonia and stop them leaving their native place.

The old masterpieces are held now in the huge airy rooms of the Palau Nacional, renovated, a second time, in the early 1990s. The Christ from Taüll, a village in the north of Catalonia, is placed, like much of the collection, in a curved recess, suggesting the apse of the church where it was originally painted. We can study the exquisite detail, the inventiveness, the subtle change of the colour. One of the animals has seven eyes, the magic number; the reclining figure of Lazarus seems desperately sad and bored; tones of blue, green and orange wash gently against each other. It is a triumph of symmetry and colour, design and detail, with Christ as the all-powerful redeemer at its centre, the eyes sharp and focused, the words *Ego sum lux mundi* written on two tablets held in His hand. Throughout the gallery, the two dimensional wields its power through tone and colour, texture and line. Some of the work has a deeply comic air, as in the twelfth-century altar-piece of Sant Quirtze and Santa Julita being boiled alive in a cauldron, their faces showing a singular lack of any sign of pain, or even mild discomfort; in the same figures being sawn in two, or having nails hammered into their heads stand in poses of Romanesque placidity.

Above all, it is the colour, the rich grainy tones, and the use of motifs and abstract shapes, which are overwhelming. These paintings are close to modern art – the work of Picasso and Miró – in the trust the artist places in paint itself, in the primitive power of tone and colour.

The museum also contains Romanesque sculpture, including polychrome wooden crucifixes, with the face of Christ elongated, the eyes enlarged and the clothing a brightly coloured mass of flourish and motif. The second half of the museum shows Catalan Gothic in painting and sculpture, the early work from the fourteenth century struggling for a third dimension, and often settling back into the flatness and simplicity of the Romanesque style before emerging again in rich gold colours and detailed realistic backgrounds, the beginnings of a new tradition.

Our footsteps echo down the corridors of the Palau Nacional on the way back to Carme Farré's office. As we look through the reproductions in her book about the museum we are joined by a man who has worked with the collection for years. The view from the window includes one of the city's two bull rings and they both talk in Catalan about their deep abhorrence of bull fighting, what a shameful thing it is, and how most Catalans feel it is something foreign which has been imposed on them.

This is 'their' culture then, this collection: the art they produced when they were left in peace, their Golden Age.

8

The Republic's Golden Age

On 15 April 1931 Pau Casals came with his orchestra and choir to the steps of the Palau Nacional on the hill of Montjuic to celebrate the new dawn of the Second Republic, by playing Beethoven's Ninth Symphony to an audience of 7000 people.

The previous year Miguel Primo de Rivera had gone into exile and died. After the victory of the Republican parties in the municipal elections of 1931, the King abdicated and left the country. In Barcelona, the Lliga, the old Conservative party, came second to a new party of radical nationalists, led by Francesc Macià, who immediately declared Catalonia a republic from the balcony of the Ajuntament building in the Plaça de Sant Jaume. Later, under strong pressure from Madrid, he agreed to become President of an autonomous body, called the Generalitat (after a medieval Catalan parliament), within the Spanish state.

Francesc Macià was in his early seventies when he took power. A lean figure from a wealthy Catalan family, he had been active on the fringes of radical politics for almost thirty years, having resigned his army commission because of his views on the Catalan question in 1907. In 1925, when in exile in Paris, he floated bonds to raise money for a small army to invade Catalonia, many of which were bought by Catalans in America. That same year a group from within his party made an unsuccessful attempt to assassinate the King.

Macià went to Moscow and tried to get support from the Soviet Government, but failed. In the winter of 1926 he led two hundred men from his party, Estat Català, towards the French border with Catalonia, where they were arrested by the French police at Prats de Molló. At their subsequent trial, which received great publicity, they were given nominal sentences and expelled from France. Two years later, Macià convened a congress in Havana which approved a provisional constitution for an independent Catalonia. In 1931, in preparation for the elections, he merged his party with that of a radical lawyer, Lluís Companys. Both men would survive in the mythology of Catalan nationalism as revered, almost sacred figures. The years when they held power, between 1931 and the beginning of the Civil War, would be seen by Catalans as another Golden Age. They won control over the police and the civil service, culture and local government, health and education. A referendum on the Statute of Autonomy was won by 562,691 votes to 3276. In the 1932 elections to the Catalan Parliament, the party of Macià and Companys won twice as many seats as the Lliga.

The Catalan language was made official by the new Government; public spending was increased on health and education. What Pau Casals would call 'a veritable cultural Renaissance' began in Catalonia. 'At last,' Le Corbusier said, 'on one living point of the earth modern times have found an asylum.' When Le Corbusier came to the city in 1932 he was received by President Macià, and when he produced his plan for the expansion of the city, two years later, he called it Pla Macià, in homage to the President. It sought to provide clinics and hospitals in the city centre, workers' flats and recreation centres in the suburbs. In 1934 work was begun on a recreation centre at Casteldefels, but the rest came to nothing because of the Civil War.

Miró came back to the city; he liked the new regime and the new atmosphere. His friend Joan Prats was becoming an important figure in the promotion of modern art through an organization called ADLAN, and another friend Josep Lluís Sert was among the principal rationalist architects in the city, founder of GATCPAC, which promoted the new architecture. Miró lived at his mother's apartment in Passeig del Crèdit with his wife and daughter until 1936 when he went back to France. During those years in Barcelona, he became an influential and fashionable figure as the city became more open to the new and the experimental in art. In September 1932 Alexander Calder exhibited in the city, Hans Arp and Man Ray had shows there in 1935. In January 1936 ADLAN organized an exhibition of Picasso's new, more avant-garde work. At the opening, which was broadcast live on the radio, Miró, Dalí and Juli Gonzalez spoke; the exhibition was seen by 8000 people.

Since Catalan had been lost as a literary language for more than three hundred years, there existed great variations in its spelling and rules of syntax. In 1913 Pompeu Fabra, an engineer turned philologist, had published his *Normes ortografiques* for the Catalan language, which were made official by the Mancomunitat, the local body which controlled culture and other local matters between 1914 and 1923. Pompeu Fabra continued his work on Catalan philology, and in 1932, with state assistance, his Dictionary was published. He became influential during the early 1930s in Catalan education, publishing many reading manuals and text-books which sought to purify the language of the tribe. Publishing in Catalan flourished during these years, and a new generation of Catalan poets emerged, influenced by French and English poetry and mostly avoiding the Castilian tradition.

'Never at any time,' Pau Casals wrote in his memoirs, 'have I been treated with such tenderness and love as by the Catalan Generalitat and the Spanish Republican Government . . . I do not believe that there had ever been before any government made up of such a group of savants and humanists . . . I had never voted before 1931, but when I heard Macià speak I said to myself: this is the man for me, and the first political vote I cast in my life was for him.'

Casals was born in 1876 in Vendrell in the province of Tarragona, where Gaudí and Miró were also born. His father was a musician who bought him his first cello in 1890. With the help of the Spanish royal family he studied in Madrid, Belgium and Paris. In 1896, three years after the Anarchist bomb at the Opera House, Casals became principal cellist in the Liceu orchestra, but left the city in 1899 to begin his international career. During his time in Barcelona, he discovered the sheet music for the six Bach suites for solo cello in a music shop in Carrer Ample (where there are still several music shops) and these became an important part of his repertoire. In the first two decades of the century he became the best-known cellist in the world. He bought a villa on the beach at San Salvador near Vendrell, now a museum, where he spent the summers.

There was a roughness in Casals' playing; the sound he produced was harsh and guttural, not lyrical or romantic. It seemed that something of the Catalan character entered into his tone when he played: that deeply reserved, gruff, earthy manner. Catalonia continued to haunt him as he toured the world. He wanted to come home, do something for his country. In 1919 he came back to the city, which was just over the boom of the war years, and bought a flat in the Eixample. He planned to start an orchestra, he wanted to devote his time and energy to assist in building Barcelona into a great European city.

When Casals formed a committee to help him in his plan, he found its members discussing politics all the time. He discovered that his project had a deeply political resonance. From now on he would be involved inextricably in the fate of Catalonia, his personality and music becoming part of the struggle for national identity. He subsidized the orchestra, of which his brother Enric would become an important member, from his personal concert tours in the winter. He worked in Barcelona as a conductor only: he did not give a cello recital in the city between 1920 and 1929. His Orquestra Pau Casals played its first recital in the Palau de la Música on 13 October 1920. Adrian Boult came as a guest conductor in 1923, Stravinsky in 1924 and 1925.

Casals wanted to go further, to attract 'the men and women from the factories and the shops and the waterfront' to his concerts. He wanted to bring classical music to the workers of the city. In 1926, after consultations with the trade union leaders, he founded the Associació Obrera de Concerts, which organized concerts by Casals' orchestra at nominal prices for those below a certain income. The concerts took place at the Olympic Theatre in Barcelona on Sunday mornings. The Associació Obrera de Concerts grew to 300,000 members, as amateur orchestras and chorus groups were founded throughout Catalonia. Arnold Schoenberg came to conduct a programme of his music for the working class of Barcelona; later, in the 1930s, he would live in the city for several years, giving his daughter the Catalan name Núria. In 1936 Alban Berg's Violin Concerto was given its world première in Barcelona with Webern conducting.

Casals became a hero in the city. At the ovations after his

concerts they would chant his name. When the King came for the Great Exhibition of 1929 he wanted Casals to play the cello. Casals agreed, but refused to conduct the *Royal March*, then the national anthem, and asked his brother to do so, a studied insult to the regime. There was scant applause for the King when he appeared, but when Casals arrived on the stage with his cello, there was pandemonium. 'Casals is our King,' the audience shouted.

In his idealism, his innocence and the determination of his efforts to represent the interests of the working class, he had a great deal in common with Francesc Macià, known as *l'Avi* (the grandfather) by the people. 'The first years of the Spanish Republic were among the most meaningful years of my life,' Casals wrote. Refusing to run for election, he was careful to keep away from direct involvement in politics, and would not allow his Associació Obrera de Concerts to be used politically. He did, however, accept a position as President of the Catalan Council of Music, a division of the Generalitat. Between 1931 and 1936, when he was on tour, he was met and looked after by a Spanish consul or embassy official in the foreign cities he visited. In 1934 the city of Barcelona named a street after him.

The Civil War would ruin his career as a musician, as it ruined so many careers. All the idealism and hope would come to nothing. Macià would die in 1933 and be replaced by Lluís Companys, and in 1940 Companys would be brought back from France by Franco and shot in Montjuic.

In the Gothic quarter during the years of the Civil War, Federico García Lorca had a street named after him. Although he came from the South, he grew to love Barcelona which he knew first in the 1920s and then during the years of the Republic. He loved the Rambla, calling it the most beautiful street in the world.

'Barcelona is something else, isn't it?' he wrote to a friend. 'There you have the Mediterranean, the spirit, the adventure, the high dream of perfect love. There are palm trees, people from every country, surprising advertisements, Gothic towers and a rich urban tide . . . What a pleasure it has been for me to meet that air and that passion! I'm not surprised that it agrees with me, because I hit it off wonderfully with everything there and my poetry was taken up in a way it didn't really deserve . . . And not alone that, but I, who am a furious Catalanist, sympathize a great deal with what those people have done, and am so tired of Castile.'

Lorca first came to Barcelona in 1925 with Salvador Dalí, whom he had met in Madrid. He gave a reading in the Ateneu off the Rambla in Carrer Canuda which was well attended by Catalan poets, and went for dinner in the old El Canario de la Garriga, opposite the Ritz Hotel. Among his companions that night was a young Catalan called Jaume Miravittles. Lorca was fascinated by his name, by the harsh Catalan consonants. He was becoming interested in the Catalan language, and constantly demanded to know the Catalan word for every object. He told Dalí's sister that *núvol*, the Catalan word for cloud, was his favourite. Over dinner in Barcelona he repeated Miravittles' name, shouting it out as though it were a poem.

Miravittles, later an important figure in the politics of the Republic, had just come out of jail. He had been arrested when he and a group of others applauded a singer in the Eldorado Theatre who sang in Catalan, and he was found to have a pamphlet by Francesc Macià in his pocket. He had been sentenced to two years in prison and was now on provisional release. In the visitors' book that night Miravittles signed his name with 'ex- and future prisoner' beside it. Dalí, ever careful, did a drawing and simply wrote 'ex-prisoner'; Lorca did a drawing too and wrote 'potential prisoner' and then *Visca Catalunya Lliure!*, which means 'Long Live Free Catalonia!' He was learning.

On St John's Day, 24 June 1927, Lorca's play *Miriana Pineda* opened with the Catalan actress Margarida Xirgu and sets by Salvador Dalí in the Teatro Goya (now the Goya cinema). After the show Lorca walked through the Gothic quarter with Margarida Xirgu, Salvador Dalí and others. Dalí's sister, Ana Maria Dalí, remembered how much Lorca liked the old quarter and wrote of Lorca in the Plaça del Rei putting on a show that night, being the mock-playwright, bowing as though to an audience in an empty square. They walked on to Plaça de Sant Jaume and then down to the Rambla, where they sat at an open-air bar and had a drink.

The following day an exhibition of Lorca's drawings opened at the Galeria Dalmau, where Miró and Dalí had both exhibited;

the catalogue was in Catalan. All his life Lorca had done drawings and doodles; now he found that he was being treated seriously as a painter as well as a poet and playwright. It was, he wrote, extraordinary. His style was naïve, funny, throwaway. Dalí wrote an article in his praise, as did several Catalan critics, including Sebastià Gasch, who had been Miró's friend in Barcelona. 'If it hadn't been for you, the Catalans,' Lorca wrote, 'I would never have continued drawing.' Before he left Barcelona, a dinner was held in his honour, attended by a great number of Catalan poets. He had learned to sing in Catalan; he had been to Sitges; he loved drinking in the bars in the Plaça Reial. He embraced Catalonia with all his energy and enthusiasm and received great warmth in return.

By the time he came back, in December 1932, to deliver a lecture at the Ritz Hotel in Barcelona, he had published *Poet in New York*. He lectured on his experiences abroad and read poems to a packed audience made up of the city's middle classes and poets. While previously he had stayed in a cheap *pension* off the Rambla, now he stayed at the Ritz. He went back to the restaurant El Canario de la Garriga with several young Catalan poets. He sang some of his poems there, accompanying himself on the guitar; the Catalan poets recited in Catalan.

The following year he came back to Barcelona from where he sailed on the *Conte Grande* to Montevideo. Before he took the boat he went to see Margarida Xirgu and told her he was writing a play for her: the title was *Yerma*. She was nervous; he hadn't given her *Blood Wedding*, which was going to be performed in Montevideo, and she knew there would be great demand from theatres for his next play.

By the time *Yerma* opened in Madrid in 1934, the political climate in the country had changed considerably. In October the Madrid Government formed a coalition with the CEDA, a right-wing Catholic party, which resulted in a general strike being declared and an uprising in Asturias. Lluís Companys, the President of the Catalan Generalitat, whose attempts at agrarian reform had been opposed by the Madrid Government and the Lliga, declared Catalonia an independent republic.

'Liberal, democratic and republican,' he said, 'Catalonia cannot absent itself from the protest that has swept the country, nor fail in proclaiming its solidarity with our brothers in the Spanish lands . . . In this solemn hour, in the name of the people and the parliament, the government over which I preside assumes all the functions of power in Catalonia.'

He refused to arm the Anarchists, now increasingly powerful and numerous in the city. Instead, he was protected and encouraged by a shadowy group of Catalan nationalist paramilitaries, the Escamots, whose bearing and philosophy were very close to fascism, Catalan-style. His position was hopeless. The army began to bombard government buildings in the Plaça de Sant Jaume. Companys surrendered and was arrested, later he was sentenced to thirty years in prison.

The new right-wing Government set about dismantling the reforms of the previous three years. A new name appeared in the politics of the country, who would be a central protagonist in the nightmare which was to come. Towards the end of 1934 forty-two-year-old Francisco Franco, the General who put down the rising in Asturias, emerged for the right as the saviour of Spain from communism.

Yerma was caught up in the polarized politics of 1934. Margarida Xirgu came under fire as the woman who had invited Manuel Azaña to stay in her house when the former Prime Minister was released from jail. (Azaña was accused of supporting the various left-wing uprisings in Spain in 1934.) Lorca, too, had made his position on politics clear in the statement to the press which began: 'I will always be on the side of those who have nothing.'

Yerma opened in Madrid in December. It was bitterly attacked in the right-wing press for its immorality. It ceased to be a play about a childless woman and became a rallying cry, like Yeats' *Cathleen Ni Houlihan*.

By September 1935, when Xirgu put on *Yerma* in Barcelona, the left was re-grouping, preparing itself for the elections in February 1936. The excitement about the play was enormous in the city. A queue for tickets formed early in the day, as the show had been booked out well in advance. Lorca managed to find a seat at the front for the sculptor Manolo Hugué, one of Picasso's old friends in Barcelona. Others just pushed their way in, filling the passage and stairways of the theatre. After the performance Lorca spoke, remembering his first show in Barcelona eight years before, and praising the work of Margarida Xirgu. Xirgu came out on to the stage and said: '*El meu cor és amb vosaltres. Visca Catalunya!*' which in Catalan means: 'My heart is with you. Long live Catalonia!' The crowd went wild.

It was a curious phenomenon: a play by an Andalusian being taken as another weapon in the arsenal of Catalan nationalism. In October 1935 the play toured the Catalan villages. Lorca was famous now, and one of the shoe-shine boys on the Rambla would recite a Lorca poem by heart as he shined his customers' shoes. (Lorca disliked the poem and avoided the boy.) He was invited to read to a workers' cultural association in Barcelona on 6 October, the first anniversary of the Asturias uprising. When Margarida Xirgu appeared, she was given red roses by the workers. Later in the month, a dinner would be held in her honour, with Pau Casals a member of the organizing committee. Everywhere Lorca went he was recognized.

It was clear which side he was on; his play and his personality were now part of the Spain which wanted freedom and progress. In Barcelona he spoke of his deep admiration for the Soviet Union. He was now a public figure, a marked man in the struggle against fascism.

In November *Blood Wedding* was put on in the Principal Palace Theatre. Lorca was still in love with the city, he often went to see the gypsies on Montjuic with Sebastià Gasch, he enjoyed eating at the 7 Portes restaurant, near the harbour. He went to hear Andalusian singing and dancing in the bars of the Barri Xinès. *Blood Wedding* had the same success as *Yerma*. In December Xirgu put on Lorca's *Doña Rosita la Soltera* in the same theatre, which received rave reviews in the Barcelona press.

Lorca stayed in the city throughout these months. Anecdotes about his favourite haunts, about his lectures on the culture of Andalusia and his conversation appear constantly in the memoirs of the Catalan poets of the time. On 23 December a dinner was given in his honour at the Hotel Majestic. The following day he left the city.

In February 1936, national elections took place. In Barcelona huge posters of the dead hero Macià appeared on the walls with the single word: *Catalans!* A popular front was formed to defeat the Lliga. The CNT, the Anarchist union, advised its members to vote in the election, which meant a left-wing victory. Manuel Azaña, to whom Xirgu had given hospitality in 1934, returned to power and fired Franco from the War Ministry, sending him to the Canary Islands in March 1936, where it was believed that he would cause less trouble.

Lluís Companys came back to Barcelona on 1 March 1936. Adolfo Bueso, a member of the CNT, described the euphoria of the day in his memoirs: 'It was a sunny morning, along the entire route hundreds of thousands of excited people were welcoming him with great enthusiasm, the entourage of covered cars regularly gave off the sound of victory on their klaxons. Companys was standing up in the first car with his hair cropped and his arms lifted in salute. On his getting out in the Plaça de Sant Jaume, a number of young people took him on their shoulders and carried him to the presidential seat. Immediately, he came out on to the balcony of the palace and saluted the crowd which filled the square and the streets all around to overflowing, but sheer emotion prevented him from pronouncing a single word.'

This time Companys got his land reform through without any difficulty. He planned an alternative Olympic Games to those which were to take place in Berlin that summer. He asked Casals to play Beethoven's Ninth Symphony once more on the steps to the Palau Nacional on Montjuic, as he had in 1931, this time to celebrate peace in the world. Casals was rehearsing the symphony with his orchestra in the Palau de La Música on 18 July 1936 when news came that there had been an uprising in Morocco.

Casals and his orchestra were advised to go home as quickly as they could. They had completed the first three movements of the symphony, and Casals asked the musicians and singers if they would finish it. They agreed. There was no audience, of course, and there never would be again for Casals and his orchestra in Barcelona. Within a month Lorca would be murdered in Granada; over the next twelve months the city of Barcelona would tear itself apart; over the next two years a dark shadow would move

across Spain. The choir began to sing the choral section of the
Ninth Symphony:

> By this magic is united
> What the harsh past held apart
> All mankind are sworn brothers
> Where the gentle wings abide.

It was the afternoon before the Civil War.

9

The Civil War

Lluís Companys, the President of the Generalitat, went out that night from his headquarters in the Plaça de Sant Jaume and walked up and down the Rambla with Ventura Gassol, the Minister for Culture. He was sure that the Army would stay loyal, but less sure about other elements in the city: the right-wing, the Anarchists, the foreigners who had come to take part in Barcelona's alternative to Hitler's Olympics which were due to open the following day. Companys was reassured by the calm in the centre of the city and went back to his office believing that his Government had everything under control.

Jaume Miravittles was by 1936 a member of Companys' administration. It was his job to organize accommodation for the 5000 athletes who were coming to the Olympics. The Army offered the administration 5000 camp beds which were to be placed in empty school buildings around the centre of the city. The Captain-General seemed enthusiastic about the Olympics, telling Miravittles that they would assist 'the cause of liberty and freedom'. Miravittles was learning to trust the Army; he reported regularly to Companys.

That night at ten o'clock he went to see the Captain-General who assured him of his loyalty, despite the uprising in Morocco and the rumour of risings elsewhere. Miravittles also spoke to Lizcano de la Rosa, an army officer with whom he had become friendly, and was told that the Army would remain loyal to democracy. He then went to the studios of Radio Barcelona and broadcast the news that there would be no uprising in Barcelona, quoting the officers to whom he had spoken.

He stayed in the radio station for a while, talking to friends, so it was late when he went out on to the street in search of a taxi. As he walked along he was arrested by soldiers and taken to the nearby university building where he found hundreds of other prisoners. 'And then it occurred to me,' he later wrote, 'that the Army had played a trick on us, and soon all of us would be put up against a wall and shot.'

The Anarchists were waiting for the uprising; they were ready. Their numbers had grown throughout the 1920s and 1930s; they were now the most significant political force in the city. Adolfo Bueso, a young journalist and member of the CNT, the Anarchist trade union, had been in the Generalitat offices that day, had heard the news of the uprising and had gone to warn his colleagues. But they already knew. They realized that the army would come to the centre of the city, seeking control of the telephone building in Plaça de Catalunya and the radio building in Carrer del Casp.

'That night,' Bueso later wrote, 'a marvellous, incredible mobilization was effected in Barcelona. Before midnight, hundreds of armed men occupied the strategic sites, ready to stand up to the rebellion.' The Anarchists still had the arms they had gathered on 6 October 1934.

The battle for the city took place on the morning of Sunday 19 July in the Plaça de Catalunya and the area around the university. The police, for the most part, remained loyal. Franco had arranged that General Goded, having taken Majorca, would fly in by light aircraft to Barcelona and lead the coup in the city. But by the time he came it was over; he and his colleagues were forced to surrender and he was taken to the Generalitat to see Companys.

In the days following, Miravittles saw a great deal of Goded, who was kept in the Palau de la Generalitat in Plaça de Sant Jaume: 'A small, thin man with grey eyes and the very fair skin to be found among Spanish aristocrats.'

President Companys wanted Goded to call on the insurgents to lay down their arms. 'They were very different,' Miravittles wrote. 'They were both in their fifties, but that is all they had in common. The General was austere and tight-lipped, the President voluble and quick-witted. Companys was a liberal, a romantic . . . Women worshipped him and the masses were spellbound by his speeches. The general looked at him from the heights of his aristocratic disdain.'

There were five of them in the room when the General gave

in: Lluís Companys, who would be brought back from France in 1940 and executed on the hill of Montjuic; Goded, who would be shot within a few weeks on the Anarchists' instructions, despite Companys' belief that he should be spared; Josep Tarradellas, who would take over as President-in-exile in the years after the Civil War, and return triumphantly to the city in 1977 as official President of the Generalitat; Ventura Gassol, poet, Minister for Culture and friend of Casals, who would also live to see the death of Franco; and Miravittles, whose memoirs of these events would appear in Catalan in 1972. Miravittles wrote how the transmitter was set up inside the Generalitat for the broadcast, which Goded made in 'a clear voice, heavy with emotion', calling for surrender.

Bueso was in the Lyon d'Or, a café in the Plaça del Teatre, at the bottom of the Rambla, when Goded made his broadcast. The Anarchists and the POUM, a Trotskyite militia, had taken over the square as their headquarters; the leaders, including Durruti and Andreu Nin, sat and listened. For the rest of 1936 and some of 1937, these people would control the city. Companys would be President only in name. He told Miravittles: 'When a revolutionary movement arises, then the chief of the Government is no longer the effective ruler. He presses a button, but nothing happens. He gives an order, but no one obeys.'

The Anarchists now had all the arms they needed; they had raided the arsenals after the defeat of the rebels. At first, they wanted no part in the Government. They were prepared to leave Companys as President. Under their influence the city began to change. It was day one of the brave new world. As Bueso walked home after the battle for the city on 19 July he found people cheering him from the balconies in the streets off the Rambla near where he lived. People who he knew would readily see him strung up were now shouting slogans of support to him.

It was clear which way the wind was blowing. Factory-owners and people with right-wing sympathies got out of the city as fast as they could. Antoni Tàpies, the painter, remembers that his father told his family to wear old clothes if they were going out in the city. Josep Trueta, a Catalan surgeon, who predicted the anti-clerical turn of the Anarchists, forced the nuns in the clinic

where he worked to destroy their habits and wear nurses' uniforms
and make-up.

A revolution was going on in the city. In the factories, wage
and management structures were being overturned. For Adolfo
Bueso it was 'like a dream from a novel, an acting out of the
books in which he had read about the activities of the Russians
in 1905 and the French in the commune of 1870.' (His memoir
was written in the third person.) All the old servility and exploitation had disappeared. All the old rules were gone. Even the rules
of the road, he noted, were being ignored as cars became anarchic,
and one-way streets were seen as part of the old regime. Bueso's
job was to take over the offices and printing works of the right-
wing *El Correo Catalan* and use them for the production of *La
Batalla*, the newspaper of the POUM. The first issue he produced
'did not just report the defeat of the military, but also that the
social revolution had begun.'

The Anarchists were never a cohesive group in the city: they
ranged from revolutionary theorists to illiterate labourers. In
Barcelona in 1936 observers noted that innocence and idealism
held sway in certain factories, where the followers of Bakunin felt
that it was enough for them to ensure that their own lives and
their workplaces were governed by a belief in the brotherhood of
man, it was not part of their principles to look any further. It was
easy, then, for other, more cruel and repressive forces to operate
within anarchism during these months in Barcelona.

The Anarchists set up their own police force, *patrullas de control*.
In each area they met to draw up death lists. Pau Casals was in
Tarragona, in his large seaside house near Vendrell. He discovered
that his name was appearing on the death lists, but each time
someone would protest that he was a good man, a great musician
and a friend of the people, even though he was rich, and he
should be left alone. But when friends of his were shot and others
threatened Casals went to Barcelona to talk to the Government,
telling them it was their duty to see that the rule of law obtained
in Catalonia. He was informed that the Government was powerless
and, when he said that the Government should resign, he was told
that if they did, then there would be no government.

The porter at Josep Trueta's hospital was an Anarchist who,

one day, 'appeared at the bed of one of my patients, flourishing an outsize revolver, which he pointed at me saying: "If he dies I am going to shoot you for being a Fascist".' The porter was called off only as a result of representations made to the Anarchist leaders. Later, one of the male nurses at the hospital was taken away, accused wrongly of being a Fascist. Trueta determined to get him back, arrived at a garage in Sant Andreu where the local committee of the CNT had installed itself and found the nurse 'more dead than alive from fear'. Trueta then met an Anarchist with an immense beard who recognized him as the doctor who had oper- ated on his sister, and led him upstairs where 'five men were sitting in the room behind a long table, each with a revolver in front of him'. When Trueta insisted that the male nurse was not a Fascist, one of the men asked him: 'And who can guarantee that you are not a Fascist yourself?' It was then that the bearded Anarchist spoke up and said he knew Trueta, and both he and the male nurse were released.

However, the Anarchist power in the city was beginning to wane. In September some of the leaders joined Companys' Government, which was now acting increasingly without any reference to Madrid, and in November a number of Anarchists joined the central Government. This came as a shock to the rank- and-file and to the idealists in the movement who were busy overturning the structures of power that had oppressed the working class of Barcelona for so long.

*

On the day after the war broke out, Adolfo Bueso was walking down the Rambla from his house towards the Anarchist head- quarters when he noticed a crowd of people outside the church on the corner of Carrer del Carme and the Rambla; they were 'desperately trying to set the church alight.' All over the city churches were sacked and burned, priests and nuns were arrested and shot, their bodies left on the outskirts of the city. 'On arriving in Barcelona,' W.H. Auden wrote, 'I found as I walked through the city that all the churches were closed and there was not a priest to be seen.'

In the last week of July 1936 one hundred and sixty priests

and nuns were shot in Catalonia, including nine nuns at Horta and fourteen St John of God Brothers at Calafell. When the parish priest of Bonanova was shot on 26 July, his two domestic servants were shot as well. When Jaume Busquets, the organist at Sant Josep in Gràcia, tried to remonstrate with the men who were burning his church he was taken away and shot.

There was no authority in the city, except the power of the Anarchist dream which sought to make a world in which the priest and his authority would have no place, which sought revenge on a Church which had consistently supported the property-owners in the city. Local committees began to search every house, hotel and *pension* in the city. Many Anarchists had nothing to do with this killing; Adolfo Bueso notes that of the seven hundred men who joined the *patrullas de control* at the beginning of the war, two hundred had left within a month, unable to stomach what was going on.

Most of the killings in Catalonia happened in Barcelona as more nuns and priests moved in from the countryside. Many were now being arrested as they searched for sanctuary. On 9 October one hundred and seven Marist Brothers were found trying to escape the city on a boat anchored in Barceloneta. They were taken to the main Anarchist prison at the Convent of Sant Elias and arbitrarily divided into two groups; those in the first group were shot, but the second survived. On the same day a Carmelite priest was taken from the Hospital de Sant Pau where he was recovering from wounds and thrown into the sea at Garraf.

The pattern of killings, which the Church documented meticulously after the war, is a useful gauge of the decline of revolutionary fervour in the city. In August two hundred clergy died; in September the total was down to a hundred and forty-six; in October a hundred and twenty-one. In November it was ninety and in December, the month George Orwell arrived in Barcelona to join the fight against fascism, it was down to fifty-two.

Orwell was shown around the city by a young Catalan journalist, Victor Alba, a member of the Trotskyite militia POUM, who was given the job mainly because he spoke French; he had never heard of Orwell or his writings. He remembered Orwell as silent and taciturn, not appearing to be very interested in the city. When *Homage to Catalonia* appeared, Alba realized that he had misunderstood his guest.

'It was the first time that I had ever been in a town where the working class was in the saddle,' Orwell wrote. 'Practically every building of any size had been seized by the workers . . . Every shop and café had an inscription saying that it had been collectivised . . . Servile and even ceremonial forms of speech had temporarily disappeared . . . There were no private motor cars, they had all been commandeered . . . In outward appearance it was a town in which the wealthy classes had practically ceased to exist.

'It was,' he wrote, 'something startling and overwhelming' for anyone coming from England, even though 'to anyone who had been there since the beginning it probably seemed even in December or January that the revolutionary period was ending.' By this time there were Anarchists in both the Catalan and the Spanish Government, and the contradictions of being 'in the saddle' and maintaining the dynamics of an Anarchist revolution were becoming apparent. By this time, Antonov Ovseenko had arrived at the Hotel Majestic in Passeig de Gràcia and he would, with the country he represented, have a great deal of influence on the fate of Barcelona.

'Ovseenko was,' wrote Josep Trueta, who treated him at the Hotel Majestic for a bone fracture, 'a distinguished-looking man, who spoke several languages including French in which he was fluent, and always dressed very smartly in the West European style. His elegant pure silk shirts had early on caught my attention.'

Antonov Ovseenko represented the Soviet Union in Barcelona. He was the man who had planned the occupation of the Winter Palace in October 1917 and later became a member of the first Soviet Government. He was close to Trotsky, but later swore allegiance to Stalin.

As the Civil War progressed Britain and France decided not to assist the loyalists, despite Germany and Italy supporting Franco. On 14 October 1936 the first Russian vessel arrived in Barcelona with food and supplies. Soon, the Soviets would seek an influence which matched their level of support.

In his early days in the city Ovssenko invited García Oliver

and Jaume Miravittles to represent Anarchist and Nationalist views
over lunch. In an interview at around the same time García Oliver
told Cyril Connolly: 'If I had to sum up anarchism in a phrase
I would say it was the ideal of eliminating the beast in man.'
Miravittles remembered how carefully the Russian listened and
how closely he argued his case. García Oliver, soon to become a
minister in the Spanish Government, argued that power must be
held by the working class as the only force which would defeat
Franco. Ovseenko disagreed, believing that a carefully organized
and disciplined broad front would be more effective. García
Oliver wanted his revolution now; Ovseenko later. Their disagree-
ment would make all the difference. Miravittles believed that
Ovseenko was seeking a way to neutralize and control the Catalan
Nationalists and the Anarchists.

But things were changing in the Soviet Union as well as in
Barcelona. The only newspaper in the city which was reporting
the show trials in the Soviet Union was Adolfo Bueso's *La Batalla*,
so much so that the Russian journalist Klitzov noted on 21 January
1937: '*La Batalla* has found one and only one object of its hate
and its daily attacks. It doesn't deal with General Franco nor
General Mola, nor with Italian nor German fascism, but the Soviet
Union.' On his way to visit Ovseenko Josep Trueta found out that
the Russian was being recalled to the USSR where he was told
that he was going to be made a commissar. When he went back
he was executed. But Soviet policy in Barcelona did not change.

*

George Orwell came back to the city in April 1937, after several
months at the Front. 'Everyone,' he wrote, 'who has made two
visits, at intervals of months to Barcelona during the war has
remarked upon the extraordinary changes that took place in it . . .
the revolutionary atmosphere had vanished . . . Fat prosperous
men, elegant women, and sleek cars were everywhere . . . A deep
change had come over the town . . . the normal division of society
into rich and poor, upper class and lower class, was reasserting
itself.'

During the previous months the Generalitat felt powerful
enough to issue an order dissolving the *patrullas de control*. The

Convent of Sant Elias was closed as a prison. In April 1937 only seven members of the clergy were shot in Catalonia; by now any priests who were arrested were held in the Modelo, the official prison. By the end of the year Alexander Werth, the *Manchester Guardian* correspondent in the city, could write that 'priests [are] allowed to say Mass in private houses, but anti-clerical feeling is still so strong in Barcelona that the authorities hesitated to allow Mass to be said in any public place of worship.' Other changes had occurred as well, and the number of those who were joining the PSUC, the Catalan Communist Party, was growing month by month.

'Those early days at the beginning of May 1937,' Jaume Miravittles remembered, 'were wonderfully clear and sunny, with crystal blue skies. Barcelona was enjoying the quiet glory of spring. The war seemed far away.

'Yet gradually and almost imperceptibly the tension was gathering. The power of the Communists was increasing, that of the Anarchists was slowly fading. Those happy people, consisting very largely of refugees from the farmlands of Murcia in the south, dreaming of fraternity and the collective life, with no one earning more than ten pesetas a day – these people with their egalitarian philosophy, their boldness, and their extraordinary courage, thought the millennium was at hand, or would come soon. And they were learning that the millennium was bitter to the taste, and their philosophy of unbridled individualism was dangerous. They were the rulers of Barcelona, but their days were numbered.'

'About midday on 3 May,' George Orwell writes at the opening of chapter ten of *Homage to Catalonia*, 'a friend crossing the lounge of the hotel said casually: "There's been some kind of trouble at the Telephone Exchange, I hear." For some reason I paid no attention to it at the time.'

The Telephone Exchange commanded an important strategic position on the corner of the Plaça de Catalunya; it had been controlled by the Anarchists since 19 July 1936. On 2 May 1937 Jaume Miravittles reports, the President of the Generalitat, Lluís Companys and the President of the Spanish Republic, Manuel Azaña, who was then living in the Parc de la Ciutadella, were

speaking to each other on the telephone when they were inter-
rupted by the exasperated voice of an Anarchist, tired of listening
in to the hated politicians: 'This conversation will have to stop.
We have more interesting things to do than listen to your stupid
conversation.'

Companys knew he could act; saw the way power was shifting
in the city over which he held nominal control. That day he
ordered his troops to take over the Telephone Exchange. In
response the Anarchists gave orders for a general uprising and took
over the city once more. It was their last stand. 'Before midday
on 3 May,' Adolfo Bueso reports, 'the centre of the city was in
the hands of the CNT [the Anarchist trade union] and the POUM.'

Jaume Miravittles had by this time become Secretary of Information in the Generalitat. He braved the streets that morning
unarmed, going from barricade to barricade, from the Plaça
d'Espanya to the Generalitat at the Plaça de Sant Jaume. He was
the first to reach Companys, who asked him what he had seen. 'I
saw nothing but the FAI [the Anarchist militia] and the POUM,'
Miravittles said. Companys nodded. 'It will change,' he said.

That afternoon Orwell saw that a 'crowd of panic-stricken
people was rushing down the Rambla away from the firing; up and
down the street. You could hear snap-snap-snap as the shopkeepers
slammed the steel shutters over their windows . . . In front of
me the crowd was surging into the metro station in the middle
of the Rambla to take cover.'

Orwell walked down the Rambla towards the POUM headquarters, where people were under the impression that the Civil
Guard who had attacked the Telephone Exchange had done so
without Government orders. There was great confusion. At dawn
the following morning Orwell watched the crowd build a barricade, 'a strange and wonderful sight,' he wrote. 'With the kind of
passionate energy that Spaniards display when they have definitely
decided to begin upon any job of work, long lines of men, women
and quite small children were tearing up the cobble-stones, hauling
them along in a hand-cart that had been found somewhere, and
staggering to and fro under heavy sacks of sand.'

Altogether in the city, according to Jaume Miravittles, Anarchists and POUM had put up 'about a hundred barricades, each

five feet high and two feet thick, all of them placed with a superb knowledge of the proper strategical position.'

The crowd knew how to make barricades, they had been making barricades with these cobble-stones for almost fifty years in Barcelona in protest at their miserable wages and insecure jobs, in protest against their exclusion from any share in the growing wealth of the city. They had come together in a philosophy which held the politician, the priest and the bureaucrat in contempt. They talked about, and believed in, human dignity and brotherly love. Once more, they held the city of Barcelona. Once more, in their innocence, they were prepared to let power slip through their fingers: power was in the Plaça de Sant Jaume, in the Generalitat building, but during those days in May they didn't take power. They battled instead for control of the streets.

Jaume Miravittles was at the corner of Via Laietana and Carrer Princesa when two Anarchist cars were ambushed. 'There have been about ten men in each car. They felt safe because the whole of Via Laietana was in their hands. But suddenly from the high balcony of a UGT [Soviet-supported Communist trade union] building at the intersection machine-gun fire broke out. The cars swerved crazily, and men jumped out. They did not jump out in any recognizable way. It was as though, in each car, an enormous compressed spring had suddenly been released. They hurtled out, they seemed to fly in the air while assuming fantastic attitudes and gestures, waving their arms and feet like dancers. It was incredible to see them spinning in the air, and then falling slowly on the road, where they assumed new attitudes, as fantastic as before. The machine-guns did not pause. They continued firing until all the men were shot to pieces.

'At that moment a small rain fell, and slowly, from each body, a red stain began to trickle over the square. The red stains met and ran into one another, and soon the entire square became a lake of blood. The funeral chant for these dead and crumpled Anarchists was provided by the wild blaring of the klaxons of the cars they had so swiftly abandoned. The rain continued to fall, and the blaring of the klaxons went on and on, without end.'

The POUM, to which Orwell belonged, did not want to take over Barcelona. They simply wanted to defend themselves. Next door to their headquarters on the Rambla was the Café Moka, which had been taken over by thirty Civil Guards. The POUM building had to be defended, but instructions had come from the leadership that the POUM militia 'were not to open fire if we could avoid it.'

Orwell was sent to the roof of the Poliorama Cinema, now a theatre, to keep watch on the Café Moka. 'I gathered,' he wrote, 'that the POUM leaders were furious at being dragged into this affair, but felt that they had got to stand by the CNT [the Anarchists].' He spent three days and three nights looking down on to the Rambla. He could see 'the glittering pale blue sea' and 'the fantastic curly roofs with brilliant green and copper tiles'. 'And the whole huge town,' he wrote in *Homage to Catalonia*, 'was locked in a sort of violent inertia, a nightmare of noise without movement. The sunlit streets were quite empty. Nothing was happening except the streaming of bullets from barricades and sand-bagged buildings. Not a vehicle was stirring; here and there along the Rambla the trams stood motionless where their drivers had jumped out of them when the fighting started. And all the while the devilish noise, echoing from thousands of stone buildings, went on and on and on, like a tropical rainstorm, crack-crack, rattle-rattle, roar. Sometimes it died away to a few shots, sometimes it quickened to a deafening fusillade, but it never stopped while daylight lasted, and punctually next dawn it started again.

'What the devil was happening, who was fighting whom, and who was winning, was at first very difficult to discover. Looking out from the observatory, I could grasp that the Rambla, which is one of the principal streets of the town, formed a dividing line. To the right of the Rambla the working-class quarters were solidly Anarchists; to the left a confused fight was going on among the tortuous by-streets, but on that side the PSUC (the Communists) were more or less in control. Up at our end of the Rambla, round the Plaça de Catalunya, the position was so complicated that it would have been quite unintelligible if every building had not flown a party flag.'

Orwell reports that a change came on Wednesday 5 May. He read Adolfo Bueso's newspaper *La Batalla*, which called on everyone to stay at the barricades. The Anarchists still controlled the streets, along with the POUM. Rumours came that the POUM was going to be outlawed; that troops from outside were going to be sent into the city. Later, these rumours would prove to be true. The Anarchist leaders, especially García Oliver and Federica Montseny, appealed to their followers to lay down their arms. They began to negotiate a cease-fire. The Anarchists, at this stage, were deeply divided about tactics.

'The end came swiftly,' Jaume Miravittles wrote. 'When it became clear to the Anarchists that there was nothing they could do with their victory, they clamoured for a cease-fire. Companys said he would discuss the cease-fire only if they came to the Generalitat.'

It was Miravittles' job to go to the Anarchist headquarters through the war-torn streets and accompany the leaders to the Generalitat. 'I could see the machine-guns on the balconies slowly turning as they followed me. The streets were deserted. There was a terrible emptiness in the air.'

The terms of the cease-fire were worked out. It was agreed that there would be no reprisals. The Anarchist leaders called on their supporters to embrace their fellow workers as brothers. But it wasn't as simple as that.

'The Anarchists had committed suicide,' Miravittles wrote. 'They had caused the bitterest fighting known up to that time in Barcelona – it was more severe than the fighting during the Rebellion of 1934, or during the uprising in July 1936. No one knows how many people were killed during those three days of fighting in May. We counted 1,500 dead but there must have been many more.'

It is still unclear whether the Anarchists caused the events of May 1937, as Miravittles claimed. It is a matter which is still disputed in Barcelona and elsewhere. Either way, they lost every-thing in those three days. Companys now had them under his control; they had taken the city for his Government in July 1936, just as the Communists helped to take the city for him now. The Communists were now free to start rounding up the members of POUM, their old Trotskyite adversaries.

By Friday there were special troops in the city, who disarmed the Anarchists and the members of POUM. Both George Orwell and Adolfo Bueso report that the troops behaved 'in a provocative manner' towards members of the CNT. Bueso saw them stopping men with CNT cards, tearing the cards up and throwing the pieces in the bearer's face. Orwell reports them stamping on torn-up CNT cards. 'The workers' militias,' he reported, 'were to be broken up and distributed among the Popular Army.' Word was spread abroad and widely believed that the POUM and the Anarchists had been operating as 'a fifth column' of fascism inside Barcelona. Some of those arrested, who weren't shot, were held in *chekas*, Communist prisons, in the city. Others were held in official prisons with Fascist prisoners for company. An Anglo-French Commission who came to inspect the prisons were rather surprised to hear prisoners singing *L'Internationale* beside others singing the Fascist hymn *Cara al Sol*.

Orwell and others report how bored the Catalans had become with the war, including the fashionably-dressed woman Orwell saw 'strolling down the Rambla, with a shopping basket over her arm and leading a white poodle, while the rifles cracked and roared a street or two away.'

'There must have been quantities of people, perhaps a majority of the inhabitants of Barcelona,' he wrote, 'who regarded the whole affair without a flicker of interest, or with no more interest than they would have felt in the air-raid.'

Elsewhere, however, there was a real war going on, with trenches and troops and two opposing forces facing each other across a landscape. Elsewhere, men were killed in battle. Elsewhere, the front shifted slowly and inexorably; Franco's army moved across Spain, making the war between the Anarchists, the Communists and the POUM seem like a faction fight, a side show, a family quarrel. By the end of July 1936 Franco had captured most of the North of Spain and some of the South, including Seville, Cadiz and Granada. By August, he had taken Badajoz and was making his way towards Madrid. By October 1937 the area around Santander had fallen to Franco, but Madrid still held out. And by July 1938 Franco had divided Republican Spain in two: Catalonia was now cut off from Valencia, Almeria and Madrid, which were still holding out against Franco. But it was only a matter of time.

In November 1936 the Republican Government moved from Madrid to Valencia, and in the autumn of 1937 it moved again from Valencia to Barcelona. There had been, since the war began, considerable tension between Companys and the central government, whose President Manuel Azaña wrote that the Generalitat 'took advantage of the military rebellion to finish with the State's power in Catalonia and then sought to explain everything by saying that the State did not exist.' The Catalan Generalitat took over the customs and the systems of transport, the Bank of Spain and the right to issue money and pardons – powers which technically belonged to Madrid. The tension increased when both governments found themselves lodged in the same city. The Spanish Prime Minister removed Companys' right to sit in the Presidential box at the Opera House. More seriously, both Governments failed to agree on any overall strategy which would help them win the war. The Catalan Government believed that the Madrid government-in-exile was involved 'in a sustained and systematic drive to diminish the authority of the Catalan Government.' Meanwhile, they were losing the war.

Both Orwell and Adolfo Bueso were forced to go into hiding in the city in the months after the events of May 1937; both were lucky to escape being arrested. 'After the summer of 1937,' Orwell wrote, 'those with eyes in their heads realized that the Government could not win the war unless there was some profound change in the international set-up', but the war continued through 1938.

On 16 March 1938 the bombing of Barcelona began. Every two hours, Adolfo Bueso remembered, German and Italian planes dropped heavy bombs. Each bomb could destroy two or three houses, killing all the inhabitants.

'All the old part of the city,' he wrote, 'the port, Barceloneta, Poble Nou, suffered terrible bombings which destroyed hundreds of houses. The area around the Palau de la Generalitat was bombed with great ferocity, but not a single bomb landed on the building, nor did any land on the Ajuntament building. Neither the Cathedral, close by, nor the Bishop's Residence, suffered any damage.'

The city was also bombarded from the sea. In the first three days of the bombings 670 people were killed and 1200 injured.

Thereafter the Generalitat didn't publish any statistics. On 31 May, the village of Granollers, just north of Barcelona, was bombed; there were 150 dead and more than 3000 injured.

'Barcelona,' one commentator wrote, 'was a city of the dead. The cause of death was demoralization. The people were tired of the war, and, long before the enemy's arrival, had only hoped for a sudden end to it.' Food was desperately short; though not for the rich and people in important positions. The American writer Theodore Dreiser was in the city in the late summer of 1938 and reported that 'the hotel at which I stayed was a big handsome structure in the most luxurious European style. Business went on as usual. In the dining room waiters served on silver platters.'

At the end of the year Louis MacNeice came to the city. The 'shops,' he wrote, 'are ghosts of shops, only open in the morning, the counters and shelves bare, one object every two yards. The cafés are ghosts of cafés – no coffee bars, spirits, or wine, people making do with coloured water which is called lemonade, or with terribly degraded vermouth.'

There was no battle for Barcelona. No trenches were dug, nobody defended the city, there was simply a slow waiting for the inevitable, and, when the inevitable came close, there was panic.

On 24 January 1939 Adolfo Bueso and some of his colleagues decided it was time to go. There wasn't a soul in the streets of the city that night; the Nationalists were just a few days away. There was no moon, there were no cars in the streets, and for the first time in months no sound of the whistling of falling bombs. They joined the convoy leaving the city: passing through the silent, dark villages on the road to Mataró: Badalona, Montgat, Canet de Mar. There was a long line of vehicles and, when the bombers came overhead, as they did constantly, everybody jumped as quickly as they could out of the cars and jeeps and lorries and got down on the ground to avoid being killed by a bomb. Ships also began to bombard the convoy slowly moving along the coast road.

Hugh Thomas in *The Spanish Civil War* gives the figures of those allowed into France from Catalonia as 10,000 wounded, 170,000 women and children, 60,000 male civilians and 220,000 men of the Republican Army. Thus almost half a million people arrived in France, including the Catalan and Spanish Government, still bickering among themselves to the very end.

Adolfo Bueso made it to the mountains and crossed into France illegally, after much adventure. It was February now, and the French were ill-equipped to deal with so many refugees. Pau Casals had spent the war in Barcelona, giving concerts, raising money and raising morale. He now found himself in the South of France, witnessing the moral and physical degradation suffered by the refugees in that freezing winter after they had lost the war. 'The scenes I witnessed,' he wrote, 'might have been from Dante's *Inferno*. Tens of thousands of men and women and children were bunched together like animals, penned in by barbed wire, housed – if one can call it that – in tents and crumbling shacks. The camp at Argelès was typical. Here more than a hundred thousand refugees had been massed in open areas among sand dunes along the seashore. Though it was winter, they had been provided with no shelter whatsoever – many had burrowed holes in the wet sand to protect themselves from the pelting rains and the bitter winds.'

Casals tried to raise money for the refugees and began to draw attention throughout the world to the plight of Catalonia and the evil nature of the new Spanish regime. He tried to get to America as the Second World War was breaking out and failed. He moved instead to the town of Prades, in the Catalan-speaking South of France. One of Franco's generals, the same man who had ordered Lorca's execution, said the Nationalists would 'cut off his arms at the elbows' if they found him.

Josep Trueta had already sent his wife and children out of Catalonia; now, when the time came, he joined the convoy himself, and arrived in France, despite relentless bombing from the air. Had he not left the city, he would have been executed: within a few hours of Franco's arrival in the city, five men came looking for him with the intention of 'paying off old scores'. He went to England, where his pioneering work on war wounds proved invaluable to the Allied cause during the Second World War. In the 1940s he published *The Spirit of Catalonia*, which he dedicated to Casals.

Miró was in Normandy living near the painter Braque when the Second World War broke out and the German bombs began.

He was married now; his only child, Dolors, had been born in 1931. He decided to leave France and go back to Spain. In Paris, through good luck, he managed to get a visa and took the train down. At Girona, his old friend Joan Prats met him and told him not to go near Barcelona. Miró had made a fund-raising poster for the Republicans and his name was known: Prats told him that he could be shot if he went to Barcelona. Miró went to Vic, a hundred kilometres to the north, and eventually managed to slip across to Majorca with his wife and child, where he stayed until 1942.

The occupation of Barcelona began on 26 January 1939; by the afternoon the main administrative buildings were taken by the Nationalists. No one knows how many people were killed in the days that followed. The commander of the Italian troops wrote to say that Franco had 'unleashed in Barcelona a very drastic purge'. The secret supporters of the Nationalist cause, who had been lying low for two and a half years, could now make themselves known, and make the names of those who had helped the Republicans known. Also, the Government in its haste to leave had failed to destroy documents which incriminated people in the city.

Hugh Thomas in *The Spanish Civil War* quotes a source which claimed that 10,000 people were shot in Barcelona between 26 and 31 January 1939, and 25,000 were shot afterwards. The source, Thomas says, 'may be right'. Executions continued right through the 1940s and 1950s; many were held in prison for years, others were forced into the army to do long periods of military service.

The repression was fierce, particularly in Barcelona. The Franco era had begun. All public use of Catalan was forbidden; Catalan books were burned. 'We are here,' one representative of the new order told a group of teachers, 'to Castilianise you and to Christianise you.' Even the Catalan bourgeois class, who had not been involved in the war, were punished. In the 1930s Antoni Tàpies' parents had been involved in every aspect of Catalan cultural life. Now they had soldiers billeted in their house, who noticed that Tàpies' father turned off the radio in the evening before *Cara al Sol*, the Fascist hymn, was played. A senior officer came to his house on Carrer de Balmes and told him that he must listen to the hymn in future.

In the prison camps a reign of terror began. The Catalan poet and future biographer of Picasso, Josep Palau i Fabre, was interned in Lleida. Every morning a name was called out at random and the person named was taken out and shot. One day the Barcelona newspaper *La Vanguardia*, then re-named *La Vanguardia Española*, was given to the prisoners. As they were looking through it, they came across a photograph of the Pope. '*Quina cara de fill de puta,*' one of the Anarchist prisoners said in Catalan, meaning 'What a face of the son of a whore'. The following morning this man's name was called. Palau realized that the executions were not random after all. Someone among them was watching, listening.

*

In the English-speaking world the Spanish Civil War has developed certain connotations. Books about it in English have titles like *The Last Great Cause, A Poet's War, A Writer In Arms, Volunteer in Spain*. It is still much talked about on the Left. It is seen as a time when writers and intellectuals believed in a cause enough to go and fight for it, or at least visit the ruined villages and cities and send home reports and poems. Hemingway, Orwell, Auden, Spender and MacNeice were all inspired by the conflict.

MacNeice wrote that the anti-aircraft defence in Barcelona was 'beautiful both to see and hear – balls of cottonwool floating high in the blue day, or white flashes at night. The searchlights also are beautiful, and the red tracer bullets floating in chains gently, almost ineptly, like decorations at a fair.' Auden wrote a poem called *Spain* in which he talked about 'the necessary murder'. (Orwell replied: 'Personally, I would not speak lightly of murder. To me, murder is something to be avoided.' Orwell, unlike Auden, had been to the Front.) In the English-speaking world the Spanish Civil War is like a folk-tale in which youth and courage and conviction and imagination are crushed by a dark, cruel, evil force. 'The police dissected/ The tongues of peasants/ To cut out the words/ The poet had made pleasant,' wrote Stephen Spender.

Among the Catalans it is different. In Barcelona, no one talks about the war: it is not romantic or heroic; it is a trauma that everybody went through, everybody fears, and nobody wants to go through again. In Barcelona, most people will tell you that it was never discussed at home, or even mentioned; most people who live in the city have no interest in the war, or their interest is so bound up with pain and fear that they don't want to talk about it. The writer Manuel Vázquez Montalbán agrees that it is fear which has pushed the memories of the war underground; his father spent five years in jail after the war but, on his release, he did not talk about what it was like. Similarly, Vázquez himself, who spent several years in prison in the 1960s, has never written about it or discussed it.

The idea that the past is intriguing, or that Louis MacNeice thought that the anti-aircraft defence was 'beautiful both to see and hear' or that the Café Moka, at which George Orwell pointed his rifle for three days in May 1937, is still called the Café Moka, doesn't interest Catalans now. It is as though there were two Civil Wars, one for the outsiders, recorded by Orwell, by *For Whom The Bell Tolls* and by *The Penguin Book of Spanish Civil War Verse*; the other for those who live in the country which tore itself apart and have suffered the consequences all their lives.

The hesitant and wounded tone in the writings of the three Goytisolo brothers catches, perhaps more than any other writing, the inward-looking, guilt-ridden feeling which people in Spain have about the Civil War. José Agustín Goytisolo became a poet, Juan and Luis novelists. Their mother, Julia Gay, was killed in the bombing of Barcelona in March 1938. The word Julia haunts the poetry of José Agustín, one of his books is dedicated to 'she who was Julia Gay'; a child's song appears in the same book with the word 'Julia' repeated over and over at the end of each verse. In another poem dedicated to her he writes:

> Where you wouldn't have been
> if one beautiful morning in Barcelona
> in my Barcelona
> full of birds and flowers and girls
> but suddenly smashed
> by the roar of bombers
> flown by men

who laughed and talked and sang
in the German language while they used their machine-guns
because all of them, every last one of them believed
 – though they deny it now –
that they were a race superior to others
while really they were just
the worst race that ever there was on the earth
worse even than desert hyenas who rot everything they touch
worse even than the vultures who live off death
right here
where you wouldn't have been
if that beautiful morning
the gods hadn't forgotten you.

His brother, Juan Goytisolo, author of *Signs of Identity*, the classic novel of the long exile in France after Franco's victory, wrote about their mother in his book *Coto Vedado* (translated into English as *Forbidden Territory*). 'On the morning of 17 March 1938 my mother set out as usual. She left the house at the break of dawn, and even though I know the tricks which memory plays . . . I have a vivid memory of having leaned out of the window of my room while she . . . walked with coat and hat on and her bag towards a final absence: extinction, emptiness, nothingness. It seems without doubt suspicious that I would have woken precisely on that day and, alerted to my mother's departure by her steps or the noise of the door, I would have got out of bed to follow her with my eyes. Nevertheless, the image is real and for some time it filled me full of bitter remorse; not having shouted after her, not having stopped her leaving. Probably it was the result of a subsequent guilt mechanism: an indirect way of blaming myself for my inertia, not having realised the imminent danger, not having made the gesture which, in my imagination, could have saved her.'

*

In October 1988 a statue of David and Goliath was unveiled in the outskirts of the city to commemorate the International Brigades who fought on the Republican side in the Civil War, on the fiftieth anniversary of their departure from Spain. Men who had fought in the war came back to the city from all over the world; others came as well, who had been too young to fight in the war but also wanted to commemorate the International Brigades.

The commemoration was being organized from a tiny, cramped office at the top of a building on Portal de l'Angel. The organizers, themselves veterans of the war, complained about the lack of official interest in the event. The Town Hall and the Catalan Government had agreed to receive the veterans only under great pressure, only when it was explained that some of the old soldiers held important positions in their own countries. The Mayor of Barcelona agreed to unveil the statue.

But the newspapers had no interest in the event, nor did the television or radio stations want to interview any of the old men. A few posters were put up, but otherwise there was nothing. Instead there were flags all over the city to commemorate the Great Exhibition of 1888, with the words *La Nostra Energia* (Our Energy) printed on them.

On the morning of the unveiling the old men gathered in the square where the statue stood. The four Irishmen who had come back after fifty years stood together and had their photographs taken. But the journalists and the photographers were from Ireland, or England, or the United States; there were no Catalans taking photographs or interviewing veterans about what it was like to leave your own country and join in the fight against fascism.

The Mayor of Barcelona, Pasqual Maragall, stood on the platform and held a replica of the statue aloft as though it were a trophy. He spoke in Catalan and French and then in English. He spoke of the need for reconciliation in his country, the need not to humiliate the other side. 'They too had their ideals,' he said in English. There was a stunned silence. One old man shouted up at Maragall, but others did nothing. Quickly, Maragall changed the subject. A Socialist, he now worked closely with Juan Antonio Samaranch, the President of the International Olympic Committee, who was responsible for the running of Barcelona during Franco's regime. In the Catalan Government, a new Minister had been appointed who had also served under Franco. The Civil War was over; its politics and its legacy were now buried.

The veterans of the International Brigades stood up at the end of the ceremony and they sang *L'Internationale*. They had fire in their eyes that morning in Barcelona, fifty years after their defeat, despite the indifference. All the old men and women of the left, who had kept the faith so long, raised their right arms and in all the languages of Europe they sang their hymn.

10

Girona

Girona is two hours' journey north of Barcelona on a slow train. Between the station and the river Onyar the town is dull and grey, a market town built in bits and pieces in the various styles of the last hundred and fifty years. Solid, commercial, a junction for roads that lead elsewhere: the motorway to Barcelona, the motorway to France, the road to the coast.

It is only when you reach the river that you realize that you have arrived in a strange medieval city: the city the Romans called *Gerunda*. The houses back straight on to the river on both sides. From any of the three footbridges which cross it you can stand and watch the colours of the houses reflected in the water, each shade looking as though it was baked hard in the sun: the mustard, the light yellow, the light brown, the white, the deep blue. Each building is painted a different colour, and each colour is made to seem richer by the matching tones in which the shutters and traditional blinds are painted. They take care of the city now that Franco is gone; they know how important it is.

I went there in the early spring when there was still a strong, cold wind coming down from the mountains. But in the mornings if you sat on the sheltered ledge at the side door of the Cathedral the sun was warm enough to keep the icy wind at bay. The Cathedral stands high over the city looking like a great old box. It can be seen from the motorway and the railway, even from the distant foothills of the Pyrenees. There was a Romanesque church on the site in the eleventh century; the Gothic Cathedral was begun in the fourteenth century and finished in 1579. The nave, completed in 1417, is the widest of any cathedral in the Gothic world. The façade was built in 1733, and makes the building look like a square iced cake, belying the solemnity and great power of the building inside.

It comes as a shock then to enter the Cathedral by the side door. The darkness inside is so rich and palpable that it seems to dazzle as the sun dazzles. There are no side columns, nothing to detract from the sweeping arrangement of stone, except the wash of light coming from one of the side windows. The air is cold. Stone upon stone rises up, each one perfectly cut and in place; this is a world ruled by the geometry of the Middle Ages. All over Europe the architects of the great cathedrals were consulted and submitted their views to the architect of the Cathedral of Girona under construction: Would it work? Would the nave stay up without supporting pillars?

The old city is built on a hill and spreads out on both sides of the Cathedral. On one side is Carrer de la Força, part of the Call, the old Jewish quarter. Before the Jews were expelled in the fifteenth century, there were four hundred Jews in a city of 4000 people. More and more emphasis is now being placed on the city's Jewish heritage. Typically, the motives are political: to make Catalonia distinct from Spain by emphasizing its non-Arab influences.

Carrer de la Força is narrow and cobbled. At night it is dimly lit; the streets which wind up to the left seem mysterious, as though they were part of a maze leading towards some Jewish heartland of the past. It seems impossible that anyone would live here, in the houses off these steep lanes leading up to the old walls of the city.

The waking dream of being there is broken only by the sound of cars and motorbikes which noisily brave these cobbled hills. All day the abiding sound is of the honking of horns as cars and bikes prepare to turn blind corners at frightening speeds. Yet at the weekend there is nobody around.

At lunchtime on Easter Saturday we wandered through the old city, which was deserted as though a new Black Death had overtaken it: no cars, no people and at each corner a breath-taking view down a side street, a Romanesque church suddenly appearing, or the mountains coming into view in the green distance.

Signs of the slow transformation from the Romanesque to the Gothic are everywhere. The squat shape of the church of Sant Nicolau to the right of the Cathedral gives way to the less modest and more towering form of Sant Pere de Galligants just beside it. The most stark version of this shift is in the Cathedral itself. In the main building there is no sign anywhere of how it was made; the Gothic construction seems finished, monumental, definitive. The Romanesque cloister, on the other hand, still preserved at the side of the Cathedral, is less imposing and more homely. The arches are lower and rougher, seeming to reflect man's humility rather than the greatness of God and the power of His church. The arches in the Cathedral are perfect in their symmetry and geometry, deeply sophisticated in their conception and three centuries away from the buildings in the cloister.

The Cathedral Museum contains old vestments and jewel-studded monstrances and thuribles, all the grandeur and wealth of the Catholic Church. In the back room, behind glass, however, is the Tapestry of the Creation, from the latter half of the eleventh century, one of Catalonia's great treasures and a masterpiece of Romanesque art. In a series of circles and squares woven in muted shades of green and orange, the Tapestry tells the story of the Creation. The text which fills the rim of the main and the inner circle is from Genesis, although the visual references in the Tapestry are taken from a variety of sources. Christ is in the centre and everything seems to radiate from Him. On one side is Adam with the animals; on the other is Eve emerging from one of Adam's ribs; below are the birds of the air and the fish of the sea, each with a different pattern and colour. The fish are almost comically two-dimensional.

The other treasure of the Cathedral Museum is a book called the *Beatus*, dating from 975, which is a commentary on the Apocalypse with a hundred and fourteen miniatures done in sumptuous colours, suggesting nothing of the sombre quality of the church beside it: all blue, pink, orange and yellow, the colours still perfect a thousand years later.

I was staying in the Hostal Bellmirall in the street of the same name, so close to the Cathedral that the bells seemed to reverberate in the room. In summer there was a huge bunch of sunflowers on the stairs, and the balconies were laden with plants. Everything had been made comfortable for the visitor without interfering with the medieval atmosphere. Two walls of the bedroom had been stripped of plaster to reveal the old stone.

We ventured one day in to L'Hostalet del Call and had turkey and prunes as a main course for lunch. Catalan cooking, in which roasting fruit and fowl together is an important element, is natural in Girona, part of the everyday fare. Another time, L'Hostalet del Call was full and we wandered down along Carrer de la Força until we came to another restaurant which advertised black rice on the menu. We had to wait half an hour for the black rice, and when it came it was indeed black. It was in a large shallow dish and looked as though it had been left too long under a grill and the top of the rice had burnt to a cinder; it was as black as charcoal. The waiter grinned at us and began to serve it. The black colour came from the ink of the squid which had oozed through the rice and hardened very slightly on the top. But the dish, full of shellfish and seafood, was moist and succulent.

*

One day in Carrer de la Força I found a doorway which led into a bar.

The bar was called Isaac el Sec, after Isaac the Blind, a medieval Jewish scholar, and it was built on the site of the Jewish synagogue. The main bar was a patio in the old building overhung by trees, the stairway was covered in ivy. The tiles on one of the eaves were the same cobalt blue and burnt orange as a page of the tenth century *Beatus* which had been open in the Cathedral that day.

In the middle of the day they played sephardic music; but at night it was jazz, the place was lit by lanterns, and spotlights on the soft stone. There were no tourists around; hidden away here, in a small space in the old medieval Jewish quarter of the city, the voices were all Catalan. The bells of midnight rang from the Gothic Cathedral while the hushed voices from the tables around the patio continued on into the night.

One day I called at the Casa de Cultura on the other side of town to see a local historian. I went around to the back door, as instructed, and through a room full of boxes, and then through a room where under a small light a woman was re-assembling the broken pieces of what must have been a large ceramic jug or pot.

The historian explained that the pieces were from an underwater excavation recently made in the sea off Cadaqués which had examined a wrecked ship from the first century. Archaeology in general, she explained, only gives you an idea of what remains; finding a ship tells you what was actually there, a minor miracle for an archaeologist. The woman in the outer room continued working on her small ceramic pieces, remnants of a cargo going somewhere in the Mediterranean in the first century.

All around in the towns and villages were similar remnants: bridges, churches, castles, roads. There were festivals as well which dated from medieval times, which were still put on, not for the tourists or for old times' sake, but for the same reason as always, for entertainment and amusement and to keep evil spirits away.

On Holy Thursday there was a sign up in one of the shops in the village of Verges, north of Girona, which announced that there was still a need for some Apostles, an Angel of the Orchard and a number of shield-holders. This was the night of *La Dansa de la Mort*, the Dance of Death, and no one knew how old it was, or when it began. There was evidence that such a festival had taken place in other towns in Girona, but this was the only one to survive.

The main square was split in two by a stage where, before the Dance of Death, a Passion Play in Catalan rhyming couplets would take place. The locals were dressing up in one of the houses off the square: Jesus was smoking a cigarette and a Roman soldier sported a fat cigar. The Passion began with Palm Sunday, Jesus arriving on a real live donkey. Suddenly, soldiers arrived from all sides carrying spears and torches. There were wild cries and drums as the cross appeared. At times the rhyming couplets took away somewhat from the gravity of the occasion, but the locals and the participants took it all very seriously.

There was a clear sky that March night and a full moon. Along one of the winding narrow streets of Verges snail-shells had been stuck to the wall, filled with oil and a wick placed inside each one, to light the procession through the town. These hundreds of small burning wicks, meticulously placed all over the old walls of houses, were like a sky full of glittering stars. After the Passion

Play, we waited for the real ritual, the dance through the town which had survived the centuries.

In the Town Hall overlooking the square through which the procession would pass, the Mayor of Verges (who belonged to Convergència, the ruling party) had invited the party faithful and various friends to drink champagne and watch the procession from the balcony. There were no priests invited to the Town Hall and there were none to be seen at the Passion Play. Before Franco died, one of the organizers said, the room would have been full of priests and church dignitaries, as well as the local police and the local schoolteacher, all representing Franco. The people of Verges would have stayed out in the cold.

Most of them were still out there now, lining the streets, waiting for the procession to pass, just as their ancestors had done every Holy Thursday for as long as anyone could remember, with the exception of the Civil War years when religious processions had been stopped by the Anarchists. The new rulers of Verges waited on the balcony, champagne glasses in hand. As it moved towards midnight, the night became colder and the sky clearer.

The procession began typically with the figure of Christ being led through the streets, and scenes from the Passion acted out by citizens of the town. Upstairs in the Town Hall we watched this in a desultory sort of way, most people moving away from the balcony to talk among themselves; it was only when the drum-beat started that the room became tense and people crowded to the balcony.

The Dance of Death. A number of figures were moving through the streets dressed as skeletons. Their costumes were black and skin-tight, the bones painted white, almost luminous against the black; the bone structure was detailed, down to toes, ankles, shins, knee joints, spine, ribs and shoulders, all in place, realistic and grotesque. The dance was to a drum-beat, a jig, a shuffle, a loose jump. One of the figures carried a scythe with the message in Latin that none shall be spared, another a sign in Catalan telling us that time is short. There were also two children, dressed as skeletons too, carrying small containers full of ashes, as well as a skeleton carrying a time-piece.

There was something melancholy and understated in the small

leaps and jumps the figures made through the streets, as though this was all that their tired bones could manage. They kept turning towards each other, and then back towards the crowd, as though looking for help or solace. The heads were painted skulls on black, skin-tight material, realistic like their bodies, and expressionless. The skeleton carrying the sign was the centre of the dance and the others moved around him in a monotonous and simple set of movements.

The drummer's hands were a skeleton's hands, but he was dressed in a black tunic, and his face was a mask rather than a skull, a mask designed to frighten and terrorize as he moved through the streets establishing the rhythm of the dance with a thick wooden stick and a drum. Around him were four hooded figures carying torches.

The skeletons' costumes were so well made that as they stopped and did their shuffle it was impossible not to be disturbed by their appearance. It was stark and direct and the sound of the drums was diabolic and mocking in its rhythm. There was an awe in the upstairs rooms as they passed and a stillness down in the square. It was hard, for those few moments, not to feel wonder and fear; the images passing along the street were so powerful, the walking dead, reminding us that to dust we shall all return.

*

The closer you move to the Pyrenees the gruffer people become, the more watchful and serious are their expressions, the less they smile unless there is good reason. The town of Berga, in the province of Girona, is two hours' drive north-west of Barcelona, a place where people seem to keep a careful eye on you if you are a stranger coming into their shop, or walking around the narrow winding streets of their town.

It is a Catalan town, as someone pointed out to me almost as soon as I arrived, and the Arabs never set foot in the place. The people of Berga have a particular way of speaking Catalan, keeping the vowel sounds to a minimum, letting the liquid 'l' sounds flow over their speech like molten lava. They frown a lot as they speak; they take things seriously.

In particular, they take their Patum seriously. This is a festival of fire which takes place on the Thursday of Corpus Christi and the following weekend. Like the Dance of Death, La Patum has its origins in the medieval world. Outsiders are not encouraged to come to Berga for La Patum on Corpus; the first night is for the people of the town, who know the dances, the jumps, and the passes, who know how to follow the fire and stay out of trouble at the same time. Visitors can come on Sunday when a special Patum is held for them. The citizens of Berga like to keep things regulated and orderly.

So on the afternoon of Corpus, there was nothing festive about the atmosphere in Berga, no shouting in the streets, no groups of young people singing and dancing. The bars of Berga were, in fact, singularly quiet; the shops were closed.

Later, a few of them would open to sell special hats and scarves and T-shirts to keep the sparks from burning the participants. I was strongly advised to invest in this special gear before setting foot in the square where La Patum would be enacted once more. It was important to be on time, I was told, because as soon as the church in the square rang half past nine, the drummer and the musicians would begin.

The dignitaries and their close friends and relations sat on the balcony of the Town Hall overlooking the square; the giants, the eagle and the dwarves were in the Town Hall awaiting their turn. On a slope above the square chairs had been provided for those who didn't want to risk getting burned and stamped on during the next few hours of music and fire. Others sat on the steps of the church near the band. The man in charge, the man with the huge drum which sounds *Patum, Patum*, sat on his own special balcony constructed on the other side of the square. Anyone who lived on the square and owned a balcony had plenty of friends and they all watched and waited for the clock to sound half past nine. Down in the square the crowds were ready, wearing red hats and red scarves and old clothes.

The first to come were the Turks on Horseback, moving through the crowd to the beat of the music and the drums. The music was brassy and jolly, but with that odd note of melancholy which characterizes the music of the *sardana*, the Catalan national dance. The crowd's job was to move around the square, following the figures in small or large groups, all the time being pushed, jostled and shoved. Those who knew the ropes, who had Berga in their blood, could move around the square without hitting into anyone.

After the Turks had done their rounds came Michael the Archangel and the devils, each carrying a sort of tambourine with fireworks attached, which spewed out sparks every time it was shaken. The square was full now, you could barely move, and the organizers worked hard pushing the crowds back, protecting the figures, directing thousands of people who were moving at considerable speed, following the fire.

It was becoming more dangerous. Now it was the monster, four or five strong men held up his back, and one took control of his long neck which led to a ferocious head with long sticks of fireworks attached. The crowd ran after him and he ran after the crowd. He took particular interest in anyone standing at the edges of the square, anyone protected by a wall, or anyone who carried an umbrella to protect himself from the sparks. The fire coming out of his mouth seemed to go on and on as the ferocious music played.

The eagle which came next was almost as big as the monster. It wore a crown and its long tail became a lethal weapon when it twirled. The music changed its measure, became solemn and ceremonious, stately and somewhat sad as the eagle careered around the square. The frenetic tone was gone, there was no shouting, no tumult, just this strange bird and the people, open-mouthed. Suddenly, the music changed, everybody waited for it, the moment at which the slow music would give way to a beat which was sudden, loud and clear. The eagle began to move faster, faster as the music speeded up. Everybody jumped up and down to the beat. All the sadness was just a preparation for this. In the last moments the eagle turned and turned and anyone close by lay on the ground to avoid a smack from its long tail. Legend says that its tail had once killed a soldier. Then the eagle was led, victorious, back into the Town Hall.

The giants who came next were placid and regal. They were followed by the dwarves whose heads were far too large for their bodies. They danced together in the middle of the square.

One by one men with their heads and shoulders covered in grass, with fireworks coming out of the grass, began to appear in the square. They mingled with the crowd. The balconies were now full, the square was packed, there was a sense of anticipation, as though the real Patum were only now about to take place. I had booked a spot at a second floor window overlooking the square, and I now moved there, as the dance of the dwarves was coming to an end. The figures covered in grass had fanned out to all parts of the square, there were more than seventy of them.

When the dwarves had finished the square became tense and crowded as more people wearing headgear to protect themselves tried to move towards the centre. Then the lights went out, all the shops and houses and the two bars in the square turned off their lights as the music started. The square was in darkness, the drum beat was more concentrated, *Patum, Patum*, the drum beat out the sound as the grass-men lit their fireworks. I could see the swirl of people down below, moving round and round the square, as though pursued. Soon the smell of sulphur from the fireworks was overwhelming, it filled the square and the only light was the light from firesticks, which was all sparks and was soon clouded in smoke. Soon, you could see nothing except smoke rising and a vast soup of human figures, doing an infernal dance, like water bubbling. The music was loud and fast and had a demonic edge to it, a sort of mocking gaiety, and it was clear as the smoke and the smell of the sulphur rose, and the crowd below seemed to suffer, desperately moving and pushing among swirls of spark and smoke, it was clear that this was a vision of hell, with all the medieval imaginings of fire and brimstone, darkness and pain. This was the devil's cauldron, the place to which you could go for all eternity, being acted out on the feast of Corpus Christi.

When it was over and I went back down to the square, everyone was exhausted. Soon, the whole thing would start again: the monsters, giants, eagles, dwarves and then the great smoke. In the meantime, the bars were serving a cocktail called *mau-mau* in big *porrons*, which had a spout from which large numbers could drink each in his or her turn as it was passed from hand to hand. It was nearly over, someone said to me, it would be done again on Sunday night, but it was never the same, as it wasn't for the people of Berga. On Friday afternoon there would be a smaller Patum, with all the same ingredients, for children, so the next generation could come to know their heritage: when to jump, when to follow the giants, and what to do when the fire began.

11

The Catalan Summer

Ana Maria Dalí, Salvador Dalí's sister, remembered how Federico García Lorca came to stay with them in the summer of 1927 at Cadaqués on the Costa Brava. She recalled the boat trips they took: to Cap de Creus, to Tudela – the calm sea and the languorous heat in the afternoons of high summer. She remembered how in one of the coves they would snooze for a while in the shade. In her memoirs she conjured up the colours of the rocks around Cadaqués, the soft shale in the light of the hard sun, and beyond, the wide transparent sea. They would row back to Cadaqués, Lorca afraid, as always, of the sea, no matter how calm it was. It would be dark by the time they arrived.

'In that time,' she wrote, 'Tudela was a solitary place, out of the world. Now, since they have built a club, it has nothing to do with the dream place of our excursions with Federico.'

Later, when the tourists had begun to come to the Costa Brava, that elegaic note would be sounded in all writing and all comment on the Costa Brava: that sense that things were perfect once, the coast untouched, the beaches deserted. In the 1950s there was nothing, a few hotels, a few summer houses, a string of quiet coves and fishing villages, a few Germans. Nothing more. It was where your parents fell in love.

Places like Tossa de Mar, Arenys de Mar, Lloret de Mar and Blanes moved in ten years from being quiet, Catalan speaking villages, where you would go from Barcelona on a summer Sunday when the city was still small, and you would find no crowds, no loud music, no foreigners, just this 'Wild Coast'. Now these villages were advertised in the windows of travel agents all over northern Europe, and came to mean cheap holidays, cheap booze, sun, crowds, 'English spoken here'.

The Catalan singer Maria del Mar Bonet comes from the island of Majorca where she was born in the late 1940s. She remembers Majorca as a paradise, *una meravella*, she can't find words to describe how beautiful the island was before they built the hotels and brought the package tours. In her songs, when she uses the word *Majorca*, she gives it an emphasis as though she could create the old place again just by singing the word and creating an aura of wonder and mystery around it: her Majorca, a dream place now, half remembered, half imagined. More and more she fails to understand the point of tourism, why they come to her island, what they want. Everywhere you go in the summer – it is the winter now and we are talking in a bar in Barcelona – you smell that awful sun tan oil the tourists use. She grimaces. *That smell.* And the drunkenness, even during the day you find them drunk in the bars. And the pain of knowing that it cannot come back, the old island, that no one can resurrect it.

But the old world still exists beside the new world of discos, high rise apartments and package tours. The old, solid, sedate world. The Catalans have repossessed the hills a few miles inland from the Costa Brava, made them their own, built houses, sheltered by the pine trees. It is, to an extent, a secret world, untouched by the mass tourism of the Costa Brava; it is a stable, traditional society. It pays no attention to what is going on a few miles away. And if you know these hills, as so many Catalans do from childhood, then you can use the old tracks and lanes to avoid the traffic which plagues the coast.

All summer, as the outsiders come for cheap holidays, cheap drink and cheap sun, the locals organize festivals of classical music in the villages on the coast. At Peralada in July and August of that summer Yehudi Menuhin played, José Carreras gave his first professional concert since his recovery from leukaemia, which the Queen of Spain and the Princess of Wales attended, and Montserrat Caballé gave a free concert in the main square. At Palamós one night we went to the local church to hear the Vienna String Quartet play Ravel and Schubert. Except for a handful of Japanese there were no tourists; the audience were all local people. As the slow movement of the Schubert Quartet proceeded, as the music rang clear in the dead silence, it was hard to remember that the month was August, the place was a popular resort on the

Costa Brava, and the tourists were all just a few yards away in the bars and restaurants.

Costa Brava means 'Wild Coast' and some of the coast is rocky and beautiful. There are no long stretches of beach, just small coves and then sheer rock falling into the sea. And all around, everywhere you go, pine trees, Mediterranean pine and white pine, covering everything that isn't built on. I watched one evening from the hill above Sant Felíu where the old church stands. Down below on the right-hand side was one of the busiest resorts on the coast; on the other side were wild rock and pine trees and a sheer drop into the sea. In that evening light the rock was a deep veined red, with purple and pink cut through it. If you turned your back to the beach at Sant Felíu, you could be in a place untouched for centuries, a strangely-coloured landscape, placid and calm in the fading light.

*

Barcelona that August was like a lost city under water, as the waves of heat went through the streets, as the temperature went into the nineties and then for a few days into the low hundreds. It was oppressively humid. But most people were away; whole streets in the city centre had closed down, and almost every shop in certain quarters had a sign saying it was closed for holidays until 1 September. Restaurants, bars, stalls in the market closed. Whole apartment buildings were left empty. No one was at home, even the politicians disappeared. When a Communist politician, Pere Portaella, gave a party, it was big news. There was no other news; the departure and the return of the holiday-makers were reported in the newspapers at the beginning and end of the month as though they were military operations.

The custom and ceremony of abandoning the city were matched by the custom and ceremony surrounding where you went. For most Catalans the idea of leaving Catalonia and going to some other part of the Iberian Peninsula was unimaginable; it was important for right-thinking Catalans to go to the same place every year, either on the coast or in the mountains. Where you went for August was like the clothes you wore, the part of the city you lived in, the restaurants or nightclubs you went to: a way of letting the world know who you were.

The further north you went along the coast the higher your credibility. Llançà, for example, could be mentioned with pride, and so indeed could Port de La Selva, but other places further south, such as Blanes, Lloret or Tossa were too vulgar, too loud, full of too many foreigners. In the months leading up to August I kept meeting people who told me that there were still coves, beautiful sandy coves, guarded by the red rock and the pine trees on either side, which nobody knew about, where you didn't find tourists, where you would find almost nobody on a Sunday in August. But you had to know such places, and that these places could only be known by Catalans – outsiders had no feel for the Costa Brava.

For many people in Barcelona the Costa Brava is too far away for a day trip: the trains don't go there and the buses don't go often enough and are too expensive. For these people the coast is the Costa de Maresme to the north, between the city and Blanes: beaches like those at Caldetes, Calella, Sant Pol, Llavaneres, Canet. On Sundays from June to September the trains to these resorts are packed. There are very few tourists on these beaches; they are crowded with city people. And there are big differences between the city people here on an August Sunday and the city people at Sant Felíu or Palamós or Roses on the Costa Brava.

The differences include such things as language, class, origin and politics. The people on the train speak Spanish, they are part of the huge wave of immigrants from the south of Spain who came to Catalonia from the 1960s onwards. They work in the factories and live in the suburbs of the city. They vote Communist and Socialist. They are well dressed, but less self-consciously so than native Catalans, less aware of the need to attend to fashion. Nearly every time I travelled on one of these Sunday trains during the years when I lived in Barcelona there would be a big woman in the carriage, who either had found a seat and wanted everybody else to stop leaning against her, or didn't have a seat and forced the poor, crushed day-trippers to move over and make way for her. Her voice offered a running commentary on the journey, and others would join in, to bicker with her first, but then initiate a general discussion. The accents would all be southern as the overcrowded train rocked back to Barcelona.

The beaches themselves would be overcrowded as well, there would be noise from radios, from youths who clapped their hands in unison to a *flamenco* rhythm, from the trains passing up and down. The pedal boats would have up to ten laughing young people balancing on them and diving off into the sea. The cheap restaurants would serve hamburgers and chips. And as the sun faded over the hills behind, people would pack up their stuff and get ready to go, standing on the railway platform, hoping that the next train would not be too full, but it always was on these Sundays, full to bursting point of the city's working class, and a groan would go up at the station when they saw how full the train was, and they would know how slow it was going to be, how it would keep stopping for no reason, how they would have to stand the whole way.

For years the beach at Barceloneta, a peninsular arm of Barcelona itself, was unused. Nobody in his or her right mind would go down there for a swim. Barceloneta was a world apart from the city, like an overcrowded fishing village, full of corner shops and local bars, and everywhere you went in the narrow, ramshackle streets there was a smell of fish. Barceloneta had become known for its seafood, especially for the fish restaurants backing on the sea, which had touts outside all night trying to entice you in. All the restaurants looked the same: long, old-fashioned dining rooms with wooden floors and board ceilings and windows which gave on to the beach. On winter nights they were wonderful places when the moon was shining on the sea, when the cold was kept out by the glass panels, with the sound of the sea pounding just a few yards away from the restaurant table.

But recently the Socialists have tried to make Barceloneta look like a seaside resort. The beach has been cleaned, showers have been installed, there are chairs and pedal boats for rent. They have built an esplanade above the beach so you can stand with your elbows on the railings and watch the crowds down below. It works. People have begun to go there rather than brave the train to the Costa del Maresme. From May onwards it is crowded at the weekend with the working class of Barcelona, who seem undeterred by the sea's pollution from the city.

The atmosphere here is totally different from that of Sitges or the Costa Brava. Along the esplanade no one is carefully dressed: the men's faces are marked and lined, and people look as though they have spent all their lives toiling at manual or factory work. On Sunday they walk along the esplanade with their wives and children, at ease.

Barceloneta is a quiet place at night; the empty streets are safer than those of the city centre. The streets are built on the same grid system as the Eixample, but Barceloneta is older, built in the eighteenth century when hundreds of houses were knocked down to make way for the Citadel, now the Parc de la Ciutadella. You can swim at night in the sea here, the beaches are lit, and some of the bars serving *tapas* and fish with cold beer are open late. During the summer it is perfect for shaking off the heat of the day.

*

In the mountains the days were hot too. The mountains were becoming more and more popular. I had first gone to the Pyrenees in the months after Franco died. It was hard then to get to the village of Llavorsí, to the west of Andorra in the province of Lleida; it took seven hours by bus from Barcelona, and then, to get to one of the villages even higher up, you had to get a jeep to take you along a precarious dirt track which corkscrewed its way around the mountain. The landscape was dramatic and exciting, and there was a sense of being cut off from the real world; no one would come up here without good reason. I knew people in one of the villages, which made it easier, as there were no hotels beyond Llavorsí.

One of the villages had been abandoned, the houses, some of them quite large and in perfect condition, left empty by the owners, who had gone to the city or moved elsewhere. In those days they could be rented cheaply, and could be bought for very little. A group of young people from Barcelona moved to this village and tried to make a living out of the land around. By 1988 some of them were still there and had succeeded.

But other changes had come. I went there now in 1988 in the height of the summer. Within an hour of leaving the city the bus had passed the monastery at Montserrat on top of the cone of melted rock and was in the pre-Pyrenees, passing fields of sunflowers and dried-up rivers. At this time in the morning – the bus left Barcelona at seven thirty – there was a low grey mist down over the fields. The bus was full, the people all around us were going hiking in the mountains. As we climbed, my ears began to pop with the rising air pressure. As the morning went on, it became hot, we passed by fields of ripe peach trees and others full of olive trees, we passed by villages stretched out over the small hills, and soon the sheer bare rock of the Pyrenees began to appear.

I remembered Llavorsí as quiet, settled, dull. Now as we arrived in the early afternoon, it was full of cars, the shops were full of locals and tourists vying for the attention of the assistants, the bars were busy. Soon I discovered that the two jeeps which could take passengers to the villages higher up were out for the day, both ferrying tourists around the mountains. There was even a queue in the restaurant in the small village. The tourists seemed to be made up of native Catalans, French and people from various parts of Spain.

Eventually, at five o'clock, the jeep came and agreed to take us up the mountain. I told the driver how many years it was since I had been here and he laughed and said that things had changed, there were tourists all summer now, his jeep was busy all day, as was the restaurant, which he also owned. I'd find the villages had changed as well, he said.

The main change was the road, they had paved the road, and they had put in metal barriers to prevent vehicles from sliding off. They had removed the inaccessibility of these villages and, to an extent, their mystery. In the first village they had also built a swimming pool, an unimaginable luxury ten years before. Now these places were normal, on the map. The highest village was no longer abandoned, the number of young people had grown. Everywhere, houses were being done up. Some of those which had been refurbished were going to be used for only a month of the year, holiday homes high up in the mountain with clean air, cool streams and a swimming pool nearby.

I spent a few days walking in the mountains. Twelve years earlier you would meet no one on these tracks. You could spend a whole day walking without seeing a car. Now, I constantly had to stand out of the way while cars passed, cars which had taken advantage of the new tarred road. Generally, the cars were full, driving slowly, going nowhere, the passengers enjoying the view, the altitude, the remoteness, but they didn't really know what to do. They arrived at a point, stopped the car, admired the view, turned the car around and went back down the mountain, forcing anyone walking to stand back into the siding once more. They seemed bemused, slightly puzzled. I was bemused and puzzled as well, by the inexorable progress of tourism. In twelve years, an area which had been cut off from the world, a magic mountain, had become part of the tourist mainstream, had joined the beaten track.

*

Figueres is the main market town north of Girona, the last place where the train stops before it reaches the French border at Port Bou. It is a solid place, business-like and quiet, largely unaffected by the tourism on the coast. But for the birth of Salvador Dalí in the town in 1904, it would be another dull Catalan town. Now Dalí's peculiar spirit infests the place: a whole square of the town is taken up with his visual jokes and morbid obsessions. There is a museum dedicated to the twists and turns of his strange mind.

Dalí's father, the town notary, sent him to Madrid to study art in the early 1920s and there he made the acquaintance of a large number of Spanish writers including Rafael Alberti, Juan Ramón Jiménez, Antonio Machado, and Federico García Lorca who became his great friend. He invited Lorca to Figueres for the Easter of 1925; later they would go to Cadaqués, where the Dalís had a summer house, and to Port de la Selva where Lorca was introduced to a number of Catalan intellectuals who were staying there. The following week he read his work in Figueres; the local newspaper called him 'a true poet'.

That summer of 1925 Dalí exhibited two paintings, including

a portrait of his friend Luis Buñuel, in a group show in Madrid. In the winter, he had his first one-man show in Barcelona at the Galeria Dalmau, where Miró had also exhibited. The following summer he refused to submit himself for examination at his art school in Madrid, telling his teachers that they were not competent to judge his work. Dalí's father became worried about his son's professional future.

The students' residence in Madrid where Dalí stayed was a centre of intellectual discussion and liberal thought: arguments would go on all night about art. Dalí wrote to Sebastià Gasch about the difference between himself and Lorca: 'I rejected every human emotion . . . my preferences only had room for purely intellectual sentiments.' He told Alain Bosquits: 'He [Lorca] was homosexual, as everyone knows, and madly in love with me. He tried to screw me twice . . . I was extremely annoyed, because I wasn't homosexual, and I wasn't interested in giving in. Besides, it hurts. So nothing came of it. But I felt awfully flattered vis-à-vis the prestige. Deep down I felt that he was a great poet and that I did owe him a tiny bit of the Divine Dalí's asshole.' Years later, when he was asked about Lorca's death he said that he was very pleased about it, it made him happy.

All his life he would revel in such remarks, in such gratuitous cruelty. His work, too, from the time he first exhibited *Blood is Sweeter Than Honey* in Barcelona in 1927, is full of shocking tricks, rotting bodies, scenes in which human bodies are rendered as carcasses. 'In his outlook, his character, the bedrock of decency of a human being does not exist,' George Orwell wrote.

In the late 1920s Paris was still the capital for an artist in Barcelona. Luckily for Dalí, both Picasso and Miró now lived in Paris where they were well established and both were interested in any new talent in Barcelona. Miró brought Pierre Loeb, his dealer, to Figueres to look at Dalí's work and wrote to Dalí's father to advise him to let his son spend time in Paris. 'I am absolutely convinced that your son's future will be brilliant.'

Dalí saw Picasso in Paris when he went with his sister Ana Maria and his step-mother. 'Each one of us knew who the other was,' he boasted in an interview in 1973. Dalí was twenty-two at the time. Pierre Loeb did not offer him a contract, but advised him to keep working. Dalí went back to Figueres and his second exhibition at the Galeria Dalmau opened on New Year's Eve 1926. He worked hard over the next several years. In his autobiography, he wrote: 'I would awake at sunrise and, without washing or dressing, sit down before the easel . . . I spent the whole day seated before my easel, my eyes staring fixedly, trying to "see" like a medium.' He would try to paint then, as realistically as he could, what his mind's eye had presented: 'the profile of a rabbit's head, whose eye also served as the eye of a parrot . . . And the eye served another head, that of a fish enfolding the other two.'

In the spring of 1929 he went to live in Paris, using Miró, once more, as his introduction. Through Miró he met Robert Desnos, Tristan Tzara and André Breton. Dalí feigned a childlike helplessness in relation to the practical world. 'He was so marvellously funny,' wrote one of the Surrealists, 'he could make everyone but himself howl with laughter.' He began work with Buñuel on *Un Chien Andalou*; both men later saw themselves as the main inspiration behind the film, Dalí, as usual, stating his case more memorably when he said that the film was a testimony to his genius and Buñuel's talent.

Dalí's biographer Meryl Secrest writes: 'Buñuel shot the fifteen-minute film in two weeks, with a skeleton crew of five or six . . . Dalí arrived on the set a few days before the end and spent most of his time pouring great pots of sticky glue into the eye sockets of rotten donkeys; he also made a brief appearance as a priest. To add to everyone's sense of what was fitting, the film's leading man, Pierre Batcheff, committed suicide on the final day. Buñuel was so emotionally involved himself that he was ill for several days after shooting the film's most ghastly sequence in which he appeared to slice a human eye with a razor.'

Dalí found a dealer in Paris and began to exhibit regularly; his work began to sell, his fame spread. In August 1929 in Cadaqués he met the poet Paul Eluard and his Russian wife Gala, who were staying at the Miramar with René Magritte and his wife. In September Eluard went back to Paris alone; Dalí had become obsessed with Gala, much to his family's annoyance. That autumn in Paris, he exhibited a version of the *Sacred Heart* with the words: 'I sometimes spit on my mother's portrait for pleasure.' It was part of Dalí's stock-in-trade, but his father was deeply offended, and, when he arrived at Figueres for Christmas with Buñuel, he was thrown out. With the money he made from a new contract with a dealer, Dalí bought a small hut in Port Lligat, near Cadaqués, for himself and Gala Eluard, who divorced her husband in January 1932.

In 1934 Dalí and his father were reconciled. The following day he was in Barcelona to give a lecture for Dalmau on Surrealism when Lluís Companys declared Catalonia an independent state. The city erupted and Dalí couldn't wait to get out. Ten years previously, under the dictatorship of Primo de Rivera, he had spent a week in jail following a round-up of Anarchist sympathizers, possibly because he was mistaken for his father. This time he found a driver and made straight for the border. He recounted what happened at a checkpoint: 'One of them, looking me in the eye, suggests we ought to be shot, there and then, as an example. I fall back on the car seat. I gasp for breath.' On the return journey, the driver was killed by a stray bullet.

Dalí went to America, where his hard work and his talent at self-promotion combined to make him famous. In 1934, when he was only thirty, Dalí had two one-man shows in Paris, one in Barcelona, one in London and two in New York. At a fancy-dress party given in his honour in New York, according to Meryl Secrest, Gala 'was sporting in the centre of an enormous black headdress . . . a baby's corpse. The doll had a wound on its forehead, carefully painted by her husband, that was filled with ants, and its skull was being clutched by a lobster.'

The Dalís kept out of Spain during the Civil War; in fact they did not return to Europe until 1948, when they re-built a number of cottages at Port Lligat. They were rich now; Dalí's images were world-famous, and he worked tirelessly on illustrations, advertisements and limited editions. Both he and Gala had become avaricious – as early as 1942 André Breton had invented an anagram for his name: *Avida Dollars*. The house at Port Lligat was extended and furnished in suitable Dalí style. In the late 1960s he bought a castle close to Figueres. By this time the Dalís had a whole court of helpers, hangers-ons, advisers, secretaries and sexual performers. Dalí began to co-operate with forgers; his surreal visions had by now become easy to copy.

In Barcelona during the mid-1970s there was a great deal of talk about the Dalís. Gala had undergone an operation for 'rejuvenation', and had developed a liking for young men. Salvador, on the other hand, liked to watch other people having sex, but nothing too strong. Anyone young and able could find suitable employment with the Dalís, it was said.

Barcelona was changing then. Many people had been abroad on holidays or business. Most movies were let in uncensored, most books were available. People lived in a free country of their own invention, despite the police, despite the dying Dictator. In September 1975, it was clear that Franco hadn't long to go; no one believed that he would execute five prisoners who had been sentenced to death. His grip had loosened on the country. The Transition had already begun which would end in democracy. I was there that horrific weekend when he went through with the executions.

Dalí sent Franco a telegram of congratulations, and then said on French radio that others who were pardoned should have been executed as well. Of all the things he did and said, it was perhaps the most callous and the most foolish. He was not forgiven. (When he died, for example, the writer, Manuel Vázquez Montalbán suggested that his paintings should be shown in the Valley of the Fallen, close to Franco's tomb.) To avoid confrontation and threats Dalí went to America, and he was there when Franco died on 20 November. From then on, Dalí would be a strange and inaccessible figure, a prisoner, some said, of Gala, or of his assistants. Jaume Miravittles, who had known Lorca and Dalí in Barcelona in the 1920s and worked for the Catalan Government in the 1930s, wrote an open letter to Gala in a Barcelona newspaper asking why her husband could not be visited by his old friends.

Gala died in Port Lligat in 1982. Dalí took her body out of the house to his castle at Puból and never returned to Port Lligat. Two years later he almost died of burns at Puból and it became clear that he was suffering from malnutrition. Those around him were becoming rich at his expense. He was lonely and unhappy, as he moved into his museum building in Figueres. Gala, his ice-goddess, his madonna, was dead. He refused to eat, afraid that the food would choke him. He had a tube up his nose all the time. He grew close to an image from his own work as he moved towards death.

The museum which Dalí built in Figueres is in an old theatre in a square off the main street of the town. The square is full of Dalí jokes: an old statue mounted on tractor tyres; the head of an old giant with a television screen set into it; a totem pole made of television sets; Dalí and Gala in cameos in the wall with angels around them; eggs in a big glass case with a man's head, a child's head as eggs and a 1950s style television set. All the old Surrealist jokes: Dalíland.

The main galleries form a semi-circle. Below is a patio with an old-fashioned car in it. Behind the patio, where the stage of the theatre might once have been, is a huge window, and behind the window is a painting of a large human figure with a cracked head. Every little corner is peopled with one of Dalí's creations. The museum, with its overwhelming sense of whim, is probably the best thing Dalí ever did. There are plaster nudes in the windows, wash-basins on the wall, paintings where two dimensions appear as three if looked at in a certain way. There is a large column of tyres with a Neptune figure on the top, then a boat with an umbrella for a sail.

There are lips for arches, breasts as drawers and knots as nipples, not to speak of knobs as navels and drawers as foreheads. There are jokes with espadrilles, there are figures made of spoons. There is a room once decorated in the neo-classical style to which Dalí has added electricity, over-elaboration and over-emphasis to make it look ridiculous.

In the patio is the big, old-fashioned black Cadillac. Inside, the driver is covered in ivy, and through the broken windows at the back you can see a woman and a man in a mask with barnacles all over him and a hole for a stomach. The car looks like something which has been fished out of the sea. If you put twenty-five pesetas into a slot, rain pours from the roof and washes all over the three inhabitants of the car. This is great fun; everybody comes to watch as the inside of the car is drenched. For once Dalí is offering value for money.

Crowning this museum full of Dalí's garish sense of party-piece apocalypse is a geodesic *à la* Buckminster Fuller and under the dome is another game you can play: a small doll has been placed inside a network of metal bars, which, when you put your money in the slot, begin to move slowly towards the centre, thereby squashing the figure to death. It is a deeply disturbing image, made more disturbing by the fact that the groups of us standing around were intrigued by the process; someone put more money in and we watched it again.

Dalí's presence can also be deeply felt in the village of Cada-qués. I took the bus there from Barcelona in the first weekend of September. Once out of the city on the road to the coast we were back in that world of soft hills and densely-packed pine trees I had known all summer. After two hours we came to Roses and then we turned left towards Cadaqués. Suddenly, everything changed. The soft Mediterranean landscape gave way to a harsh, arid, mountainous world. The day was hot and windy, the sky completely blue. At certain moments as we moved up the steep roads and then down again, we could have been in the west of Ireland – Clare, or the Dingle Peninsula – on a high, windy summer day.

Much of the landscape seemed charred, having suffered badly from forest fires. It looked as though nothing would grow again. The land was harsh and grey against the glinting blue of the sea at Port de la Selva, and then Cadaqués, which we had begun to glimpse down below.

When I got out of the bus and asked directions, I could smell the smoke. And as I walked along a narrow winding road on a hill above Cadaqués, it was almost choking. Then I realized that one of the nearby hills was on fire, its whole shoulder burning and smouldering; the smoke was being blown towards the sea by the fierce wind. So black and dense was the smoke that at times I couldn't see more than a few hundred yards ahead. The whole effect was like a Dalí joke, heightened as I approached the hotel and found two large egg-shaped structures and a life-size camel in the building next door, with this acrid, black smoke whirling past.

I did not know that the house I was looking at was his house, the house in which Gala had died, nor did I know that the hotel where I was to take shelter from wind and fire was in his style. But I might have guessed when I saw that the entire lobby of the hotel was showing an exhibition of toilet seats, all transformed in one way or another, given surreal new dimensions. I looked at them for a while until a man appeared at the desk. I asked him in Catalan for a room. We played our various parts, he telling me I could have the room for a few nights only and the price, I handing him my passport and telling him the price was all right. We ignored the toilet seats. I was shown to my room.

There was such a wind over the sea, such a wind howling that when I opened the balcony shutters they were nearly blown off their hinges and when I stepped out onto the large tiled balcony the wind whistled in my ears and blew so hard that I had to go back in and shut the window. I went back into the room, relieved by the quiet and the calm. It was a day for staying indoors.

The wind, I learned, was called *La Tramontana*; it usually lasted for three days, but it could last longer and had already been blowing for two days. Who knew when it would end? For lunch I met some friends who were also foreigners and they confirmed what I had already suspected: the people of Cadaqués were gruff and surly. In a bar, a restaurant, even on the street you felt like an intruder into their strange, mountainous world. I had come across Catalan surliness before; but the manners of the populace of Cadaqués were something startling, which none of us could properly decipher.

The landscape was bare and inhospitable as well; altogether there was something dark and forbidding about Cadaqués which seemed to affect everybody, not just the natives. The tourists too, who were mostly Germans, seemed depressed and low; in the morning people sat at the bars beside the shore and looked out to sea, read the papers, talked quietly.

As the days went by, I almost came to believe that I was on an island, far apart from the rest of Catalonia. It was like suddenly finding the dreamed-of seaside resort which is quiet, cheap and remote, where the fish for dinner is fresh and well cooked in the small restaurants, where the bars are open late, where the small coves are completely deserted, where pleasure boats and fishing boats come and go, where there are paths over the hills and along the cliffs that you can walk along and meet nobody.

Cadaqués is built on a small slope, the buildings are white and perfectly kept. There is a plaque on the house where Picasso stayed in the summer of 1910 when André Derain was also brought here by Ramon Pitxot, who had married Carlos Casagemas' beloved Germaine. There is a plaque in the bar where Marcel Duchamp played chess.

The weekend was coming, the first weekend in September, and the man at the reception desk told me my room was needed and I would have to go. I didn't want to move hotel. Port Lligat was a good distance uphill from the town, I enjoyed walking back at night in the dark, with the view in the moonlight of the bare mountain against the sky. I liked the view from my window. I liked the beam of light from the lighthouse coming and going.

He told me there was only one thing he could give me: it was called *La Barraca* (which meant 'The Hut') and a lot of people didn't like it. It was where Dalí's personal guests always stayed. He told one of the waiters to show it to me. It was an old fisherman's hut below the hotel, just off the beach. The door and windows were painted a dark blue and the outside was whitewashed. Inside was a large bedroom with stairs up to a bathroom. There was a telephone and table and chairs. I pulled up the blind and looked straight out at the sea. I went back and told the man that I would take it. He mentioned a particular friend of Dalí's, half man, half woman, who loved it and often came here. As I lay in bed that night I wondered what strange things they got up to.

The next morning the wind had gone. There was a dull grey light over the sea. There was no one around. I left the door of *La Barraca* open, crossed the beach and had a swim in the steely cold water.

Sunday came. There were more people than usual in the bars at the seafront for morning coffee. I walked over towards Cap de Creus, thinking that I could make it in a few hours, since at night the lighthouse seemed quite close. There were paths all along the cliffs; I stood still in surprise at one point when I saw below me a cove of shale with more than a dozen Germans lying there completely naked. They were young, in their early twenties, lying on rocks at an incline, or flat out on towels, or standing up paddling in the water. Most of the women were pink and busty and fleshy, I noted as I looked down at them; it must have been their first day in the sun; the blokes, on the other hand, seemed skinnier than the general run of Germans, but perhaps they simply looked strange in this light.

Because of the number of coves and inlets, Cap de Creus was much further away than it seemed. The afternoon sun grew hotter as I moved along the cliff. Most of the rock here was slatey shale, fragile and easy for the sea to cut into. After a while there was no one in sight. I moved away from the edge of the sea and walked along a path over a hill, and for the next half hour I met nobody. It was the first Sunday in September on a coastline which had been transformed in twenty-five years from empty coves and fishing villages to bustling tourism and overcrowded roads and beaches. Here, completely unexpectedly, was the deserted resort I had been looking for.

★

Dalí died in January 1989. To the end he refused to see Ana Maria, his sister, whom he had banished in 1949 after she wrote a book about their childhood, just as Buñuel and Miró had refused to see Dalí because of his support for Franco. In his last years there was much speculation about what would happen to his fortune and his collection, and he was courted by the politicians of the new Spain. Dalí had developed a devotion to the King and Queen, and wrote poems to them; they were, he said, one of the reasons why he wanted to live.

He enjoyed being ill, looked forward to the news bulletins about his state of health, waited for them avidly. His face on television was that of a deeply bewildered, frightened old man. During his last illness in December 1988 he was visited by the King and Queen, and the King told television reporters that Dalí had expressed a wish to begin painting again; but the only paintings done in his name now were by forgers. As a final twist in his long career, he gave his paintings to the Spanish State and left nothing to Catalonia. He was buried with great pomp and ceremony in the museum in Figueres, his grave a further exhibit among the surreal objects.

12

Food and Sex

Where did you eat? they would ask, and I would mention L'Egipte at the back of the Boqueria market; I would say that I usually went there on Saturday at lunchtime. And that would meet with general approval. L'Egipte was in then; it's still there and cheap at lunchtime, but it's no longer part of the trendy city. Or I would say that I went to El Pla de la Garça on Carrer Assaonadors for cheese and pâté and a bottle of red wine. And that too would provoke a positive reaction. That, too, was trendy in the Barcelona of 1988, a time when fashions moved fast. In the 1990s, for example, superb Basque tapas bars opened all over the city centre; the best of these is in Carrer Cardinal Casañas, near Plaça del Pi.

But doubts would be cast on other places. It wasn't that the food was bad or the prices exorbitant, it was just – and here the citizens of Barcelona would curl their lips and shrug – it was just that they weren't really where people went now. Maybe tourists went there, and in the trendy city, the city ready to make a killing out of 1992, tourists would be the kiss of death for a restaurant.

So I would mention other places I went to in the city and be met with stony silence. Years ago, someone would mumble before changing the subject, years ago maybe, but not now.

The Boqueria market off the Rambla, however, is not open to trends or changes in fashion. It is fundamental to the city's conception of itself. The Boqueria is above politics and petty snobbery; it has its own rules and habits – the central aisle, for example, much featured in postcards, is colourful and worth inspecting, but the regular shopper at the Boqueria never buys anything there, it is for show. It is for out-of-season lettuce and rare fruits; it isn't for serious shoppers.

Serious shoppers first have to discover who is last in the

queue at each stall by shouting out '*Qui és l'últim*' in Catalan, or
'*Quien es el último*' in Spanish. Some people behave aggressively
in the queue, but this is accepted, nobody minds. Most of the
stall-holders speak Catalan and, even if they speak Spanish to a
customer, they will do the calculations in Catalan.

This is where the seasons' movements can be seen at their
most intense: the melancholy progress of the year. More than the
changes in light, or the heat which fades in September and
October and comes back in April and May, more than these, the
market marks time.

After a few days' absence in February or March you wander
through to discover that the strawberries have arrived, not just the
early ones for high prices, but on every stall heaped in piles are
the cheap strawberries. It is a surprise, so early, the first sign that
spring is coming. And then two months later they will be gone
and the market will be full of peaches, plums, red cherries. For
two months they will make up the colour of the market. It is
warm then, the sun shines on the Rambla and the nights are full
of the pleasure the heat brings.

And the first sign that this will change, the first shock of
approaching autumn, comes when summer is still at its height:
the first black grapes for low prices, the first tangerines, the
pears, the figs. The summer coming to an end. Another summer gone.

Certain things remain, untouched by the caprice of seasons.
At the back of the market, the fish-sellers operate. Some of the
fish I had never seen before; I couldn't imagine that there was, or
even could be, a word in English for some of the shapes and
textures of sea-life on sale. The cod stalls have done everything
you can possibly do to cod: salted it and soaked it, cut it into long
strips, covered it in batter. Things we throw away in Ireland are
delicacies here and are laid out proudly on ice beside the trout
and the salmon and the sardines and the hundreds of other fish.

One fish-seller in the Boqueria market came to regard me as
her personal property: she made it clear that I could only buy fish
from her. She would lie in wait for me as I wandered from stall
to stall and then pounce, demanding to know what I wanted, and
insist that she had it at the best price. If I hinted that the prawns she
wanted me to buy had been frozen, she would protest vociferously,

calling people over to attest to the freshness of all the fish and seafood on her stall. She had me hooked.

The women in the market dress like queens and behave like duchesses. If you touch any of the fruit, or try to break the queue, you are in trouble. But if you ask how best to cook the many varieties of mushrooms which grow in Catalonia, and are on sale in late November, they will go to great lengths to explain. Most of them wear make-up, and have the appearance of women who go to the hairdresser every day.

In the market I developed, as did many other of the customers, an intense relationship with the three women who sell ducks. They run a side-stall, with a window in which their ducks are displayed with long necks neatly folded. Duck pâté, duck breast and many other duck accessories are also on sale. Since I knew nothing about ducks, the women in the duck shop took me to their hearts. It was like going to a kindly and efficacious How many was I cooking for? Two, I said. Then I should buy a breast and they would make it into two big steaks, one of them said. Another watched me carefully, and nodded agreement. A third, younger woman was consulted as well, and she added that the steaks should be cooked very lightly; she seemed concerned that I might overcook the duck.

The doctoring of the duck began, careful cutting and snipping, incising and unfolding. They were like heart surgeons, these women. And every time I came back they wanted to know how the last duck had turned out, and was I sure that I hadn't over-cooked it? One day they moulded the breast into three piec another day into four. Another day they sold me a whole duck. Their attitude towards food, like that of the rest of the stall-holders in the market, was deeply serious; it was not something they had learned, or been told about; it was in their blood, it was in their eyes when they turned to you, next in the queue, and asked what they could do for you. (So too Senyor Lopez, who had a poultry stall, will bone and stuff a turkey with any amount of fruit and nuts and meat, all done with artistry and flair and the suggestion that nothing in the world is more important.)

Where do you eat? I would be asked, and I would mention Senyor Perallada on Carrer Argenteria, and that would always meet with approval. That was, and remains, real Catalan chic: a cool modernity in the core of an old building near Santa Maria del Mar, bright new furniture, with old chandeliers hanging from the ceiling, but nothing old-fashioned or musty. The owner, Ramon Perallada takes your order with a certain humility and is somewhat owlish in his general bearing.

His family have been in the restaurant business for ten generations. He told me that his grandfather had built up the 7 Portes into one of the best-known eating houses in the city. His ancestor had also invented the *pijama*, a popular dessert dish. His family is steeped in the restaurant business; they own the Hotel Europa in Granollers, an hour away from Barcelona.

He took me there one Thursday, which was market day in Granollers. He had talked about part of the Catalan culinary tradition known as *la cuina de la misèra*, in which cheap ingredients such as tripe, brains and pigs' feet were used. But nothing he said had prepared me for breakfast at Hotel Europa in Granollers at half past nine that Thursday morning. Three hundred farmers, in Granollers for the market, were having breakfast. The noise of conversation filled the air; everyone was wide awake, animated, full of life. On every table there was a bottle of red wine and a bottle of white; on most tables there was also a bottle of brandy or a bottle of rum. Baskets of bread lay in the middle of each table as waiters came from the kitchen with plates full of *la cuina de la misèra*: brains, lungs, tripe. Three hundred farmers sat relishing the food that others throw away, some of them had three separate plates made up of these ingredients. They dipped the bread into the sauce and gravies, they took the pigs' feet up in their hands, drank back the wine. And when they were finished they started on the brandy. The noise of conversation became louder as the morning went on.

These are the backbone of Catalan society, industrious and prosperous. Barcelona is a world apart – Barcelona, Ramon said, is where their sons go to become 'poets and professors'. This scene in the Hotel Europa seems like a flash-back to the years before the Civil War: the faces, the clothes and the traditional food could be from an old photograph. But it is easy to recognize it as a Catalan scene: these are not peasants working the land for an absentee lord but strong farmers, well-off and independent. They are not part of the Anarchist agrarian tradition in Spain, but conservative Catalans in their local town on a market day.

*

In Barcelona the poets and the professors, the designers and the rest of the generation of 1992 have taken champagne to their hearts. In Barcelona they call it *cava*, and they take it as seriously as they take most things. *Codorniu* and *Freixenet* are local brews, for everyday use like wine from a barrel. Dotted throughout the Catalan countryside, but mainly in the province of Tarragona and the southern parts of Barcelona province, are the small champagne makers, the families who only sell to the specialist wine and liquor shops. The best of these in the city centre is Vins i Caves de la Catedral in Plaça Ramon Berenguer.

Over a lunch of pasta, then, or with fish or even chicken, it is acceptable to drink dry *cava*, their beloved *cava*. On Sunday at family gatherings, a bottle of *cava* is drunk with dessert. It is part of their great tradition, like *sardanes*, or Torres wine, or the Catalan language. Drinking *cava* is an integral part of being a Catalan.

The phone rang one day; it was a friend from Dublin. She was coming to Barcelona on business, she would be on expenses, she assured me, and wanted to take me to the best restaurant in the city. Money was no object, she said nonchalantly: the choice was mine. But she had heard that there were good restaurants in Barcelona.

Lists were drawn up, lengthy consultations held, deep discussions ensued. As a result, we found ourselves in a Galician restaurant in Gràcia the following Friday called El Botafumeiro. The people around us were fancy-looking, the prices were high, the bottle of Galician white wine we had while we waited for our table was delicious. We ordered a platter of seafood, and my friend demanded a bottle of really good Galician wine. The platter which came was the size of a coffee table. It contained an entire lobster, the usual types of prawns and crayfish you found in the Barcelona market, oysters, clams, mussels. It also contained a number of small objects which we had never seen before nor imagined.

The waiter came over, noticing our deep puzzlement over a

black object with an orange tint at the edges. I had squeezed mine and a pinky-coloured juice, the texture of washing-up liquid, shot into my face, almost blinding me. My partner was afraid even to touch it. The waiter explained that it was simply a *percebe*, a barnacle, and you didn't squeeze it, you pulled it apart and ate the tender piece inside. The whole restaurant was now looking at us as I sampled the inside part of our former enemy the barnacle. It was strong and juicy. I told my companion that it was safe, but she was busy mangling the lobster claws with the extraordinary utensils we had been given.

The waiter began to point at all the objects he had brought us when I asked what sea they had been found in. They were all fresh, he said, as he pointed to the prawns, from Sant Felíu on the Costa Brava, or crabs which had been flown in that day from the Cantabrian Sea, so that we and people like us could enjoy the fruits of two seas, the wild Atlantic and the calm Mediterranean.

We cut our way through the rich food of two cultures; prawns were ripped apart and devoured; the firm white flesh washed down with the northern wine which was cold and subtle. The battle was fought to scoop out the lobster and there was dead silence at our table as chewy chunks of it were swallowed. We tried everything. We ordered another bottle of wine, and it lay in its bucket of ice beside our table as we found, under everything, lurking there untouched, an enormous crab which was full of soft, juicy meat. We worked away at the barnacles, pulling them apart now like experts. And then we were done. My companion shrugged, unable to finish everything, but I kept trying to eat more. I knew it would be a long time before I would eat so well again in Barcelona.

When it was my turn to buy dinner I thought my companion should experience the other end of the market in Barcelona – namely the Portalón on Carrer dels Banys Nous which still looks like an old, dilapidated garage in bad need of repair. The prices are low, almost unbelievably so, and on good days the food is reasonable. Over the years it has increasingly become a haven for tourists; its sister restaurant on Carrer de Regomir, off the Plaça Sant Jaume, is now more authentic and less full of outsiders.

The Portalón is one of the places where you can take visitors and watch them hold their breath when they see the huge barrels of wine at the door, the dark, musty atmosphere, the lack of paint, the bustling waiters and the low prices. The Portalón isn't fashionable, although it is much frequented. Finding someone there from the city's trendy overworld is like bumping into an acquaintance in a brothel who insists that this is his first visit, he has only come to see what it is like.

There are other places, other points off the beaten track, in the city's web of pleasure. There is Boades, on Carrer Tallers off the Rambla; on Fridays after about six in the evening, it is the nearest thing in Barcelona to a bar in Dublin: everyone standing owing to lack of space, half the clients involved in a desperate attempt to gain the waiters' attention, loud voices coming from all sides. But in Boades everyone is drinking lethal concoctions. The waiters are not pulling pints but mixing cocktails. The place is unusual in Barcelona, for its low lights, its good wood, its speakeasy atmosphere.

The area around Santa Maria del Mar has a number of new bars, where the music is loud and hours are late and the prices are high. Hidden away from them, but close by, at an intersection of narrow streets between Princesa and Argenteria, is a bar called El Nus. It is almost impossible to find, much to the delight of those who frequent it. If you come across it by accident, it is a shock, the bar you have dreamed of finding in the medieval city, full of posters and paintings, with a balcony upstairs. It is carefully decorated and dimly lit. Here the music is cool and low, the glasses are frosted, the waiters are knowing and good-looking and just as smart as you are; if you come after twelve they won't let you in unless they know you, and if they know you they'll keep you in drink until three or four in the morning. Llúis, the owner, has drawings of himself all around the walls, just as the owner of Bar del Pi, in the Plaça del Pi, has a drawing of himself printed on the sachets of sugar.

But the most precious jewel in the city's treasury of bars is the Paraigües in the Plaça de Sant Miquel, behind the Ajuntament building in the Plaça de Sant Jaume. This is turn-of-the-century Barcelona at its most respectable, its most solid. The wood and mirrors have been re-mounted from an earlier establishment near the Cathedral; the wood is carved in Art Nouveau shapes and designs, but the bar has nothing of the excesses of Gaudí or Domènech. It is not loud or overdone. The service is always impeccable, just as the prices are high. In the early 1980s they opened a cocktail bar downstairs in the cellar which is like the crypt of a church, its brick arches left bare with mirrors placed all around, classical music on the speakers. In summer, it is air-conditioned but at any time of the year it is one of Barcelona's havens.

*

The devil looks down on Barcelona. The city is a bowl surrounded by hills: Montjuic, Monterols, Putget, la Creueta, Collserola, Tibidabo. The devil looks down from Tibidabo where he brought Jesus, during His forty-day fast in the desert. This is where he tempted Him with all the kingdoms of the world. 'To thee I will give: *Tibidabo*.' And he showed Him Barcelona.

Jean Genet came here too, to the city of temptation, and set the opening of his novel *The Thief's Journal* in the Barri Xinès. His hero lived here in the dangerous sub-culture of the whores, the pimps, the transvestites, the drag artists, the thieves and the down-and-outs who inhabited the streets between the Rambla and the Paral.lel (there is a dot between two 'l's in some Catalan words).

'1932,' Genet wrote in *The Thief's Journal*. 'Spain at the time was covered with vermin, its beggars. They went from village to village, to Andalusia because it is warm, to Catalonia because it is rich, but the whole country was favourable to us . . . In Barcelona we hung around the Carrer Migdia and the Carrer del Carme. We sometimes slept six in a bed without sheets, and at dawn we would go begging in the markets. We would leave the Barri Xinès in a group and scatter over the Paral.lel . . .'

In the 1970s the Barri Xinès was still thriving: on Sunday afternoons there would be queues of men outside certain buildings, a look of tense expectation on their faces; the streets were seedy, populated with characters who could have figured in Genet or in Picasso's 'Blue' paintings from the turn of the century. I used to frequent a bar named after the city of Marseilles which specialized in cheap absinthe; most of the regular clients had seen better days, some of them talked to themselves, or stared straight ahead. The floor looked as though it hadn't been swept since the Civil War. In those years, too, there was a bar further down towards the port where an old woman served *pastis* and played Edith Piaf records all night; in general her expression was deeply mournful, as though the music reminded her of something she would rather forget.

I was sitting happily in one of the bars in the heart of redlight Barcelona one night in 1976 when my companion pointed at the tall, elegant woman behind the bar and whispered that she was a man; not exactly a man, but a *travesti* (transvestite or transsexual). 'She' heard us talking about her, and smiled. I studied her face and realized it was true. I wasn't long out of Ireland, and this came as a bit of a shock. Soon I noticed *travestis* all around the city centre, but mainly on the Rambla and Barri Xinès. All of them had long, thin legs and bodies like models. They moved in twos and threes, walking with great pride and nonchalance down the Rambla. Some of them, I was told, did great business, better than the male and female prostitutes who also hung around the Rambla.

Years later, a friend fresh from Liverpool stood in his local bread shop one morning watching a lone *travesti* discuss her domestic life with the other women in the queue. All of them talked naturally to her, as though she were one of themselves, even though they were Catalan and she was Andalusian, even though they were settled housewives and she, clearly, was not. When she had bought her bread and departed, my friend thought that the women would comment on her, or perhaps snigger at her clothes, but they said nothing, her presence for them was perfectly normal. *Travestis* were a part of the city's fabric, its sexual heritage.

I was new to the idea of *travestis*, so I asked somebody about it, a friend who took a rather personal interest in the sexual mores of the city. And he explained. They were cheaper, he said; that was the first thing. And they were safer, or at least he thought they were safer. But these, he said, were minor factors compared to the real allure of *travestis* which lay in the shape and texture of their breasts. My friend went cross-eyed as he explained the joy to be found in the breasts of *travestis*. There were married men all over Barcelona who went home smiling to their wives after twenty minutes in the company of a *travesti*, he assured me.

By 1988 there were no married men to be found in the Barri Xinès. Half-way through the year the bar named after the city of Marseilles closed. The mournful woman who played Edith Piaf records had died, but Piaf played on; someone took over the bar, put up the prices and captured a fashionable clientèle. The naughty shows carried on as well on the Paral.lel which offered a mixture of sleaze and glitz. But the streets, which once had throbbed with desire, were now deserted. A cold wind blew up Carrer dels Robadors, no longer notorious, now simply empty, its years of passion spent. The clients had moved elsewhere.

During 1988 more than a hundred heroin addicts would be found dead from overdoses in the city, many of them in squares and the narrow streets of the Barri Xinès. They made no secret of their addiction. All over the city centre you could see people injecting the heroin into themselves in broad daylight. They didn't bother to move away if anyone came. Their presence and the constant activity of those who supplied them made the centre of the city dangerous, and made the Barri Xinès too risky for men in search of sex. And in the 1990s this, in turn, changed and the streets became safer, almost too safe.

There are still prostitutes on the Rambla, the younger women stand down towards the port and the older women, some of them in their sixties and perhaps their seventies, hold the corner of the Rambla and Ferran and use the *pension* buildings off Ferran when they get clients. But most of the business has moved elsewhere, in particular to the area around the University off Diagonal, where there are quiet side roads and dark corners. One section is reserved exclusively for the *travestis* and their clients. Even on weekdays there are cars circling all day and during the night, and at the weekend it is wild.

Yet all this is only a tiny part of the huge business of prostitution in Barcelona. The days are gone when businessmen would stalk through the dark streets in search of a brothel. Most of it now happens indoors, by arrangement. And those who wish to make an arrangement buy *La Vanguardia*, a conservative daily newspaper published in Barcelona. At the back, in the small ads section, under the heading 'Relax', sex in all its variations is freely advertised.

Carlos, for example, is 'virile' and his telephone number is 237–12–25. Losmen at Urgel 156 in the Eixample promises fifteen girls, beautiful and young. A mulatto *travesti* 'apetitosa' can be telephoned at 418–44–51. Mara is a dominating mistress and she will initiate you in sadism, she is at 347–81–40 from eleven in the morning until ten at night.

The advertisements have developed their own shorthand. Thus Mara can place *Econ* at the end of her ad to signify that she is cheap. Roselló, a brothel close to the Sagrada Família, has a display ad. in Catalan saying that it is the oldest in Barcelona, takes Visa cards and is open from ten in the morning until half past nine at night. Visitors should ring the red bell. Nacho at 425–41–40 promises a penis twenty-three centimetres in length.

At 246–8–26 there is a little rabbit who is looking for a sweet carrot. Martha, on the other hand, offers 'exquisite cruelty' at 352–38–54. She also takes Visa cards. Laura at 349–94–26 is available twenty-four hours a day and will travel to your house or hotel, as indeed will many of her companions, male, female and *travesti*. Thus the small advertisement section of *La Vanguardia* appears day after day; no attempt at discretion about phone numbers or addresses, nothing coy or discreet, simply a huge sex industry in the city offering its clients temptation.

The Barri Xinès is still where poverty in the city is at its most desperate, where the houses are insanitary and where many old people live alone under an inadequate system of social welfare. There has always been intense poverty in Barcelona, even during the great waves of wealth which came to the city. In the 1940s, during what are called 'the years of misery', more than 100,000 emigrants from the south arrived in Barcelona; there was nowhere for them to live. Only 15,000 houses were built in the fourteen years after the Civil War; during those years one third of the city's population was living in slum conditions. It was another Barcelona: far from the grandiloquence of Gaudí and his contemporaries, and distant, too, from the more earthly plans of Francesc Macià and Le Corbusier in the 1930s. No one was planning the city, as 400,000 more people came looking for work between 1953 and 1958; families were living wherever they could find space.

Building was no longer a way of glorifying the new mercantile order in the 1950s and 1960s; building was an emergency. It had to be done quickly and cheaply. Thus, all around the city, sky-scrapers began to rise, and all of the people who moved into them were from the south. The immigrants are now a solid block which votes Communist and Socialist in elections.

'To put Barcelona in order,' the architect Oriol Bohigas has said, 'you would have to knock down almost everything which was built during the Franco years.' This is still the uncharted city, in official eyes, where you hear *flamenco* music and Andalusian accents. The size of some of the districts, the extent to which the high buildings go on and on, would probably have frightened Jean Genet more than the Barri Xinès ever did.

Deep in the heart of Genet's Barcelona, one of the old dance-halls still survives. It is called La Paloma and it has old-fashioned décor and an old-fashioned band. It is cheap and respectable; even the waiter service at the upstairs balconies is cheap. It is perfectly preserved, the paintwork still shines, the players' uniforms are spick and span. People come here to dance the night away, wedding parties come, the bride still in her white dress, and trendy people mix with middle-aged couples, the men in shirt sleeves sweating copiously as the band moves from a gentle ballad into a frenetic version of *La Bamba*. The place is vulgar and loud; there is nothing cool or chic here, and during the fast dances there isn't room to move. It must have sorely tempted Jesus when the Devil stood with him that day on the hill of Montjuic and offered him a good time.

13

A Fragile Country

I was on the steps of the Cathedral in the early evening, the hour before twilight one day during the last week of April, when I saw the first swifts diving and darting across the sky. I watched how they suddenly seemed frenetic and out of control, and then how they glided calmly for a while over the Hotel Colon and the Via Laietana.

I remembered seeing them for the first time during the April of 1977 when it was still unclear how things would work out here, when everybody held their breath, united in wanting autonomy for Catalonia. It must have been the feast of Sant Jordi, and there were crowds of people in the Plaça de Sant Jaume. The stone plaque announcing that the Civil War was over and the 'red army' had been defeated by Franco was still on the wall of the Town Hall. I remember someone saying that it would be easy now to take it down or deface it, since the square was so full.

They called out for sweet liberty that day, a few months before they broke into factions and political parties. The same day the first brave swifts came back to the city.

Eleven years later, that week in April 1988 was a good lesson for me, in case I had forgotten, that everything was still political here, that politics was the mould in which everything was shaped: from art to religion, from football to a visit by the King of Spain.

He was scheduled to come to Barcelona on 23 April, the eve of the feast of Sant Jordi, the patron saint of Catalonia whose killing of the dragon was depicted on tapestries, stained glass windows and paintings all over Catalonia. His visit was to celebrate the Millennium of Catalonia at a function in the Palau de la Generalitat. No one believed much in the historical veracity of the Millennium, and it was perhaps no coincidence that within five weeks Jordi Pujol, President of the Generalitat, and his

Government would seek a third term in office, which they would win.

There were posters all over the city protesting against the visit. Some depicted Pujol, a small man at the best of times, sitting on the King's knee. These were put up by La Crida, an extreme nationalist group; La Crida also broke into the Palau de la Generalitat and took down the Spanish flag, returning it with great ceremony the following day. They announced that they would disrupt the King's speech with fireworks from a nearby rooftop. That same day two men from Terra Lliure, a small Catalan terrorist army, were found with explosives in a car outside the city.

The following morning there were security men everywhere. Montserrat Caballé, the reigning queen of culture in Catalonia, was to sing; there would be medieval music; there would be speeches. It was a tense morning. Pujol later told journalists that when the drums began for the medieval music he thought it was a bomb. He and a historian spoke in both Catalan and Spanish, Pujol extolling the greatness that was Catalonia, the historian outlining its independent spirit in the tenth century. When the King began to speak the fireworks started.

It was like gunfire, or the sound of a small bomb, and it seemed close at hand, dead close. The sound shook the building. Everyone ignored it, pretended it wasn't happening, looked straight ahead. Everyone knew that it was the sound of fireworks, parodying another sound which these streets had known so well just fifty years before. It came at intervals, like a taunt, seeming to say: look what we could do with you if we wanted.

It didn't stop until the rooftop on Passeig del Crèdit was identified and the culprits arrested. By that time the King had begun to speak in Catalan talking about the 'art and the industry' of the Catalan people; he referred to the language, which Franco had banned, as 'the live expression of a great culture'; he referred to the Catalans' sense of solidity, their closeness to Europe. He seemed pleased with his Catalan subjects, and happy to use their language, even though his accent was heavy and foreign.

Later there was champagne and smoked salmon in the patio of the orange trees in the middle of the Palace. The day was becoming warm as the King moved from group to group, escorted by Pujol.

All around the peculiar grammar and morphology of the Catalan language filled the air, as its ruling class talked to each other. Those clipped, harsh sounds, that intense seriousness, that pride in modernity and progress. The King smiled and grinned, a gamey, amused look on his face. Artists and significant figures in the society had been invited, as well as politicians, but no trade unionists. Pujol's party was dedicated to representing bourgeois values, conservative forces. This was the day for showing strength and establishing stability. The King was on their side.

The following day was the feast day of Sant Jordi and one of the anti-King demonstrations on the Rambla had a large photograph of the King in his former incarnation as Franco's heir, wearing a military uniform marching alongside the old Dictator. *Fora el Rei Borbó*, their posters said, meaning 'Out With the Bourbon King'. They also had a life-size model of Jordi Pujol with various anti-Spanish slogans around his neck. The Trotskyites, the Green Alternative, the Gay Liberation Movement all had stalls. Boys who wanted to raise money for fireworks at a forthcoming football match also had a stall.

But the main point of the day was not to protest, but to celebrate love and culture. It was the day of the book and the rose, the day when every male gave his girlfriend or wife or live-in companion a rose and got a book in return, or vice versa. The city was one big bookshop; the publishers, both Catalan and Spanish, had new titles launched. All the roses had little Catalan flags attached. The newspapers had published special literary supplements. By the afternoon there were stalls on both sides of the Rambla from the Plaça de Catalunya down to the port, all of them selling books, some specializing in political books, children's books, picture-books, new books, novels in Catalan, new Spanish novels. Authors were in great demand for signing sessions at the various stalls.

Everybody seemed to take the day seriously; boys walked in the streets on the way to meet their loved ones with roses in their hands. A rich-looking old man had a large art book under his arm, while his wife walked beside him with an opulent rose. There were two streams of people moving up and down the Rambla perusing all the new books. You couldn't move. I sat for a while outside the Bar del Pi in the Plaça del Pi and watched three boys and three girls in their early twenties who had neither rose nor book between them. Eventually, the three boys went off and came back with roses. They kissed the girls formally and then handed them the roses. It was a serious occasion. The girls then went to the Rambla to buy books; all of the books they bought, when unwrapped, turned out to be about sex, including a book in Catalan on how to make love to a woman, as well as a new pornographic novel in Spanish. No one giggled or laughed about the books. They passed them from one to the other, showing each other significant passages.

All over the city that day the Catalan flag, the four red bars on a yellow background, had been put out on the balconies to make clear that this was a specifically Catalan occasion. They danced *sardanes*, the national dance, that afternoon, in front of the Boqueria market on the Rambla. Salvador Dalí did a special drawing, his first in five years, for the Sant Jordi edition of the Catalan-language newspaper *Avui*. The other Catalan-language newspaper ran a survey which showed that forty per cent of Catalans supported complete independence from Spain.

A few days later it was the feast of the Virgin of Montserrat, the patron of Catalonia. Vast numbers left the city in cars and buses on the morning of the feast, 27 April, to visit Montserrat, one of Catalonia's sacred places. It has been a place of pilgrimage since the twelfth century when the famous Black Virgin was carved, but the significance of Montserrat is not simply religious; it stands as a beacon outside the city, the very soul of Catalonia. Over the last fifty years, through the work of its liberal abbots, it had become something of a symbol of hope and freedom for Catalans. Jordi Pujol's party had its first meeting there in 1973 and Miró was among those who marched there as a protest against the Franco regime in 1970.

It was a misty morning as we set off for Montserrat from the Plaça Universitat; the windows of the bus were steamed up with condensation. The other passengers were middle-aged; I was the youngest person on the bus. Everyone spoke to me in Catalan. These, my fellow-passengers, were very different from the Catalans at the reception for the King who had oozed power and money and satisfaction. They were different, too, from the crowds on the Rambla buying books on the feast of Sant Jordi, who were younger and emphatically post-Franco in their clothes and manners and opinions. These people were the conservative, lower-middle-class Catalans, the bedrock of Pujol's support, who had office jobs, owned small shops, who kept the faith, both Catholic and Catalan. Montserrat, for them, was Mecca, although, like good Catalans, they remained discreet and reserved about this as about all else.

The mountain comes as a shock when you first see it from the road, its rise is so sheer, the rock so white and smooth, the shape so conical. It looks artificial, as though someone had built it. The bus began the slow ascent, hampered by all the other traffic making its way up the mountain in time for Mass.

The buildings around the church are functional and straightforward; the whole place looked grey and uninviting that morning as the mist turned to a light rain; this meant that the cable cars, which went further up towards the summit, weren't working. We crowded into the church where, by now, there was standing room only. The Mass was in Catalan and everyone knew the responses. People listened attentively to the sermon which declared that the Catalan identity and the Christian faith were synonymous, and emphasized the importance of religion in the life of Catalonia. It was a nationalist sermon for an audience well used to the transforming of even religion into another facet of the self which Catalonia was in the process of re-making.

The Black Virgin was behind the main altar; a queue began of those who wanted to kiss her hand. She would not be paraded down the mountain, as the Spaniards did with their Virgins, she would be left in her place, stately and sedate. As the rain softened back to mist, the crowd got ready to dance *sardanes* in front of the church, celebrating once more their sense of nationhood on the feast day of their patroness.

I started to walk down the corkscrew road which wound around the mountain. The day was clearing now although the sky was still watery and grey. I stopped for lunch some way down the mountain, at the Hotel Colonia Puig, which stood as a monument to the past: the huge rooms dated from the 1920s and 1930s, all untouched, just as the people in the church and on the bus seemed to belong to a time which had gone.

As I walked further down the mountain I noticed a woman in a field picking flowers, and later I met a man who asked me in Spanish if I had seen a middle-aged woman. When I told him where he would find her, he asked me where I was going; I said I was going to Barcelona, but I wasn't sure how. He told me he would pick me up in his car when he was going down, once he had found his wife.

They both spoke Spanish and were from Madrid. They were retired now, they said, and had come especially for the feast of Montserrat. But they didn't want to stay any longer: they didn't like what they saw. The mountain was beautiful and they had enjoyed the journey. The problem was the language: they couldn't understand a word of the Mass, nor a word of the sermon. And they were in their own country, they emphasized. And to make matters worse, the wife had tried to buy some holy pictures with prayers printed on them but they only had them in Catalan, and she left without buying anything. She shook her head and sighed. Imagine, she said, imagine.

Was everything like that now? they asked me. It was, I said. There was a television station in Catalan, several radio stations, two daily newspapers, signs in shops; in Barcelona, I said, the street names were in Catalan only. The husband said that he was first in Barcelona in 1939 and it was a great city. I wondered what he was doing there in 1939. He didn't know things were as bad as this now. He had never imagined, he said.

What do you Catalans want? the wife asked me. Why do you want to have everything in Catalan? The husband turned to her and said he didn't think the passenger was Catalan. But the wife was sure, until I told her I was Irish. My Spanish was clearly that of a foreigner but she had assumed that my accent was merely part of the new order in Catalonia, which she and her husband found so puzzling and offensive. She stopped for a moment and then went on. She didn't understand, she said, why they couldn't use Catalan just among themselves; surely for big occasions, like the feast day of Montserrat, they could use Spanish, which was the language everyone understood. They said nothing more and for a second I felt as powerless and upset as they were, sensing their hardness and hostility.

We remained silent until we discovered that they had taken a wrong turn. They were going back to Madrid and planned to drop me at a train station, but they had gone too far. They were desperately apologetic and genuinely concerned as to how I would get back to the city. We parted then, using the Spanish language which they knew and loved so well, and I found myself at the entrance to the toll road to Barcelona, where I was picked up by one of the first cars which came.

The driver was alone, in his early forties and Catalan. When I told him where I had been, he looked at me as though I was mad. There was rock music on the car stereo, he was wearing trendy clothes; he had put Montserrat and all it stood for way behind him as we drove fast towards the city. He had bought a bar, he told me, in one of the posh suburbs of the city in the late 1970s. He had seen a gap in the market. The Catalan kids were a new generation, they wouldn't go to old-fashioned bars or loud, vulgar discos: they needed places which were modern and cool, which were subtle mixtures of old and new. He designed this bar, spent a lot of money on it, and it worked. Once Franco died, he said, Barcelona changed, everyone's habits changed, the market changed. The young people were different now.

So different, he said, that everyone picked up his idea, new places opened all over the city. He saw another gap in the market, he sold his bar (it still did great business, he said, and told me I should go there some time) and he began to design and make trendy furniture for bars. He was doing well and employed a lot of people. Barcelona was changing every day. You had to keep up with the changes. He was enjoying talking like this, and I was enjoying listening to him, as he went on, with confidence and innocence, seeing the arrival of democracy and the death of the old Dictator in terms of gaps in the market, new ways to go in there and make a killing.

It was that week in April when chance encounters with Catalan businessmen seemed to take on political nuances and reverberations. It was also the week when a huge exhibition of recent work by Antoni Tàpies went on show in the two medieval buildings on the Plaça del Rei: the Sala Tinell and the Church of Santa Àgata. The exhibition, entitled *Tàpies els anys 80*, was sponsored by the Ajuntament, the Town Hall, who had also produced a sumptuous 274-page full-colour catalogue.

Tàpies' name, too, stands for something other than art: for the spirit of resistance to Franco and Fascism in the 1960s and 1970s. His paintings, however abstract and philosophical in their origins, often had a directly political message. His actions, as well, have frequently been overtly political, such as his part in the occupation of the Capuchin Convent at Sarrià in 1966 for which he was arrested and fined, his involvement in the march of protest to Montserrat in 1970, and his involvement after 1975 in the campaign for amnesty and democracy.

'Tàpies' Catalan identity,' one of the essays in the catalogue reads, 'has been viewed as a constant in his career that gave unity and continuity to his art . . . Many motifs appearing in the work of Tàpies have been recognized as references to his Catalan roots, but his Catalan identity has also been explained on a deeper technical and formal level. The significance of craftsmanship in his work, especially his profound knowledge of the materials he employs, has been associated with Catalonia's traditional craftsmanship. Ultimately, Tàpies' intellectual attitude towards mysticism, the esoteric and the magical has been explained through his Catalan identity.' The catalogue was produced in Catalan with translations at the back in small print into Spanish and English, but at the exhibition the titles were in Catalan only.

He is a diffident man, Tàpies. At the press reception on the day of the opening, he shrugged a lot, kept his distance, answered questions in a bemused and self-deprecating tone. At one stage he slipped away and stood on his own while others who organized the exhibition answered questions. The work in the two big halls was a retreat from the public Antoni Tàpies back into the private artist. The paintings were big, big enough for the large Gothic space they had come to fill in the great square of Tàpies' native city.

In an interview in the catalogue he had said that 'there was a time when the Franco regime was at its height, that I believed that certain clearer political messages could contribute to a general revulsion for the regime. These messages have not reappeared for some years now.' Politics had freed him then from having to paint about politics; now he was free to be playful and obscure, if he so wished. Franco was thirteen years dead now, and this was his legacy; that an artist would no longer need to protest, he could look inwards.

The fashionable people came that night to the big opening. Tàpies now looked slightly frightened but stayed on, even after the Mayor of Barcelona had left. Tàpies was watching everyone, his hair tousled and untidy, looking owl-like, mildly sceptical. 'The artist,' he had written, 'has always been something of a solitary bird, a perturbing spirit that constantly rocks the boat . . . he will continue to be so even under socialism.'

The fashionable people were wearing designer clothes, designer shoes, designer glasses. They were moving slowly, elegantly and carefully from painting to painting. They found nothing strange about the work, there was no beckoning over of a friend to come and look at this extraordinary object on the wall in which the artist has stuck two halves of a broken chair to a canvas; they were equal to this work, the use of old foam, old doors, old book covers, the use of glue, newspaper, numbers, squiggles, daubs and crosses. If you didn't know the city, you would wonder where they could possibly be from: they couldn't be Spanish, there were too many blond people and people with fair skin. They had to be from somewhere which valued design and modernity, Milan perhaps, except that several faces were too swarthy, too earthy, and there was a prudence in their watchfulness and their self-consciousness. Two girls arrived wearing skintight leggings; no one ogled them or stared at them. The sexual tension was carefully controlled and was not based on the macho ideal. Some of the conversations were deeply animated, people listened carefully, curled their lips, gesticulated with their arms, shrugged, touched each other, no one spoke in Spanish. This gathering was quintessential Catalan chic, as though everything – the paintings, the occasion, the building, the clothes – had always been thus. This was a gathering of those who had not simply recovered from Franco, or forgotten about him, this was a gathering of those who had shrugged him off.

It was the last week in April, and I was beginning to imagine that life in the city was one long set of symbolic occasions from which morals could be drawn about the state of the national psyche, in which politics sucked in everything that happened and spewed it back out again in the colours of the Catalan flag. It was like Ireland. But here, like nowhere else, the game of soccer meant everything. Barça, the richest football club in the world, was the most potent symbol of the city's greatness and of Catalonia's destiny. It was more powerful than the Liceu, the Sagrada Família or Montserrat because its fortunes could change, its team could lose, it could undermine the city and the country. And when it won, then the whole of Catalonia, its great traditions, its glorious future, would win as well, would shine like a light.

I remembered a Saturday in the early summer of 1981 when I had come to the city, left my bags in a hotel, bought no newspapers and contacted nobody, simply gone for a walk and ended up by chance at the first showing in a cinema in Barcelona of Fellini's *La Dolce Vita* which Franco had banned. The film had dated, but it was still worth seeing after all these years. When I came outside, after that mild encounter with heat and sex, it was as though the city was on fire. I walked over towards the Rambla, where the cars were blocked on both sides of the street, with their klaxons honking over and over the eleven-note rhythm of victory. In a frenzy of zest and celebration young fellows were attacking each car, hitting the car on the roof, beating the windows with their fists, and the people inside were laughing, and the driver was honking the horn. And then that car would be let go, and they would attend to the next one, standing in front of it to make sure that it couldn't go by until it got the treatment. A few of the cars were driven by people who, like myself, were unaware of what was happening, who looked frightened and tried to speed up and get past without any trouble, but these too were detained and then released, the driver by this time in a rage.

Barcelona had won the cup. And not just that, but Barcelona had beaten Madrid in the Camp Nou, Barcelona's own football ground. The top of the Rambla was full of people cheering and shouting, waving Catalan flags, wearing them around their shoulders. Some cars were circling the city, the passengers shouting out victory slogans, waving flags and proclaiming themselves the victors. Beating Madrid was a special pleasure.

Young Catalans brought bottles of cheap champagne and poured it over themselves and their companions, and then went back to stopping the cars. Not once over the next two hours was there any violence in the city, none of the cars was damaged. It was pure, unconfined joy, going on and on into the night.

Seven years later the atmosphere surrounding the Barça and the Camp Nou was darker. There were internal dissensions in the Club, difficulties between players and management. Some blamed the players, others blamed the club's President Nuñez. The games at the Camp Nou were no longer packed, the crowds weren't coming. Below the press box were the men who ran soccer in the city, the owners of the club. You couldn't avoid seeing them, in their sombre suits or blue blazers and slacks, they stood out against the crowd. Some people said that things would never be right until Nuñez left; other commentators wrote that football was merely a sport, the Camp Nou merely a football field, the Barça were merely eleven players, and, until the Catalans realized this and stopped using the Barça as a symbol, things would never be right. Everyone had a view on what should be done with the Barça.

In the last week of April, the players issued a statement of no confidence in Nuñez. They had won the King's Cup in Madrid, which had resulted in mild celebrations on the Rambla. But they were badly down in the League, which they now had no chance of winning and they were playing Madrid in the last round on the last day of April, and even if they won it would mean nothing. Some people said that the players should concentrate on the game.

The nearest Barcelona got to soccer hooliganism came from a small bunch at the front of the Camp Nou in standing room only, who cheered and whistled and banged a drum, threw cheap fireworks and bangers when the going was good. Tonight, when they moved too close to the field, or threw petards which let off coloured smoke, the police came after them, but it was a game; what was serious was the level of insult they roared up at Nuñez. He sat there surrounded by his henchmen, as they pointed their finger at him all through the game, as though it was he who had lost the matches, as though he was a politician, as though he ran the country.

And so he did, someone told me, he did run the country. The club was as important as the Government. You had to understand that.

On the last day of April in the week when the first swifts appeared in the sky over the city, I watched the football, watched our team winning as night came down, but it wasn't football, it was another piece of pageantry, the vast parade which a fragile country was making of its sacred symbols.

14

The New Regime

On the night he died I was in a house in the Eixample. I remember asking what would happen now. The two Catalans in the room shrugged: nothing would happen, they said. Things would go on the same. They changed the subject then, as though they didn't care, as though his death didn't bother them. Elsewhere in the city that night, people drank the champagne they had saved up for years for this very night, when they would be free of Franco. Elsewhere, too, others refused to celebrate, ignored his death, as they had tried to ignore his life.

I walked down the Rambla that night, looking for signs of something, but there was nothing strange. Juan Carlos would become King and there would be no change. Everywhere I went, people told me that.

Two months before his death, Franco had ordered the execution of five political activists. They were shot by military firing squads in their towns of origin. Franco was relentless, right to the end. He did not give up. A few months after his death I was talking to a friend who imagined how good it would be if the regime just dissolved and democracy came, without years of suffering and struggle, without executions or prison sentences or baton charges. In the end, though, he said that it couldn't happen. It would take years to unseat them. And he was wrong.

For those of us who lived in the city in the years after the Dictator died, for those of us who were in our twenties then, who remember the first demonstrations and the first rock concerts under the new dispensation, and remember, too, the hot nights in the summer of those years when the Plaça Reial was full, when every table was taken up, there are several voices which now conjure up what it was like in Barcelona then.

They were the singers, the representatives of *La Nova Cançó*, the movement in Catalan singing which began in the early 1970s. To sing about love in Catalan was to sing about politics: the audience understood what lay between the lines. For the new generation of Catalans, Spanish was the language of the police and the Government, the military and the school authorities. For them Spanish was not the language of Lorca's *Yerma* but of the people who made arrests and carried out executions, the language of the cruel, dark, inflexible state. In the 1970s in Barcelona Catalan was the language of freedom; it was trendy to speak Catalan in the city, just as it was to smoke dope and own Bob Dylan records.

Sex, drugs, rock'n'roll and Catalan; it was a peculiar mixture. Most of the young people couldn't read or write Catalan, and that made it even trendier. Singers came to represent political desires more than any political party or election manifesto. The new songs were the first public life the Catalan language had been given since the Republic.

The singers were all young and good-looking; the idiom owed more to Woody Guthrie than the Catalan choral tradition, the style was more in tune with Woodstock than the holy mountain of Montserrat. And some of the songs, too, were openly political. Lluís Llach was perhaps the most popular among the new singers. He came from Verges, where the Easter procession of *La Dansa de la Mort*, the skeletons' dance of death, had been preserved. His song 'L'Estaca' became the battle-hymn of Catalonia in the last years of the old regime.

It was about a stake in the ground, and how if you beat at it for long enough it would fall. The chorus repeated the word fall, and everybody knew what the stake was, and everybody who sang the song wanted it to fall, fall, fall. On Sunday nights in the mid-1970s the *sardana* would be danced in the Plaça de Sant Jaume, and afterwards they would join hands in the square and sing 'L'Estaca'. Sometimes the police would come in jeeps and attack people; but most of the time it was quiet and orderly, there was just the fervour of the chorus: *Segur que tomba, tomba, tomba.*

But nothing fell; things simply began to shift over a period that came to be called the Transition. The programme for the Saturday night and Sunday morning concerts at El Palau de la Música began to appear only in Catalan. One morning in 1976

new plaques appeared throughout the Gothic quarter with the
street names in Catalan; the Spanish names, for the moment, were
left in place. The King came to Barcelona in the spring of 1976
and made part of his speech in Catalan. A newspaper – *Avui* –
appeared in Catalan. But still no one was sure what would happen.
The King appointed Adolfo Suarez as Prime Minister; Suarez was
not known for his democratic views.

Llibertat, Amnestía, Estatut d'Autonomía became the cry in demonstration after demonstration. It was a time of innocence, before
party enmities formed and solidified. As the possibility of significant political change appeared more real, the meetings and the
marches became euphoric. It culminated in the march on 11
September 1977 when one million people gathered in the city
shouting for autonomy. September 11 was the day in 1714 when
beleaguered Barcelona finally fell, the day of the final Catalan
defeat.

It seemed at times as though nothing was solid in the Catalan
politics of that time, as though any party or faction could rise and
take power, as though any leader could emerge from the one
million marchers and lead the Catalan people to the Promised
Land. But it wasn't like that; these appearances were deceptive.
By 1976 political alliances had been carefully formed; political
profiles had been carefully worked out. A number of people had
been poised for some time to take over power in the new Catalonia, and in the new Spain.

Throughout the Franco years very few opposition forces had
operated with any success against the dictatorship. It is still possible,
however, to trace networks of contacts and influence within the
business community in Catalonia during the 1950s and 1960s
which would later lead to the ruling party Convergència i Unió,
led by Jordi Pujol. It is also possible to trace Pujol's shadow as he
moved through various Catholic organizations in the same years,
but there are gaps, years when very little happened.

Pujol's fame arose from an event which took place in the Palau
de la Música Catalana on 19 May 1960. Franco was in the city
on that day and a number of his colleagues were to attend a
concert at the Palau. The organizers that night forbade the choir
to sing *El Cant de la Senyera*, one of Catalonia's sacred hymns.

Pujol and others decided to sing the song at the moment when it should have come in the programme. They were arrested and Pujol was sentenced to four years in prison, later released after two, but banished from Barcelona and forced to live in Girona. El Palau de la Música, the choral tradition and *El Cant de la Senyera* were sacred things to Catalans. Pujol had chosen his ground with care.

Only one other major force worked against Franco in the last two decades of the dictatorship in Barcelona and that was the Communist Party. The Party was powerful, particularly in the universities, so powerful and well organized that many social democrats joined it in the 1960s, seeing it as a useful vehicle for political change. A great number of its adherents were also arrested and imprisoned in those years.

In the months after Franco died, it was clear that a party situated between Pujol and the Communists would be needed. Pujol's politics were nationalist and conservative; his party, in certain ways, was the old Lliga come to life again, but more populist, closer to a European Christian Democratic party.

When the third force emerged, it was led by a number of young Catalan academics and intellectuals. This was the PSC – el Partit Socialista de Catalunya – which would merge with the PSOE – Partido Socialista Obrero Español – led by Felipe Gonzalez in Madrid. As the elections loomed, the two parties on the right, one led by Adolfo Suarez, the other by Franco's former minister Manuel Fraga, refused to recognize Catalonia as a distinct area on the electoral map, and suffered accordingly. The Communists did as the Socialists: they had a separate party organization to represent their interest in Catalonia.

The most striking characteristic of the parties on the left, particularly the Socialists, was that all the leaders were Catalans, most of them from the Eixample, and many from the old ruling families of the city. Pasqual Maragall, for example, who later became the Mayor of the city, was the grandson of Joan Maragall, the poet and friend of Gaudí. These men who emerged to represent the interests of the working class were from the generation which had filled the nightclub Zeleste in the early 1970s, were well educated, the best and the brightest of their generation. They had suffered only the dullness of the dictatorship; none of them had lived in the new suburbs, worked in factories, or organized trade unions.

In December 1976 the referendum was held which made way for the first general elections. A few months later the Communist Party was made legal. The elections were held on 15 July 1977. Adolfo Suarez formed the first Government. In Catalonia the Socialists and Jordi Pujol's Convergència Party emerged as the two main forces.

The pressure for autonomy continued in Catalonia; it was a violent and tense time in the city. The old President-in-exile of the Catalan Generalitat, Josep Tarradellas, who had served with Macià and Companys in the 1930s, moved from the South of France into French Catalan-speaking territory, and waited. The Catalan newspaper *Avui* collected signatures calling for his return as President. In October he flew to Madrid to negotiate the terms for his return. It was the most unlikely scenario in that time of unlikely scenarios: this old man, so long out of the country, so removed from what Catalonia had become since its Government went into exile, was ready to return, to take power once again. And yet it was agreed, and in October 1977 he came back to the city as the President of the Generalitat.

Manuel Vázquez Montalbán wrote in his book *Barcelonas*: 'Nobody will ever know what democracy is who hasn't lived through those times which came before the fall of fascism.' It was as though the sun moved closer to the city and the temperature rose. Graffiti began to appear everywhere; posters were plastered on the walls of the city; the battle was on now for power. In a few months Franco had been forgotten, within a year everything had changed. The simple right to vote had changed the face of Barcelona: the communal euphoria moved swiftly into party politics, people became Communists or ultranationalists, everyone formed a view, everyone argued. Mass meetings were held, rallies followed by long speeches. Later, it would be called history, but then it was sheer joy.

I was there the day Tarradellas came back to Barcelona. I stood in the Plaça de Sant Jaume and watched his car weave through the cheering crowd. It was to be a day of great emotion for

Catalans. He went to the balcony of the Generalitat building in the square and began to address the crowd. He had had forty years to write the speech, a long time in politics, perhaps too long, and his rhetoric came across as bloated and vague. *Ja sóc aquí* he told us at the beginning of each sentence, as though he were Martin Luther King saying 'I have a dream'. But *Ja sóc aquí* simply means 'I am here now', and nobody was impressed. That Sunday afternoon, less than two years after Franco's death, the old man droned on from the balcony and the specially invited audience in the square began to laugh at their new President. Each time he said *Ja sóc aquí* further mirth broke out and in the weeks afterwards *Ja sóc aquí* became a joke, something you said as you arrived in a bar.

Nobody wanted rhetoric, they wanted progress, they wanted power. Nobody knew what Tarradellas' return meant. The laughter that day was instructive: nobody would win votes in Catalonia by looking to the past, or using vague phrases; the Catalan middle classes had been working hard during the dictatorship, making money, looking after their businesses, educating their children to be the new ruling class, and they wanted a leader who was pragmatic, hard-headed, who would offer action, who would stand up for Catalonia in deed as well as word. They wanted Jordi Pujol.

The country accepted reform, fast and effective, rather than rupture. In December 1978 a new Constitution was passed, and in March 1979 Adolfo Suarez won his second general election. In April the Communists took all the working class suburbs of Barcelona in the local elections, and the Socialists took power in the city of Barcelona. In the first elections for the Catalan Parliament in 1980, Jordi Pujol's Conservative Nationalist Party won, and Pujol replaced Tarradellas as the President of the Generalitat.

These were the years of change and consolidation. In 1982 Gonzalez became the Socialist Prime Minister. In Barcelona the Socialists continued to hold the Town Hall where they would have the task of preparing for the Olympic Games, and Pujol continued to rule Catalonia. There would be continuing friction between Pujol and the Madrid Government, between Catalan demands and Spanish centralism, which Pujol would consistently aggravate by behaving like a head of state on his trips abroad.

Pujol today exudes competence and shrewdness. He doesn't miss a chance. In his speeches he doesn't wait for applause or cheap cheers, but rattles out facts at machine-gun pace. He stands for economic progress, for getting things done, the tradition of working hard and giving nothing away. His politics are Catalan to the core. He is capable, certainly, of playing the nationalist card, of exuding sheer sentiment, but he is always careful. His style, the leader as manager, is just right.

The man across the square, Joan Clos, the Mayor of Barcelona, like Pasqual Maragall whom he replaced, is younger, more stylish, of a different generation. He and his supporters find Pujol's nationalism too heavy and old-fashioned. Pujol is a fervent Catholic; the guys who run the Town Hall are products of the 1960s, post-Christian in their style.

These were the years when the Catalan language came into its own, when it became compulsory in the schools, when the commentary on the football matches was in Catalan only, when the second television channel was mainly in Catalan, and when TV3, the all-Catalan station, controlled from Barcelona, showed *Dallas* dubbed into Catalan. The street names are now in Catalan only; there are two daily newspapers in Catalan; there is a flourishing Catalan publishing industry. Signs in shops and on the metro are in Catalan, menus in restaurants are in Catalan.

Yet Barcelona is less of a Catalan city than it was in 1930 when the population reached a million. Now the population of Greater Barcelona is almost four million, of which more or less half speak the language – although the vast majority claim to understand it. There is now a considerable difference between the language as used in Barcelona and the language spoken in the villages, the latter being much purer and more difficult for an outsider to understand. Because of television, radio and the education system, the number of people who speak the language in Catalonia is rising by 20,000 every year, while in Valencia, to the south, the number of Catalan speakers is decreasing by 5000 a year. Overall now, Catalan is spoken by more than six million people, most of them in Catalonia, Valencia and the Balearic Islands, but up to 100,000 in the South of France (or what Catalan nationalists called

Catalunya del Nord), 50,000 in Aragon to the west, and a few
thousand in the town of L'Alguer in Sardinia.

On 11 September 1988, the day in 1977 when a million
Catalans demonstrated for autonomy, the ruling class had its own
wreath-laying ceremony in the Eixample and reception in the
Parliament building while those who wanted complete independence from Spain walked the streets, shouting slogans of support
for Terra Lliure, the Catalan paramilitary force, rubbing out any
Spanish words they found on the route of their march. Later
that evening, they would attack McDonald's hamburger joint, the
traditional target of Catalan separatists on 11 September.

Lluís Llach, whose song *L'Estaca* had united Catalans in the
1970s, moved into the separatist camp. He became an influential
figure once more, his concerts important focal points in the
struggle for a completely independent Catalonia. The crowd
singing his songs are young, as the crowd singing *L'Estaca* had
been young; now they cheer and roar as we had done in the
seventies, but this time the middle class Catalan youth applauding
Lluís Llach want independence from Spain. In November 1988 a
survey published in *El Pais*, the Madrid newspaper, showed that
44.5% of Catalans would vote yes in a referendum on complete
independence, 28.4% would vote no; the rest would abstain or
didn't know.

Many Catalans still feel under siege, living in an occupied
country. But slowly, as military service is abolished and a Catalan-
speaking police force is established, things are changing.

A Catalan, Jordi Pujol insisted, is anyone working and living
in Catalonia with a view to permanence. However, for many who
were born elsewhere, the new Catalan institutions, the increasing
use of the language, and the rise in nationalist feeling makes them
deeply uncomfortable. The professional classes in particular see
Pujol's politics as dangerous and threatening. Most of them have
no time for the language and very few have bothered to learn it,
but now things are being made difficult for them: two out of three
of their television stations are in Catalan, and their children are
being forced to study Catalan. They, too, see themselves as living
in an occupied city, a city occupied by Catalans, Catalans who are
becoming, in their view, increasingly powerful and arrogant. And

if you come from Castile, and your language is the language of
Cervantes and Unomuno, Alberti and Lorca, and your country
has colonized most of South America, then you have very little
patience with the pretension of the Catalans, their insistence on
the antiquity and importance of their culture.

In 1981 2300 'intellectuals and workers' living in Catalonia
signed a manifesto which complained bitterly about the increasing
use of Catalan and the denial of rights to those who spoke only
Spanish. Their protest had little effect. On 24 June 1981 the Camp
Nou, the playing ground of the Barça, was filled with 100,000
people calling for further recognition of Catalonia's existence as a
separate entity. The slogan they shouted that day was *Som una
Nació*: 'We are a Nation'.

15

Barcelona 1992

In the first months of 1992 the city held its breath. Everywhere you went, you noticed changes. Gaudi's great building La Pedrera on Passeig de Gràcia had been cleaned; it seemed lighter and more beautiful now that all the grime of the city had been washed from the stone, more wave-like in its shape, more ethereal and more intriguing. The house in Carrer de la Palla where I used to live had been painted a light ochre, but the stone around the windows and the door had been cleaned and left unpainted. In the light of the early afternoon, the stone-work stood out, bright and glistening. In all the years, I had never noticed it before.

I never knew that a great stretch of the Roman wall lay intact within a building on Carrer de Regomir, even though I had passed it every day. Now the building had been restored, painted a salmon colour, and plate-glass windows had been put into the ground floor so you could see the huge cut stones of the Roman wall from the street. These were minor compared to the great Olympic buildings, but they mattered to people who lived in the city; they were part of the city's effort to show off its history and heritage now that it was going to host the Olympic Games.

On the first of January 1992 the Barcelona newspapers carried the usual headlines, but they also informed their readers that this was the city's great year. Everybody knew the importance of the Great Exhibition of 1888 in establishing Barcelona as one of the dynamic and thriving cities of Europe, how statues and monuments and buildings had been created for the occasion, most of which still stood in the area around the Parc de la Ciutadella. They knew, too, that the Exhibition of 1929 had created the public parks on the hill of Montjuic as well as the Palau Nacional. Now 1992 was another great opportunity to reinforce the city's infrastructure and to add to its heritage. At the beginning of 1992, they started to count the days to July 25, when the Games would begin.

As excitement increased, memories shortened. When I marched with the first post-Franco demonstrators in 1976 in Barcelona, one of the constant slogans was '*Samaranch, fot el camp*', a rather rude way of calling for the dismissal or resignation of Juan Antonio Samaranch from the city's administration. He was to remain one of the three or four top figures in the demonology of those seeking free elections and Catalan autonomy in the years after the death of Franco. Now he was a hero in Barcelona, he was photographed smiling with young people or Socialist politicians or trendy architects. He had become President of the International Olympic Committee and he was given credit for guiding Barcelona and the Olympic Games towards each other. A few times in the couple of years before the Olympic Games as I watched him being cheered and applauded, I wondered if I was the only person in the crowd who remembered that he had once represented Franco's regime in the city.

In Barcelona, as 1992 approached, the past did not interest people very much. Most Catalans saw the Games as a great political opportunity, another way of consolidating their political and cultural autonomy, another way of establishing the idea of a Catalan nation, separate from Spain. Since the death of Franco, without resorting to violence or terrorism, they had won a degree of autonomy from Madrid. They had their own parliament, the Catalan language was now taught in the schools. But Madrid still controlled taxes, foreign policy and defence. Many Catalans were uneasy about Madrid's degree of power and control.

Thus when the Olympic Stadium on the hill of Montjuic above the city was inaugurated in September 1989, they booed and jeered the King of Spain, Juan Carlos, when he appeared. Executives from NBC, who had bought the television rights to the Games, were puzzled and disturbed by the antics of the crowd at the inauguration. Surely this was a proud day for the people of Barcelona? Surely the King, who had fought to preserve democracy, was a popular figure? Surely it was right that he should be there?

They whistled and cat-called and shouted abuse. Some of it

seemed to be organized, as though groups of nationalists had block-booked seats in the stadium to make their protest against the King's presence all the more effective. The President of the autonomous Catalan government sat on the platform, but, as one newspaper reported, the youth section of his party seemed to be the best-organized group among the spectators, as they booed the King and shouted slogans in Catalan. They did not want the Spanish King in their city.

And this is the key to understanding the 1992 Olympic Games in Barcelona: they are a way for Catalans to put their capital city and their nation on the map. They will not throw bombs, and they will strongly disapprove of the Basque nationalists who will do so, but they will use every method available to let the rest of Spain and any others who will listen know that they are a separate nation with a great capital city.

Much of the impulse in Barcelona now to make the Games successful, to make them run smoothly, is political. The pride is not simply that the attention of the world is on Barcelona. The pride is that the Catalan character and way of doing things has once more triumphed. Traditionally, the Catalans and citizens of Barcelona see themselves as progressive and European against the rest of Spain, which they view as backward-looking. Catalans believe in hard work and profit, in getting things done. They are happier making deals than throwing bombs. They spent the years of Franco's repression (and Franco had a special loathing for them) building up their businesses and staying out of trouble. Now they will forget the past, and forgive Juan Antonio Samaranch his sins, if it suits them.

And this is their *annus mirabilis*, their apotheosis after centuries of struggle to build a nation and preserve a fragile culture. They will also use the Games to show the world how deeply rooted their culture is. In the early days of 1992 they began to flood-light the facades of their great Gothic churches as darkness fell each evening. Barcelona's power in the Mediterranean and beginnings as a great metropolis are rooted between the eleventh and fourteenth centuries, between the Romanesque and the Gothic, long before Spain even became powerful.

All over Catalonia are the small, perfectly preserved Romanesque churches. These are the buildings that Catalans associate with their heritage, built at a time when the rest of Spain was under the control of the Moors, at a time when Catalonia was closer, in cultural terms, to Provence than to Andalucia. The wall paintings were removed from those churches in the early decades of the twentieth century, and these, as well as the Gothic churches, are the first things which the Catalans want to make sure that most visitors see during the Olympic Games, not just as beautiful works of art (although they are beautiful, some beyond belief) but as examples of what Catalans did in the centuries before the rise of Castile and the notion of a unified Spain with Madrid as its capital.

The collection of Catalan Romanesque and Gothic art was preserved in the Palau Nacional, built to house the ceremonies surrounding the 1929 Exhibition. But it has always been felt that not enough fuss was being made of the collection, that visitors to Barcelona knew about Gaudi's unfinished Sagrada Família and the Picasso Museum, but hardly anyone outside the city was aware that the best collection of Romanesque wall paintings in the world was housed at the top of the huge number of steps which led from the Plaça d'Espanya to the Palau Nacional.

It was essential that these be on show during the Olympic Games. Spain had Goya and Velázquez and El Greco, but Catalonia's heritage was best represented by this collection. As usual, in times when Catalans seek ideas and innovation, they looked to France, and they saw what had been done to the Gare d'Orsay by the Italian architect Gae Aulenti. They wanted something similar done to their Romanesque collection and they employed her to redesign the Museu d'Art de Catalunya in the Palau Nacional, taking in the Romanesque and Gothic collections as well as the paintings in the Museu d'Art Modern, housed beside the Parliament building in the Parc de la Ciutadella.

These, too, were important paintings, many of them done by contemporaries of Picasso and Miró and Dalí. There was even some interesting early work by Dalí. But most were by the painters who did not go to Paris and become famous or have American dealers. Many of the painters worked on the Catalan landscape and became quietly distinguished figures such as Joaquin Mir –

much valued among Catalan collectors but hardly known in the outside world.

The Palau Nacional was built as a neo-classical palace. As architecture it was a piece of pastiche, only half serious. But its Grand Salon was the second-biggest enclosed space in Europe, smaller only than the Albert Hall, in London, and this, for Catalans, was important. It had been derelict for years. When I went to see it in 1988, there were pigeons flying around it and the roof was leaking. The first plan was to flood it, to make the floor space into a lake and to build mock Romanesque churches on islands and put the art back into the churches, into the spaces for which it was originally made. This would surely attract visitors to the Museum.

But then the purists began to worry. This was, after all, their heritage, like the Catalan language or their Gothic churches. This was to be handed down to Catalans of the future. What if the water began to affect the tones and colours over a thousand years? Luckily the project was deemed too expensive. The Town Hall simply did not have the money to make it a showcase of Catalan art in time for the Olympic Games.

The Town Hall faces the headquarters of the Catalan government across Plaça de Sant Jaume. It is run by Socialists, who have had special responsibility for the Olympic Games; the Catalan government, on the other hand, is run by conservative nationalists, and throughout the 1980s the two hated each other and tried to outdo each other in every possible way.

But suddenly, on the issue of the Palau Nacional and the collection of Catalan art, they joined forces and persuaded Madrid to pay a third of the cost for the restoration of the Palau Nacional, while they would pay the rest. The Town Hall and the Catalan government would share the costs of running the Museum, and it was agreed that spending on its annual upkeep should increase ten-fold.

These negotiations took time, and a new design had to be commissioned, and this took time, and it seemed for a while that the Museum, the modernized showcase of Catalonia's heritage, would not be ready for the Olympic Games. So in the autumn of

1991 a three-shift day began at the Palau Nacional: they literally worked twenty-four hours a day to have it finished for June 1992.

When I went to see the work in January, they were aware that the Museum would not be fully completed by June, but the entrance hall would be done and the Grand Salon would be ready and enough exhibition space would be completed for them to mount a showcase exhibition of Catalan art from the Romanesque period to the 1940s. A team was working day and night preparing posters, calendars, postcards and books about the collection. The art would be exhibited in other rooms in the huge palace.

The newspapers reported regularly on progress at the new Museu d'Art de Catalunya, but as the winter progressed they began to concentrate on the huge sock which had been commissioned from Antoni Tàpies to stand in the middle of the Grand Salon. Tàpies had been using socks in his work for years, as an example of the objects which are considered beneath the interest of the artist. Now this stuffed sock he had designed was going to stand eighteen metres high in the Salon. The photograph of the maquette in the newspapers showed that Tàpies's sock had three huge holes in it just above the ankle, and visitors could go inside and climb up the sock.

There had already been huge publicity around the design of the roof of the Tàpies Foundation, which many thought looked like a huge toilet brush. The sock now became a matter of public debate, meaning that the new Museum was being discussed months before it was due to open.

The Palau Nacional was just beside all the main Olympic buildings. It was clear that the city authorities and the Catalan government were determined that it would become a major attraction during the Olympic Games. A series of escalators had even been added, running from the Museum down to Plaça d'Espanya. At the bottom, to the left as you walked down, Mies van der Rohe's German Pavilion for the 1929 Exhibition, complete with his Barcelona chair, had been reconstructed and could be visited.

The architectural rhetoric of the Palau Nacional is so bloated and artificial that the delicate angles and purity of the German Pavilion come as a great relief. It still remains one of the most interesting and oddly comforting spaces created by an architect, and its reconstruction is part of Barcelona's effort to leave no stone unturned as July 1992 approached. Even the Spanish Pavilion in the 1937 Paris Exhibition designed by Miró's friend, the Rationalist architect Josep Lluis Sert, who designed the Miró Foundation and Miró's studio in Majorca, was being reconstructed in Barcelona in the early months of 1992. This was the building which originally housed Picasso's *Guernica*.

In January 1992 the first police reinforcements came to Barcelona and stood around the old city, the streets off the Ramblas and around the port, looking at us as we passed, searching our faces. Thus the streets became safer, and one night I ventured down Carrer de Sant Pau by the side of the opera house, something which I would not have done alone late at night a year earlier. The streets were quiet, the pimps and the heroin dealers had moved elsewhere. Several police cars passed me as I walked towards a bar I had loved in the past – Bar Marsella, which had been closed for some time, but had now, I was told, re-opened. There was a uniformed guard at the door who sized me up and let me in.

Nothing had changed; all the old signs which forbade singing and spitting and spending all day mulling over the same drink were still there, but now it was full of young people, the sort of people who would not have dared walk down Carrer Sant Pau in the past. At least half of them were foreigners – English, Americans, Irish. A band began to play. I stood against the wall and watched: One of my old haunts, which, ten years earlier was frequented by people straight from Picasso's Blue Period, was now in vogue again.

I walked back down Sant Pau that night and across the Ramblas to Plaça Reial. On the first floor of one of the buildings there was a party going on. I stood once again and watched. All the people at the windows could be seen clearly, as there were no curtains. They were well dressed, polite and bourgeois. This was, I knew, the flat which the architect Oriol Bohigas had bought and decorated for himself. He, more than anybody else, was the leader of what was called 'the generation of 1992'. His firm of architects had designed the Olympic sites on Montjuic and many of the new buildings in the city. He had worked as a consultant with the city council in the years after the death of Franco to draw up a plan for the development of Barcelona. And now he had become head of the culture section of the Barcelona city council. His curriculum vitae fitted into the recent history of Barcelona like a hand into a glove.

The following day I telephoned Oriol Bohigas's office and made an appointment to see him and also David Mackay, one of the partners in the firm, who is half-Irish and has been working as an architect in Barcelona since 1958. In the 1950s, Mackay explained, an effort was made in Barcelona to hook up with the architecture of the years before the Civil War. Franco viewed modern architecture as part of the legacy of the left, and thus the design of public buildings during his rule was deeply conservative.

But the architects who were to become influential in the design of the Olympic buildings in the 1980s did very little work in the public sector until after Franco's death. They experimented with brick and tiles and reinforced concrete. In attempting to reassert the modern movement in architecture in the city, they realized that their aims were essentially political. They wanted to open up the city to European influences, and they wanted to use or refer to native Catalan sources in their work.

Their work represented, as David Mackay is quick to point out, only a fraction of what was built in Barcelona in the 1960s. Most of the buildings were put up as quickly and as cheaply as possible for the huge influx of immigrant families seeking work in Barcelona. But the teachers in the University of Barcelona tried to keep up with what was happening abroad in architecture, economics and politics and relay it to their students, who would thus be ready to take over power once Franco died.

Many of those who came to rule over post-Franco Barcelona had been to university together and came from the old middle-class Catalan families. They understood the importance of culture and they understood the importance of creating public spaces and putting up serious, modern architecture in their brave new city. David Mackay is sure that no Catalan firm of architects ever worked for the public sector in the Franco years. His firm, Bohigas, Martorell & Mackay, did not get their first job in the public sector until 1975, the year of Franco's death. But by the late 1970s, 90 per cent of the firm's work came from the public sector.

By that time there was a strong neighbourhood movement, and the city authorities began to work closely with local groups to create parks, public sculpture and a better environment in the city. For David Mackay and for Oriol Bohigas, who in the early 1980s combined a private practice with a position as policy maker on planning in the Town Hall, opening the city to the sea became a priority.

Thus the beach at Barceloneta was cleaned up and a new esplanade built. Some of the empty warehouses were knocked down. But the big change came in 1988 when a new road was built along the seafront, but sunk underground, and over it an esplanade was constructed with access to the waterfront. This was called Moll de la Fusta, and the new designer bars there became immensely popular on hot summer nights. You could park your car safely in the underground parking lot and look out over the city's old port as you sipped your gin and tonic.

This road was already in place when Bohigas, Mackay and their team began to design the layout of the Olympic facilities. Now it would be used to connect the Olympic Village, which would face the sea at Poble Nou, to the hill of Montjuic, where the main stadium and some of the smaller stadia would be built. It was decided that the winners of the main architectural prize in Barcelona over the previous thirty years would each be asked to design a block of the Olympic Village, thus veteran architects and architects in their twenties got an opportunity to work on the Village. Bohigas and his team decided to extend the grid-shaped city, the Eixample, right down through the new Olympic Village to the sea.

David Mackay is happy about the Olympic Village apartments which were being sold off to private investors in the early months of 1992. They had produced a bit of genuine city, he believes, full of variety, some 'very nice, some ugly', reflecting the state of the profession rather than 'an over-designed architectural exhibition'. Perhaps it was the very extent of the variety which was making the new apartments difficult to sell.

All this development in Barcelona, David Mackay emphasizes, will service the Olympic Games and then make Barcelona one of the best-planned cities in Europe. All the new roads and tunnels and train systems, with the new telecommunications network, and the sports and cultural facilities will make Barcelona an attractive place in which to site a factory or set up offices. The new Europe will be made up of cities rather than countries. Mackay is full of rhetoric of hope, energy, dynamism, as he extolls the virtue of Barcelona in 1993.

He does not mention the new airport. It has been designed by Ricard Bofill as a light-filled space, which exudes the colours and tones of the Mediterranean, using a reddish marble floor, huge palm trees and glass. Of all the new buildings in Barcelona, it is easily the most impressive, remaining simple and symmetrical and warm. But with architects in Barcelona you have to be careful; it is like dealing with politicians. They seldom like each other. Mackay dislikes the layout and design of the new airport, sees no sense in making an airport building symmetrical when both sides, leaving and arriving, have different needs. 'The space effect is very well handled,' he says.

But he had nothing good to say about Bofill's other Olympic building, the Sports College. 'Indescribable,' he says. When I mention Neo-Georgian, he replies, 'Messed-up Georgian.' He has not been inside, he says, but he believes it is worse inside.

A few days later I sat talking to Oriol Bohigas in his office in the Virreina Palace, overlooking the flower-stalls on the Ramblas. He is suave, polite, more like a politician than any politician I have ever come across. He is businesslike, even when it comes to the matter of Ricard Bofill's buildings. Bofill likes neo-classicism, and Bohigas doesn't. He shrugs. It's like tonal or atonal music: you choose one or the other, he says. He goes on, then, to talk about the group of politicians, architects and administrators who got to know one another in the last years of Franco's reign, and how lucky it was that the politicians were intellectuals who understood the need to use the best ideas to rehabilitate the city of Barcelona. His joy now, he says, is to improve the cultural infrastructure in the city in the 1990s. Luckily, his old friends the Socialists are still in power in the Town Hall.

The main Olympic Stadium sits at the top of the hill of Montjuic, close to the Palau Nacional and the old city cemetery. The old facade from a stadium constructed for the 1929 Exhibition has been left in place, and the inside has been refurbished using that raw concrete which you see in such stadia all over the world. Close by is the Palau Sant Jordi, designed by the Japanese architect Arata Isozaki, which has multi-purpose indoor sports facilities. All the support comes from the sides, so the view is perfectly clear from every seat in the auditorium. It is a squat, light building. Its roof was literally raised one miraculous day in 1989 by a set of computer-controlled, hydraulic forces stiffening the columns at the side and holding the roof in place. Below this is Bofill's new Sports College, which seems clean, old fashioned, remaining apart from all this experiment and modernity.

Beside the Olympic Village in Poble Nou two new high modern buildings punctuate the skyline. One, a new luxury hotel, is one of the ugliest buildings in Barcelona, and the other, an office block, is not far behind. And as you move around the new Olympic buildings in the city you realize that no new architectural style is on display or has been developed for Barcelona 1992. This is not the city of a century earlier, forging its own identity through its buildings. The style is international now, a bit of Japanese here, a bit of neo-classicism there, but there is no flagship building in the new Barcelona which is original in concept and will be influential in the future.

Some of the new buildings in the city are beautiful, however, such as the post-modern police building beside the Hotel Oriete on the Ramblas or some of the sports buildings outside the city.

All day as the Olympics approached the digging and building went on. It was now clear that the two large sites on the Ramblas would not be finished in time for July. But new tunnels were inaugurated to relieve the terrible traffic congestion at the exits to the city. It was announced that the problems at the control tower in the airport, which had been caused by the design of Bofill's building, could be rectified in time for the Olympics.

Some of the restoration work was as disastrous and ugly as some of the new buildings. The old cobblestones were taken up from the square in front of the Cathedral and flagstones put down. But they were too bright against the dark stone of the Cathedral facade, and they stained easily, and as you walked past you wondered why the city could not leave well enough alone. Around the corner on Carrer de la Palla the city authorities had cleared a space so the Roman walls could be seen, just as they had in Carrer de Regomir. But this time they had left the space open and surrounded it with huge bright steel bars, like a cage, to keep the locals out in case they might use the space to sit in, or as a place to take the sun.

In the early months of 1992 more plans for the city were discussed, as though Barcelona were going to remain as restless in 1993 as it had been the previous few years. There was going to be a new Museum of Contemporary Art. There was a possibility that the top three floors of the modern building attached to the old Town Hall in the 1960s would be removed. Nothing was going to stay still, remain certain. Day after day new surprises came. One afternoon I took the train to Sitges, the seaside resort south of the city, only to find a new, cool, modernized ticket office, and a double-decker train which formed part of a new rail network and got you to Sitges in half the time.

There was no need for demonstrations in favour of nationalism, or slogans, or new graffiti. Everything planned for the Olympics, every improvement in the city's fabric, was a way of making Catalonia great. Thus Barcelona was going through a sort of post-nationalism in which much had been consolidated and taken for granted, especially by the young. Barcelona was also, in its night life, going through a post-designer phase. The new trendy bar did not look like an expensive art gallery, complete with high-tech toilets and fancy lighting. It was called the San Francisco and it was on Carrer de Casanova in the Eixample. It looked as though it had been built in a day, thrown together using any old leftover material available. It had no cool credentials. But it was where everybody wanted to go, where the doorman had to turn most people away in the early hours of the morning. It remained open until five o'clock.

All day you noticed changes. But the city itself did not change. In the morning at a quarter past nine a man wandered along the street where I lived, banging a piece of metal against an empty gas cylinder, indicating that he had full gas cylinders and would deliver one to you if you would stick your head out of the window and shout down to him. He came back twice more before lunchtime. One morning every week a knife sharpener came to the street and alerted us to his presence by playing a melancholy three-note sound on a whistle. The wonderful old shops which had seemed so old-fashioned in the 1970s when I first came to the city were still there, the knife shop in Placa del Pi; the hat shop where Carrer de Boqueria meets Carrer d'Avinyó; the traditional craft shop on Carrer d'Avinyó close to Carrer Ferran where you could buy hand-made espadrilles.

And most of the old bars were still thriving; even the Portalon on Carrer dels Banys Nous, which looked like a Stone Age cave, was alive and well. But the owner wasn't happy. People had been in to see him from the Town Hall, he said, people who were concerned about the image of the city during the Olympics and who wanted him to paint the walls and tart the place up. He was indignant. He pointed at the walls. They had never been painted, or if they had been painted, it had not occurred in living memory. The place looked seedy or medieval, depending on your point of view. The people from the Town Hall thought it looked seedy; the owner and myself agreed that it looked medieval. It was as though the people at Oriol Bohigas's party that night when I stood watching in the Plaça Reail had come down into the old city complete with their taste for the modern and the cool, complete with the power, and ordered the old bars to be modernized. The owner of the Portalon said that he agreed to have the whole place cleaned, but he wasn't letting any paint near the walls.

In Barceloneta, they knocked the old beach restaurants down, as part of a general scheme to clean up the coast. They were old fashioned, wooden structures, redolent of the 1940s and 1950s. They were not part of the new Barcelona; they went against the spirit of 1992. A few palm trees were put up instead of them. The seafront looked bare and strange without them. I remembered all the things which had happened to me in those restaurants; some of the best nights of my life. These restaurants were gone now, a memory, something you would point to in the future and tell how there used to be restaurants there and they were old fashioned and the food was good, but they were knocked down in the months before the Olympic Games.

But there was too much of the old city left for the Olympic spirit to affect it much. For me, it was still so old fashioned, the signs over the shops, the way the windows were decorated, the grey stone and the scarce light in the narrow streets, the custom and the ceremony surrounding the serving of food and drink. Every evening at around eight in the early months of 1992 I walked across Plaça de Sant Josep Oriol and along Carrer del Pito to La Pineda, which was still perfectly preserved as a delicatessen–cum–bodega from the early years of the century. Cured meat hung from the ceiling; olives and anchovies soaked in oil, and cheeses matured. There was wine in bottles all around the walls and sherry and brandy and Catalan champagne. But the place was not a museum, even though the owner, now in his nineties, had been there since the 1920s. He and his two young assistants were busy slicing meat, making sandwiches, cutting cheese and deciding what wine you should try next.

If you were lucky on those winter evenings you could find a free table at the back of La Pineda and take on the smells, watch the people passing in and out of the shop, lean against the old presses where the bottles of good wine were kept, wait for your olives and anchovies to be served and shake your head in wonder at the sheer pleasure of being in Barcelona now, or any time.

*

Picasso died in 1971. He had left a large collection of his work to the Picasso Museum in Barcelona, from his very first efforts (two cut-outs of a dog and a dove done in Malaga when he was nine) to the technical exercises of his early teens. In the rooms of the two palaces where the collection is housed we can watch his early development, his first complete portraits of peasants and members of his family, his first large canvas, *Science and Charity*, his paintings of the city of Barcelona: the sea, the port, the Cathedral cloister, the café concerts he attended with his friend Pallarès, Barceloneta, the moon over the rooftops of the city, the dome of a church at dusk. The Museum follows his route to Madrid in 1897 and from there to Horta de Sant Joan. And then his life in Bohemian Barcelona; Pere Romeu, the owner of *Els Quatre Gats* appears; Carles Casagemas, his doomed friend; Jaume Sabartés, who became Picasso's secretary more than thirty years later and established the Picasso Museum in the early 1960s using his personal collection as its base.

Then there is Picasso's work done in Paris in 1900 and the 'Blue' paintings done on his return to Barcelona when he lived in Carrer Nou de la Rambla. There is nothing from Picasso's time at Gósol, and nothing from his return visit to Horta de Sant Joan in 1909; but his work from Barcelona in 1917 such as *The Harlequin* or *The Balcony* fills a room of the palace.

During 1917 the Russian Ballet, for whom Picasso had designed *Parade*, devised a show based on Velázquez's *Las Meninas*, which Picasso saw at the Liceu. Forty years later the painting would come to obsess him, and in Cannes in 1957 he began to make his own versions of the painting, and these would be his last donation to the Museum before his death.

In 1937 he gave the title *Dream and Lie of Franco* to a work in which Franco was depicted as a monster, 'a grotesque and loathsome figure', in the words of Roland Penrose. Picasso was asked to exhibit at the Spanish Pavilion at the International Exhibition in Paris in 1937 which was being designed by Miró's friend Josep Lluís Sert. Miró made a poster and a painting for the exhibition. Picasso agreed to take part as well, and wanted to make clear his sympathy for the Republicans in the Spanish Civil War. On 29 April 1937 the Germans bombed the Basque town of Guernica, and in passion and anger Picasso set to work first on sketches and drawings, all of them with a wounded horse as the central focus. He then began work on a canvas eleven and a half feet high and nearly twenty-six feet long. Within two months this painting, *Guernica*, hung as the main attraction in the Spanish Pavilion. Picasso made several statements about what was happening in his country: 'I have always believed', he said at the end of 1937, 'and still believe, that the artists who live and work with spiritual values cannot and should not remain indifferent to a conflict in which the highest values of humanity and civilisation are at stake.' Later, when the war was lost, he was generous in helping refugees from Spain.

As Franco's regime sought respectability in the outside world, it made overtures to Picasso. His work was included in the Spanish Pavilion at the United States World Fair in 1964 and 1965. The Museum in Carrer de Montcada was at first called The Sabartés Collection, when it was set up in 1962, but soon afterwards it was given Picasso's name. They were courting his favour. But he would not come back to Spain and, more importantly perhaps, he would not allow *Guernica* to be seen in Spain until the dictatorship had come to an end and democracy was restored. The painting stayed in exile for more than forty years, graphic and forceful in its depiction of the pain and horror of war. Its presence in Madrid, where it now hangs in the Centre de Arte de Reina Sofia, offers a sort of atonement, a sense of something put right.

In 1983 Barcelona built its monument to Picasso in Passeig de Picasso, beside the Parc de la Ciutadella. It was designed by Antoni Tàpies as a glass box in a pool of water, containing some old chairs and an old hall-stand, old ropes and sheets with indecipherable messages written on them. All the furniture is cut through with iron grids. It is an astonishing piece of work. It stands there as a monument to the mind's ability to create images, to our freedom to imagine. It is hard not to feel that if the Fascists ever took this city again it would be one of the first things to go.

*

Pau Casals died in 1973 at the age of ninety-seven. After the execution of Lluís Companys, he had refused the offer to become President of the Catalan Generalitat, but he never managed to stay out of politics, and all his life the plight of his country would haunt him. The concerts which he organized at Prades in the Catalan-speaking South of France were attended by large numbers of Catalans, and became an important symbol of Catalan dissent from the Franco regime.

Josep Trueta, the surgeon from Barcelona now at Oxford, met Casals in March 1939 in London, when he gave a concert at the Royal Albert Hall in aid of refugee children. In 1945 Trueta saw him playing the Elgar Cello Concerto at the Royal Albert Hall again, and met him a few days later in Reading where he was playing with Gerald Moore. During the interval he turned to Trueta and his wife 'in a state of utter despondency' and said: 'You know what they have decided? They are going to do nothing to remove Franco, nothing; it is incredible, but true. Nothing – they are even going to help him, and our poor Catalonia will be destroyed! This is the end of everything – I have lost all hope.' He wrote to Trueta three years later: 'With the discovery of the word "realist", all ideals have gone overboard; all that is most noble . . . Deception, resignation, despair: these are our only reward for having sacrificed everything.' He refused to play his cello in the countries which helped to keep Franco in power.

In the end, however, there was nothing he could do. Music would not move Franco, nor move foreign governments to take action against the dictatorship. Casals added a Catalan tune to his repertoire, and he played it wherever he went. It was not a marching song or a national anthem; it was a sombre and melancholy Catalan folk-song called *El Cant dels Ocells* (The Song of the Birds). He played it at the end of each concert to remind the world of the plight of his country. (He would have winced, perhaps, had he heard it used as background music in 1988 for a commercial on TV3, the all-Catalan station.)

He married in his old age, and moved to Puerto Rico, where Trueta visited him. 'Look,' he said, pointing out to the landscape, 'doesn't this remind you of Tarragona, see how the green and blue blend together.' The two old exiles watched some peasants cutting cane: 'They are not like our peasants,' Casals said. 'Ours would cut the cane close to the root.'

*

December came to the city from which Casals and Trueta fled in 1939. The traditional Christmas market opened in front of the Cathedral, selling Christmas trees, figures from the crib and toys; all around the Cathedral there were stalls full of artisan work. At the weekend you couldn't move among the crowds wandering around the Gothic quarter. In the Plaça de Sant Jaume a huge crib had been placed in the middle of specially imported trees and grass so that there was barely space for cars to get through. It had taken days to build; the life of the square had been disrupted just for this. The three Kings bearing gifts arrived in mid-December, rather earlier than usual, a tribute to the optimism in Barcelona now, part of the general feeling that all things would come to pass.

*

Miró died in the winter, on Christmas Day 1983, at the age of ninety. His body lay in state in the Palau de la Generalitat and people queued in the Plaça de Sant Jaume to pay respect to him.

He had moved away from the city in the 1950s, spending most of his time in Majorca where Sert built him a big studio. In 1968 the city authorities put on a retrospective in the Hospital de Santa Creu; he was at last forgiven by the winners of the Civil War. But he would not forgive and refused to attend the opening. As a protest, too, he painted on the glass front of the architects' headquarters in the Plaça Nova and wiped it off some weeks later, in an ephemeral protest not just against Franco but against capitalism and the commercial world of art. In 1970 he marched to Montserrat with Antoni Tàpies and other artists and intellectuals in protest against the Burgos trials.

He was relieved when Franco died. 'We can breathe more freely now,' he said to an interviewer. He did a poster for the Barcelona football club, for the new Catalan newspaper *Avui*, and he designed record sleeves for singers of *La Nova Cançó*, including Maria del Mar Bonet. He designed a set of tiles on the Rambla at the Plaça d'Os, with the colours and shapes he had played with all his life. He worked with a young theatre group, La Claca, designing costumes. He loved the new graffiti in Barcelona, but he found the air in the city humid. He wasn't sure that fascism had come to an end with Franco's death, but as the elections took place he came to feel that his country had been saved, that the dark forces which filled so many of his paintings had been defeated.

The city had abandoned him for so long. He was back now, watching over the new Foundation. When he asked them for this space, the best site in the city, the authorities didn't know how famous he was; they had to make enquiries. They were told that he was important and they gave him this piece of land on Montjuic, overlooking the city, overlooking the Mediterranean, where he could put his life's work.

Nobody knew him in Barcelona in his last years, nobody recognized him in the street. He enjoyed being incognito but, also, he remembered how, one day when the Foundation had just opened, the young people, the new generation who would not know life under a dictator, started to come up to him. He was standing there with Sert, his old friend and architect. He had taken so much of his inspiration from their world, from Catalonia, its light, its contours. All his life he had used it. He had shown his work all over the world; it was dispersed. He had shown so little here. It was hard, he said. Can you imagine how hard it is? For fifty years not being able to exhibit in your own country. That day they started to come up to him, and he could feel the warmth from them and the affection, and he couldn't bear it, he had to turn away crying. He knew that Catalonia had come through.

Select Bibliography

Los anarchistas en las crisis politicas española, Jose Peirats (Buenos Aires, 1964).

Barcelonas, Manuel Vázquez Montalbán (Barcelona, 1987).

The Catalans, Jan Read (London 1978).

Catàleg del Patrimoni Arquitectònic Històric i Artístic, Ajuntament de Barcelona.

Conversaciones con Miró, Georges Raillard (Barcelona, 1978).

Conversations with Dalí, Alain Bosquet (New York, 1969).

Episodis de la guerra civil espanyola, Jaume Miravittles (Barcelona, 1972).

The Essence of Catalonia, Alaistair Boyd (London, 1988).

Federico García Lorca: De Fuente Vaqueros a Nueva York, Ian Gibson (Barcelona, 1986).

Federico García Lorca: De Nueva York a Fuente Grande, Ian Gibson (Barcelona, 1987).

Federico García Lorca: A Life, Ian Gibson (London, 1989).

Forbidden Territory, Juan Goytisolo (London, 1989).

García Lorca en Cataluña, Antonina Rodriguez (Barcelona, 1975).

Gaudí His Life, His Theories, His Work, Cesar Martinell, trans. J. Rohrer (Cambridge Mass., 1975).

Gaudí The Visionary, R. Descharnes, C. Prevost (New York, 1971).

George Orwell: A Biography, Bernard Crick (London, 1980).

Homage to Barcelona, Arts Council of Great Britain (London, 1985).

Homage to Catalonia, George Orwell (London, 1938).

Joan Miró y Cataluña, Juan Perucho (Barcelona).

Joan Miró, Sebastià Gasch (Barcelona, 1963).

Joys and Sorrows, Pablo Casals (London, 1970).

Memoria Personal, Antoni Tàpies (Barcelona, 1977).

Modern Architecture in Barcelona, David Mackay (Sheffield, 1985).

Museu D'Art de Catalunya, Carme Farré (Barcelona, 1983).

Pablo Casals: A Biography, H. L. Kirk (New York, 1974).

La Patum de Berga, Jaume Farras (Barcelona).

Picasso i els seus amics catalans, Josep Palau i Fabre (Barcelona, 1971).

Picasso His Life and Work, Roland Penrose (London, 1958).

Picasso Retratos v Recuerdos, Jaime Sabartés (Madrid, 1953).

Picasso Vivent, Josep Palau i Fabre (Barcelona, 1980).

Recuerdos de un cenetista, Adolf Bueso (Barcelona, 1976).

Salvador Dalí Visto por su hermana, Ana Maria Dalí (Barcelona, 1983.)

Salvador Dalí: The Surrealist Jester, Meryle Secrest (London, 1986).

The Spanish Civil War, Hugh Thomas (London, 1961).

Spanish Front: Writers on the Civil War, ed. Valentine Cunningham (Oxford, 1986).

The Spanish Labyrinth, Gerald Brenan (London, 1943).

The Spirit of Catalonia, Josep Trueta (Oxford, 1946).

Trueta: Surgeon in War and Peace, trans. Amelia and Michael Strubell (London, 1980).

Index

Spanish/Catalan compound names are indexed by the first word not a preposition that follows the forename(s), e.g. Puig i Cadafalch, Josep

Acràcia (magazine) 41
ADLAN 97
Agut (restaurant) 5, 65
airport 201, 202
Ajuntament *see* Town Hall
Alba, Victor 112–13
Alberti, Rafael 148
Alfonso XIII, King 96, 100
Almeria 120
Anarchists 10, 18, 20–21, 38, 40,
    41–2, 43, 45, 57, 59, 107–20
    passim
Antiga Botiga Bruno Cuadros 4
Antiga Casa Figueres 4
Antonioni, Michelangelo 55–6
Aragon, Louis 87
Aragon (province) 13, 190
Arc del Teatre 83
Arc de Triomf 35, 48
architects' building (Plaça Nova) 23,
    209
Arenys de Mar 141
Argelès, camp at 123
Argenteria (street) 165
Arp, Hans 88, 97
Arsenal buildings (Catalan Parliament)
    79
Artaud, Antonin 87
Art Nouveau 4, 30, 32, 33, 66
Arts and Crafts Movement 30

Arxiu de la Corona d'Aragó 12
Associació Obrera de Concerts 99,
    100
Ateneu 101
Athens 14
Auden, W.H. 111
   Spain (poem) 125
Autozut (nightclub) 24
Avui (newspaper) 17, 174, 185, 187,
    209
Azaña, Manuel 103, 105, 115–16, 121

Bakunin, Mikhail 41, 110
Balearic Islands 13, 189
Bar Agustí (Horta) 75
Bar del Pi 165, 174
Bar Joanet 18
Bar Manolo (Horta) 75
Bar Marsella 198
Bar Mundial 18
Bar Navarro 83
Bar Roure 83
Barça football club 37, 45, 180–81,
    191, 209
Barceló, Miquel 56
Barceloneta 112, 121, 145–6, 200,
    204, 205
Barcino (Roman city) 12–13
Barraca, La (Dali's 'hut') 156

Barri Xinès 82–3, 104, 166–8, 169, 170
Bases de Manresa (document) 38
Bassegoda i Nonell, Joan 61
Batcheff, Pierre 150
Beatus (book) 132
Berg, Alban 99
Berga 76, 136–40
Besalú 13
Bishop's Residence 121
Black Virgin of Monserrat 174–6
Blanes 141, 144
Boades (restaurant) 165
Bocabella, Josep Maria 53, 59
Bofill, Ricard 201–2
Bohigas, Martorell & Mackay 199–200
Bohigas, Oriol 170, 198–9, 200, 201, 204
bombing of Barcelona 41–2, 121–2
Bonanova 112
Bonet, Jordi 61–2
Bonet, Maria del Mar 5–6, 25, 141–2, 209
Bonet, Ramon 58
Boqueria market 159–61, 174
Bosquits, Alain 149
Bot (village) 89
Boult, Adrian 99
Braque, Georges 123
Brenan, Gerald: *The Spanish Labyrinth* 40, 42, 44
Breton, André 87, 150, 151
Bueso, Adolfo 105–6, 108–12, 114, 116, 118–21, 122–3
Buñuel, Luis 149, 150–51, 157
Burgos trials (1970) 209
Busquets, Jaume 112

Caballé, Monserrat 46, 49, 142, 172
Cadaqués 148, 150, 151, 154, 155–6

Café Moka 118, 126
Calafell 112
Calder, Alexander, 91, 97
Caldetes 144
Calella 144
Call, the (Girona) 131
Camp Nou football ground 180–81, 191
Canadiense, La (electrical company) 44
Canet 144
Canigó, the 36
Cannes 206
Cap de Creus 141, 156–7
Capmany, Aureli 22
Cara al Sol (Fascist hymn) 124–5
Carcassone 51
Carrer Ample 98
Carrer Argenteria 161
Carrer Assaonadors 18, 20, 159
Carrer Canuda 101
Carrer Carders 18, 20, 93
Carrer Cardinal Casseñas 159
Carrer Carme 22, 166
Carrer Carme & Rambla, church on corner of 111
Carrer Corretgers 18
Carrer d'Aragó 35
Carrer d'Ausiàs Marc 35
Carrer d'Avinyó 65, 204
Carrer de Balmes 125
Carrer de Bruc 32
Carrer de Buenos Aires 32
Carrer de Casanova 32, 203
Carrer de Corcega 32
Carrer de Jupi 18
Carrer de Boqueria 204
Carrer de la Força (Girona) 131, 133
Carrer de la Mercè 64, 65, 71, 80
Carrer de la Palla 12, 192, 203
Carrer de la Plata 65

Carrer de la Reina Cristina 64

Carrer de Montcada 18, 19, 20, 33, 78, 207

Carrer de Montsió 33, 68

Carrer de Paradís 13

Carrer de Regomir 80, 164, 192, 203

Carrer de Sant Oleguer 83

Carrer de Sant Pau 34, 93, 198

Carrer de Santa Monica 83

Carrer del Bisbe 21

Carrer del Bon Dia 18

Carrer del Call 12

Carrer del Casp 108

Carrer del Cid 83

Carrer del Comerç 71, 72

Carrer del Consultat 72

Carrer del Migdia 83, 166

Carrer del Oli 18

Carrer del Pito 205

Carrer dels Banys Nous 164, 204

Carrer dels Canvis Nous 41

Carrer dels Comtes 12

Carrer dels Escudellers 64, 65

Carrer dels Escudellers Blancs 65, 72

Carrer dels Robadors 168

Carrer Ferran 47, 80, 92, 168, 204

Carrer Flasserders 18

Carrer Gignàs 5

Carrer Hospital 34

Carrer Jaume I 80

Carrer Lauder 64

Carrer Mallorca 34

Carrer Nou de la Rambla 35, 52, 65, 71, 72, 206

Carrer Petrixol 70

Carrer Portaferrissa 84

Carrer Princesa 80, 117, 165

Carrer Sant Pere més Baix 71, 82

Carrer Tallers 165

Carrer Wellington 29

Carreras, José 5, 46, 48–9, 142

Casa Amatller 33

Casa Antoni Roger 35

Casa Battló 33, 55

Casa de Cultura (Girona) 133

Casa de l'Ardiaca 23

Casa de la Canonja 23

Casa de la Ciutat 12

Casa de les Punxes 32

Casa Iglesias 34

Casa Juncadella 35

Casa Lleó i Morera 33

Casa March 4

Casa Maria Robert 35

Casa Meca 19

Casa Milà (Pedrera) 55–7, 66, 192

Casa Padellas 18

Casa Serra 32

Casa Thomas 34

Casa Vicens 51, 52

Casagemas, Carles 67, 69–70, 72, 156, 206

Casals, Enric 99

Casals, Pau 96, 97, 98–100, 104, 105, 110, 123, 207–8

Casas, Ramon 46, 66–7, 68–9, 70–71

Casteldefels 97

Castell dels tres Dragons 35–6

Castile 15, 16, 17, 195

Catalan Council of Music 100

Catalan Employers' Federation 41

Catalan language 2–3, 36, 45, 97, 98, 101, 124, 173, 183–4, 189, 190–91

Catalonia, history of 3, 12–18, 30–31, 36, 42, 96–129

Catalunya del Nord (France) 189–90

Cathedral 3, 6, 11, 12, 18, 20–21, 22–3, 51, 69, 91, 121, 171, 202, 205, 208

Cathedral of Girona 130–32, 133

Catholic Church, the 43, 112

Cau Ferrat 67
Cézanne, Paul 68, 84
CEDA (right-wing Party) 102
Centre de Arte de Reina Sofia 207
Centre d'Escursionistes de Catalunya
     13
Cercle Artístic de Sant Luc 82
Cerdà, Idlefons 31
Cerdagne 13
Charlemagne 13
Christ of Taüll 92, 94
Chronicle of the Abbey of Moissac
     13
Ciurella 79
Ciutadella fortress 16
Civil War, Spanish 7, 10, 46, 59,
     107–29, 199, 206, 209
Claca, La (theatre group) 209
Clarke, H. B. 41
Clavé, Josep Anselm 36
Clos, Joan 189
CNT (Anarchist trade union) 44–5,
     105, 108, 111, 116, 118, 120
Cocteau, Jean 73
Collserola (hill) 166
Columbus, Christopher 11
     statue of 8, 11, 35, 63
Communist Party 7, 115, 120, 186–7
Companys, Lluís 93, 97, 100, 102–3,
     105, 107–21 passim, 151, 207
Connolly, Cyril 114
Consell de Cent 15, 21–2
Constance of Sicily 14
Constantinople 14
Convent of Sant Elias (used as prison)
     112, 115
Convergència i Unió (political Party)
     28, 185, 187
Cornudella 79, 81
Corpus Christi (1896) 41
Corpus Christi celebrations 136–40

correfoc 5, 10
Corsica 14
Cortes of Madrid 38, 39
Costa Brava 141, 142–3, 144, 146,
     164
Costa de Maresme 144, 145
Counts of Barcelona 13, 15
Creueta, la 166
Crida, La (nationalist group) 172
Cuba 38, 43
Cubism 83

Dada movement 84
Dalí, Ana Maria 101, 141, 149, 157
Dalí, Salvador (father of painter) 42,
     148–9, 151
Dalí, Salvador 42, 67, 82, 84, 98, 101,
     148–54, 157–8, 174, 195
     Blood is Sweeter than Honey 149
     Sacred Heart 150
Dalí, Señora (step-mother of painter)
     149
Dalmau, Josep 83–4, 86
Dansa de la Mort (Dance of Death)
     134–6, 184
David & Goliath, statue of 127–8
Davies, John Langdon: *Dancing
     Catalans* 22
Derain, André 156
Desnos, Robert 87, 150
Despuig, Ramon 20
Diada (National Day) 16–17, 58, 185,
     190
Diaghilev, Sergei Pavlovich 84
Diagonal (street) 32
Documentos (artist) 83
Domènech i Montaner, Lluís 32–6,
     38, 39, 48, 51, 166
Domingo, Placido 46
Drassanes (shipyard) 22
Dreiser, Theodore 122

Duchamp, Marcel 83, 156
  Nude Descending a Staircase 83
Durruti 109
Dylan, Bob 184

Ebro river 74
Eden Concert (music hall) 71
Eixample, L' 30–49, 99, 183, 186,
  200, 203
El Botafumeiro (restaurant) 163–4
El Canario de la Garriga (restaurant)
  101, 102
El Cant de la Senyera (hymn) 185–6
El Cant dels Ocells (song) 208
El Correo Catalan (newspaper) 110
El Libre del Consolat del Mar (book) 15
El Nus (bar) 165
El Pais (newspaper) 190
El Pla de la Garça (restaurant) 159
Eldorado theatre 101
Els Quatre Gats (artists' centre) 33,
  68–9, 71, 72, 73, 205
Els Quatre Gats (magazine) 70–71
Els Segadors (national anthem) 17
Eluard, Gala 150–51, 152–3, 155
Eluard, Paul 87, 150–51
Empúries 13
Ensanche *see* Eixample
Ernst, Max 88
Escamots (paramilitaries) 103
Escola Moderna 42
Estat Català (political Party) 44
Excursionisme 36

Fabra, Pompeu: *Normes ortografiques*
  98
FAI (Anarchist militia) 116
Falla, Manuel de 67
Fanelli, Giuseppe 40
Farré, Carme 92, 94–5
Fellini, Federico 180

Ferdinand & Isabella 11, 14
Ferrer, Francesc 42, 43
Figueres 148, 149–51, 153, 158
Ford, Richard 14–15
Fraga, Manuel 186
Francis, Sam 91
Franco, General Francisco 2, 7, 23,
  103, 120, 123, 124, 152, 183,
  185, 186, 193, 194, 195, 198–9,
  201, 206, 207–8, 209
Fundació Miró *see* Miró's Foundation

Galeria Dalmau 85, 101, 149, 150
Galeria Maeght 19
Galerie Georges Bernheim (Paris) 88
Galerie Vollard (Paris) 71
Galí, Francesc 81–2
García Lorca *see* Lorca
Gargallo, Pau 86
Gasch, Sebastià 82–3, 102, 104, 149
Gassol, Ventura 93, 107, 109
GATCPAC 97
Gaudí, Antonio 32, 33, 35, 50–62, 63,
  68, 82, 84, 166, 169, 192, 195
Gauguin, Paul 71, 84
Gay, Julia 126–7
Generalitat 96, 98, 107, 115, 116, 119,
  121, 187–8, 207
Genet, Jean: *The Thief's Journal* 166
Germaine (girlfriend of Casagemas)
  69, 70, 156
Girona 13, 39, 93, 130–40
Goded, General 108–9
Gonzalez, Felipe 186, 188
Gonzalez, Juli 98
Gósol (village) 74, 76–8, 206
Gothic quarter 11–23, 31, 208
Goya cinema 101
Goytisolo, José Augustín 126
Goytisolo, Juan 126
  Coto Vedado 127

Goytisolo, Luis 126
Gràcia (suburb) 27, 31, 51, 163
Gran Hotel International 35
Gran Via 35, 58
Granollers (village) 122, 162
Great Exhibition of 1888 34–6, 37,
    45, 48, 128, 192
Great Exhibition of 1929 92, 100,
    192, 195, 197, 201–2
    German Pavilion 197–8
Gropius, Walter 60, 61
Güell, Eusebi 52, 54
Guernica 206
Guston, Philip 91
Guthrie, Woody 184

Hannay, David 41
Hemingway, Ernest 87, 125
    For Whom the Bell Tolls 126
Herzen: *Bell* (journal) 40
Horta de Sant Joan 64, 68, 74–6, 89,
    112, 205, 206
Hospital de la Santa Creu i Sant Pau
    34, 112, 209
Hostal Bellmirall (Girona) 132–3
Hostalet del Call (Girona) 133
Hotel Colon 23, 171
Hotel Colonia Puig 175–6
Hotel España 34
Hotel Europa (Granollers) 162
Hotel Majestic 104, 113
Hotel Oriete 202
Hotel Rialto 80
Hugué, Manolo 103

Impressionism 84
Institute of Catalan Studies 39
International Brigades 128–9
Ireland (influence of) 44
Isaac el Sec (Isaac the Blind) 133
Isozaki, Arata 202

Jacob, Max 71
Jamboree (nightclub) 24
Jaume I, King 13–14
Jewish heritage 14, 131
Jiménez, Juan Ramón 148
jocs florals (poetry competition) 36
Jou, Victor 25–6
Jove Catalunya, La (nationalist group)
    38
Joyce, James: *Ulysses* 87
Juan Carlos, King 29, 157, 171–3,
    183, 185, 193–4
Juncosa, Pilar (wife of Miró) 88

Karma (nightclub) 24
KGB (nightclub) 24
Koklova, Olga (wife of Picasso) 73

L'Alguer (Sardinia) 190
L'Egipte (restaurant) 159
La Batalla (newspaper) 110, 114,
    118–19
La Boite (nightclub) 24
La Dolce Vita (film) 180
La Huelga General (periodical) 42, 43
La Paloma (dance hall) 170
La Pineda (bodega) 205
La Traviata (opera) 49
La Vanguardia (newspaper) 125, 168–9
Le Corbusier 22, 60, 61, 90, 97, 169
Léger, Fernand 83
Lerroux, Alejandro 42, 43
Liceu Opera House 4, 34, 36–7, 41,
    46–7, 53, 73, 206
Liceu Orchestra 98
Llach, Lluís 184, 190
Llançà 144
Llavaneres 144
Llavorsí 146–8
Lleida 39, 125

Lliga Regionalista 38–9, 43, 44, 45, 96, 105
Llorens i Artigas, Josep 82, 85, 86
Lloret de Mar 141, 144
Llotja (Stock Exchange) 12, 21, 63, 64, 81
Loeb, Pierre 87, 149–50
Lopez, Senyor 161
Lorca, Federico García 4, 67, 82, 100–102, 105, 141, 148, 149
  Blood Wedding 102, 104
  Doña Rosita la Soltera 104
  Miriana Pineda 101
  Poet in New York 102
  Yerma 102, 103, 184
Los Caracoles (restaurant) 65
Lyon d'Or (café) 109

Machado, Antonio 148
Macià, Francesc 96–7, 100, 101, 105, 169
Mackay, David 199–201
MacNeice, Louis 122, 125–6
Madrid 31, 37, 38, 39, 40, 42, 120–21, 195, 196
Magritte, René 150
Majorca 13, 79–80, 90, 124, 141–2, 198, 209
Malaga 69, 205
Mancomunitat 39, 98
Manzana de la Discordia 33
Maragall, Joan (poet) 66, 78, 186
Maragall, Pasqual (Mayor of Barcelona) 128, 186, 189
Marca hispànica (Spanish March) 13
Mariscal, Javier 28–9
market building (Passeig del Born) 19
market complex (Carrer d'Aragó) 35
Martínez de Campos, General 41
Masson, André 87
Matamala, Llorenç 58

Mataró 122
Matisse, Henri 84, 88, 91
Matisse, Pierre (son of Henri) 88, 91
McDonald's hamburger joint 190
McGahern, John: *The Beginning of an Idea* 5
Mediterranean 194, 201, 209
Memorial de Greuges 38
Menuhin, Yehudi 142
Mercè festival 3, 6–9
Metge, Guillem 20
Milà family 57
Milà, Rosario 57
Mir, Joaquin 195–6
Miramar Hotel 150
Miravittles, Jaume 101, 107–9, 114, 115, 116–17, 119, 152
Miró, Dolors 88, 124
Miró, Joan 4, 51, 58, 63, 79–92, 97–8, 123–4, 149, 150, 157, 174, 195, 198, 206, 209–10
  The Farm 86–7, 90
  The Fireworks Triptych 91
  Harlequin's Carnival 87
  Her Majesty the Queen 91
  His Majesty the King 91
  The Nude by the Mirror 86
  Ploughed Earth 87
Miró's Foundation 80, 90–91, 198
Modernisme 30, 32–3, 34, 38, 45, 48, 68
Molas, Isidre 38–9, 44
Moll de la Fusta 28, 200
Monet, Claude 84
Montagut, Berenguer de 20
Montalbán, Manuel Vázquez 29, 152, 187
Monterols (hill) 166
Montjuic (hill) 9, 10, 41, 92, 104, 109, 166, 192, 193, 198, 200, 201, 209

Mont-roig 79, 81, 84–5, 86, 87–90
Montseny (mountains) 36
Montseny, Federica 119
Montserrat monastery 147, 174–6,
    177
Moore, Gerald 208
Moore, Henry 91
Moors 13, 14, 195
Morera, Enric 22
Morocco 42–3
Morris, William 30, 54, 68
Museu d'Art de Catalunya 92, 195–7
Museu d'Art Modern 86, 195
Museu de la Historia de la Ciutat 12
Museu Marés 12
Museum of Contemporary Art 203
Museum of Romanesque Art 79
Museum of Shoes 18
Museum of Sport 32

Naples 14
National Library 22
Nationalist Party *see* Convergència
Nic Habana (nightclub) 24
Nicholson, Jack 55–6
Nin, Andreu 109
Nonell, Isidre 71, 82
Nosaltres Sols (political group) 44
Noucentisme 85
Nova Cançó, La (singing style) 183–4,
    209
Núñez (President of the Barça) 181

Odette (friend of Picasso) 69, 70
Olivares 16
Oliver, Fernande (girlfriend of
    Picasso) 75, 76, 77, 78
Oliver, García 114, 119
Olympic Games 1936 107
Olympic Games 1992 28, 29, 48, 188,
    192–205 *passim*

Olympic Stadium 193, 200, 201–2
Olympic Theatre 99
Olympic Village 200, 202
Onyar river 130
Opisso (friend of Picasso) 52, 53–4,
    57–8
Orfeó Català (choral society) 30, 37,
    45
Orquestra Pau Casals 99
Ors, Eugeni d' 58, 85
Orwell, George 4, 21, 112–13, 114,
    115, 116, 117–18, 120, 121,
    125–6, 149
    Homage to Catalonia 113, 115, 118
Osona 13
Ovseenko, Antonov 113–14

Palamós 142, 144
Palau de la Generalitat 12, 107, 108,
    115, 121, 171, 188, 209
Palau de la Música Catalan 30, 32, 37,
    45–6, 68, 99, 105, 184, 185–6
Palau Güell 35, 52–3
Palau i Fabre, Josep 73, 125
Palau Marcet 35
Palau Montaner 34
Palau Nacional 92–4, 105, 192,
    195–7, 201
Palau Sant Jordi 202
Pallàs, Paulí 41
Pallarès, Manuel 64–5, 69, 70, 74–5,
    82, 205
Parade (ballet) 73, 206
Paraigües (bar) 165–6
Paral.lel 166, 168
Parc de la Ciutadella 25, 34, 37–8, 48,
    51, 64, 79, 80, 115, 146, 192,
    195, 207
Paris Exhibition (1937) 198, 206
    Spanish Pavilion 198, 206
Paris Trade Fair (1938) 90

Park Güell 50, 54–5
Passeig de Colom 8, 35, 63
Passeig de Gràcia 4, 24, 31, 33, 35, 47, 55, 56, 66, 68, 113, 192
Passeig de Lluís Companys 35
Passeig de Medoz 80
Passeig de Picasso 36, 207
Passeig de Sant Joan 51
Passeig del Born 19
Passeig del Crèdit 80, 86, 88, 97, 172
Passenger, The (film) 55–6
Passion Play *see Dansa de la Mort*
patrullas de control (Anarchist police) 110, 112, 114
Patum (festival of fire) 136–40
Pèl i Ploma (magazine) 70–71, 73
Pedra Força 77
Pedralbes monastery 20
Pedrera, La (Casa Milà) 55–7, 66, 192
Penguin Book of Spanish Civil War Verse 126
Penrose, Roland 78, 206
Peralada 142
Perallada, Ramon (restaurant owner) 162
Philip V 16, 34
Picabia, Francis 84
Picasso monument 207
Picasso Museum 19, 78, 93, 195, 205–7
Picasso, Pablo 4, 23, 33, 52, 63–78, 79, 82, 84, 97, 149, 156, 166, 195, 198, 205–7: Blue Period 52, 198, 206
 The Balcony 73–4, 206
 La Celestina 72
 Les Demoiselles d'Avignon 75, 77, 78
 Dream and Lie of Franco 206
 The Factory at Horta del Ebro 75
 Guernica 74, 78, 198, 206, 207

The Harem 78
Harlequin 73, 206
Houses on the Hill 75
Life 70
The Old Guitarist 72
Parade (ballet) 84, 206
The Reservoir 75
Science & Charity 63–4, 205
Woman with a Mantilla 73
Picasso, Señora (mother of Pablo) 80, 84, 85
Pitxot, Ramon 156
Plaça d'Espanya 92, 116, 195, 197
Plaça d'Os 209
Plaça de Catalunya 1, 4, 9, 31, 72, 108, 115, 118, 173
Plaça de Sant Agustí Vell 18
Plaça de Sant Felip Neri 18, 51
Plaça de Sant Iu 11
Plaça de Sant Jaume 6–7, 10, 18, 21, 80, 101, 103, 105, 107–8, 116, 117, 165, 171, 184, 187, 196, 208–9
Plaça de Sant Josep Oriol 205
Plaça de Sant Miguel 165
Plaça del Palau 52
Plaça del Pi 159, 165, 174, 204
Plaça del Rei 10, 11, 12, 18, 21, 101, 178
Plaça del Sol 27
Plaça del Teatre 109
Plaça Nova 209
Plaça Ramon Berenguer 12, 163
Plaça Reial 9, 12, 52, 65, 80, 183, 198, 204
Plaça Universitat 174
Poble Nou 121, 200, 202
Poliorama Cinema 118
port of Barcelona 1, 3–4, 121, 173, 205
Port de la Selva 144, 148, 154

Port Lligat 151, 152, 156
Portaella, Pere 143
Portal de l'Angel 128
Portal de Santa Madrona 83
Portalón (restaurant) 164–5, 204
POUM (Trotskyite militia) 109–20
    passim
Pound, Ezra 87
Prades 79, 123, 207
Prat de la Riba 39
Prats, Joan 90, 97, 124
Primo de Rivera, Miguel 44–5, 58,
    96, 151
Princess of Wales 142
Provençal language 2
PSC (Partit Socialista de Catalunya)
    186
PSOE (Partido Socialist Obrero
    Español) 186
PSUC (Catalan Communist Party)
    115, 118
Puból 152
Puerto Rico 208
Puig i Cadafalch, Josep 32–3, 35, 39,
    44–5, 51, 68, 93
Pujol, Jordi 14, 28, 29, 171–3, 174–5,
    185–7, 188–9, 190
Putget (hill) 166

Queen Elizabeth II of England 29
Queen Sofia of Spain 29, 48

Radical Party 42, 43
Raillard, Georges 89
Rambla de la Catalunya 4, 32, 35,
    47, 90
Rambla, the 1, 3, 4, 9, 18, 22, 35,
    36–7, 64, 80, 83, 100–120
    passim, 198, 201, 202, 209
Ray, Man 97
Reading 207

Red Lion, The (bar) 83
Reed, Jan: The Catalans 14, 42
Republican Government at Barcelona
    121
Ricart, Enric 82, 84, 86, 91
Riera de Sant Joan 69
Ritz Hotel 102
Roger de Llúria 35
Rohe, Mies van der 92, 197
Romeu, Pere 68, 205
Rosa, Lizcano de la 107
Roselló (brothel) 169
Roses (resort) 144
Roussillon 13
Royal Albert Hall 196, 207
Rusiñol, Santiago 66–9, 71
Russian Ballet 84, 206

Sabartes Collection see Picasso
    Museum
Sabartés, Jaume 66, 72–3, 206
Sagnier i Vilavecchia, Enric 35
Sagrada Família church 50–51, 53,
    57–62, 91, 195
Sala Bikini (nightclub) 24
Sala Pares gallery 70
Sala Tinell 21, 178
Salvador, Santiago 41
Salvat i Papasseit 86
Samaranch, Juan Antonio 128, 193,
    194
San Francisco (bar) 203
San Salvador 98
Sant Boi 17
Sant Felip Neri 58
Sant Felíu 143, 144, 164
Sant Jordi, feast of 171, 173–5
Sant Josep (Gràcia) 112
Sant Just 7, 12, 18, 58
Sant Marcus 93
Sant Nicolau (Girona) 131

Sant Pau del Camp 93
Sant Pere més Baix 18
Sant Pere de Galligants (Girona) 132
Sant Pol 144
Santa Àgata 12, 178
Santa Creu (National Library) 22
Santa Creu (in Carrer Hospital) 58
Santa Llúcia 12
Santa Maria del Mar 12, 18–20, 21,
    26, 31, 41, 91, 162, 165
Santa Maria del Pi 12, 18, 21
sardana (dance) 22–3, 184
Sardinia 14
Sarrià 31, 178
Satie, Erik 67, 73
Schneider, Maria 55
Schoenberg, Arnold 99
Schoenberg, Núria 99
Secrest, Meryl 150, 151
Sert, Josep Lluís 90, 97, 198, 206, 209,
    210
Setmana Tràgica, La 43, 57
7 Portes (restaurant) 104, 162
Sicily 14
siege of Barcelona 34
Sinn Fein 44
Sitges 67–8, 146, 203
Spender, Stephen 125
Sports College 201, 202
Stock Exchange *see* Llotja
Stravinsky, Igor 99
Suarez, Adolfo 185, 186–7, 188
Sutherland, Joan 46

Tàpies, Antoni 82, 91, 109, 124,
    177–9, 197, 207, 209
Tàpies, Señor (father) 124–5
Tàpies Foundation 197
Tarradellas, Josep 109, 187–8
Tarragona 36, 39, 51, 64, 79, 80, 81,
    93, 98, 208

Teatro Goya 101
Telephone Exchange 108, 115–16
Temple of Augustus 13
Terra Lliure (terrorist army) 172, 190
Terrassa 43
Thebes 14
Thomas, Hugh: *The Spanish Civil War*
    122, 124
Tibidabo (hill) 33, 166
Torras i Bages, Bishop 54
Tortosa Cathedral 93
Tossa de Mar 141, 144
Toulouse-Lautrec, Henri 68, 71, 84
Town Hall 5, 6, 7, 10, 21–22, 128,
    165, 178, 196, 200, 201, 203,
    204
Tramontana, La (wind) 155
Transition, the 26, 152, 184–5
Travessera de Dalt 54
travestis 167–8
Treaty of the Pyrenees 16
Trueta, Josep 109–11, 113, 114, 123,
    207–8
    The Spirit of Catalonia 14, 15, 123
Tudela 141
Tzara, Tristan 150

UGT (Communist trade union) 117
Un Chien Andalou (film) 150
United States World Fairs (1964,
    1965) 207
    Spanish Pavilions 206
University 16, 199
Up & Down (nightclub) 24
Urgel 13
usatges (code of laws) 15

Valencia 28, 120–21, 189
Van Dongen 71
Velázquez, Diego 195, 206
Vendrell 98, 110

Verges (village) 134–5, 184
Via Laietana 7, 12, 17, 18, 68, 117,
171
Vic 124
Vinçon (design shop) 28, 66
Vins i Caves de la Catedral 163
Viollet-le-Duc, Eugène 51
Virgin of Montserrat, feast of 174–6
Virreina Palace 4, 201

Wagner, Richard 37, 46
War of the Reapers 16
War of the Spanish Succession 16

waterworks building 31
Webern, Anton von 99
Werth, Alexander 115
William Tell 41

Xirgu, Margarida 101, 102, 103–4,
105

Yeats, W. B.: *Cathleen Ni Houlihan*
103

Zeleste Nou (nightclub) 24, 25–6, 29,
186

picador.com

blog
videos
interviews
extracts